D1604035

HEDGE HOGS

HEDGE

HOGS

THE COWBOY TRADERS BEHIND WALL STREET'S LARGEST HEDGE FUND DISASTER

BARBARA T. DREYFUSS

RANDOM HOUSE

NEW YORK

Published in the United States by Random House, an
imprint of The Random House Publishing Group, a division
of Random House, Inc., New York.

RANDOM HOUSE and colophon are registered trademarks of
Random House, Inc.

Library of Congress Cataloging-in-Publication Data
Dreyfuss, Barbara.
Hedge hogs : the cowboy traders behind wall street's
largest hedge fund disaster / Barbara T. Dreyfuss.
p.   cm.
Includes bibliographical references and index.
ISBN 978-1-4000-6839-5
eBook ISBN 978-0-679-60501-0
1. Hedge funds.   2. Investment advisors.   I. Title.
HG4530.D73 2013   332.64'524—dc23   2012015889

Printed in the United States
of America on acid-free paper

www.atrandom.com

9 8 7 6 5 4 3 2 1

First Edition

For Anna and Justin, who light up my life

To fight, to prove the strongest in the stern war of speculation, to eat up others in order to keep them from eating him, was, after his thirst for splendour and enjoyment, the one great motive for his passion for business. Though he did not heap up treasure, he had another joy, the delight attending on the struggle between vast amounts of money pitted against one another—fortunes set in battle array, like contending army corps, the clash of conflicting millions, with defeats and victories that intoxicated him.

—EMILE ZOLA, *Money*

CONTENTS

INTRODUCTION

This book was sparked in a roundabout way by my twenty years on Wall Street. It was an accidental career. I started out as a social worker at a foster home program for abandoned and abused children in New York City, then worked in various positions at area hospitals. When I moved to Washington, D.C., my experience in the health care system led to a job at a newsletter company writing about government health policy. Most of my subscribers were executives of hospitals and other health providers.

One day a guy named Mark Melcher rushed into our office to hand-deliver a check for a subscription he insisted must start immediately. He was opening a research office for a large brokerage house, Prudential-Bache Securities, to provide information about Washington to Wall Street clients. He was going to focus on health care and politics. Others would look at tax and budget policy. Wall Street was abuzz with questions about new hospital payment policies and regulations, he explained, and my newsletter provided little-known information about them. He subscribed for a couple of years and we discussed health policy over many lunches. When he learned I was looking for a more challenging job, he offered me a spot as a health policy research analyst.

I didn't really see it as the start of a Wall Street career when I went to work for Prudential-Bache in 1984. After all, I wasn't in New York and the pay was only slightly better than what I was already earning. Rather, I thought Mark a fun person to work with and an experienced, astute analyst who could help me hone my writing and research skills and my understanding of health care policy.

When he hired me, Mark already had over a dozen years' experience on Wall Street, writing and speaking about Washington policy on pharmaceutical and other health issues. He was highly regarded by clients—portfolio managers and health care analysts at mutual funds, insurance companies, banks, and money management firms. Like Mark, many had a decade or two of Wall Street experience and were probably closer to fifty than thirty. A few had started their careers working in pharmaceutical or other health care companies or had business school degrees. Although friendly and ready to laugh, they were serious, smart professionals and asked detailed, thoughtful questions.

Wall Street seemed a bit formal back then. Institutional investors, mostly men, dressed in monogrammed white shirts with gold cuff links, fancy suspenders, and suits. Their offices sported conference rooms with lots of mahogany and paintings.

I kept in close phone contact with our firm's top clients and traveled around the country to meet them. A large number managed money at mutual funds, firms such as Fidelity and T. Rowe Price, which were exploding as a result of 1980 tax changes allowing employees to put money into 401(k) pretax retirement savings accounts. Others worked at money management firms investing corporate, union, municipal and state pension funds, along with the fortunes of families such as the Rockefellers and Mellons.

These portfolio managers were long-term investors, maintaining the same holdings for weeks, months, years. Each mutual fund and money management company had rules for determining which stocks or bonds to buy or sell, along with parameters for how much to invest in each. Pension plans and wealthy clients also imposed restrictions on money managers. The emphasis was cautious, methodical money management, not speculative, risky activity.

At some firms, committees decided investments and okayed changes in holdings. At others, a portfolio manager had to consult colleagues before buying a hot new stock. The discussion might cause a portfolio manager to reassess his action, or his co-workers might endorse the move and piggyback onto the purchase. Often money managers had firm-wide caps on the number of shares held in one stock. Some firms controlled the number of transactions per manager per quarter. Others regulated the number of stocks, so if a portfolio manager bought a new stock, the firm might need to simultaneously sell something. Some firms limited cash on hand, so when managers sold they also needed to buy. These portfolio managers were known as the buy side of Wall Street, because they bought services from the investment banks and brokerage houses. The banks and brokerage firms handled the actual trading of stocks and bonds and were paid commissions. They also provided research on companies and industries to guide portfolio managers in their investing. This is where I came in. My job was to look beyond the hype of corporate CEOs and public relations professionals and determine what legislation or regulations were in the works that might impact drug companies, hospital firms, and medical device manufacturers.

The federal government was a dominant player in health care through Medicare, Medicaid, and the Veterans Administration. It accounted for a third to half of most hospitals' income and paid doctors, labs, and X-ray technicians. Many nursing homes depended on Medicaid revenues. Federal regulators set the rules governing health care providers. The Food and Drug Administration approved all new pharmaceuticals and medical devices. Surprisingly, given the significant impact Washington had on health care, there were only two or three Wall Street analysts in Washington at the time, following developments in Congress and administrative agencies.

The Internet as we know it didn't exist back then. C-SPAN and twenty-four-hour television news broadcasts were in their infancy. There were no telephone hookups to FDA meetings. Only a few investors came to Washington to watch FDA and congressional meetings firsthand. But decisions by the FDA and revelations at Capitol Hill hearings moved stock prices. So my on-the-scene reporting was much in demand.

I attended FDA meetings on specific drugs, arriving early to peruse handouts that often revealed their concerns. Many times I telephoned our worldwide sales force from an FDA meeting to convey breaking news, often negative for a company—an FDA review panel unexpectedly turned down a widely hyped drug for approval, or medical reviewers saw dangers in a new device. Within minutes our salesmen called hundreds of clients and the drug or device company's stock price tanked.

But going to hearings, meetings, and conferences was only part of my job. Another was to analyze how interest groups hoped to shape legislation or regulations. Washington is a chatty town; most jobs revolve around Congress or regulatory agencies. Everyone wants to discuss who is pressing for what amendment, proposal, or policy and the likelihood of their success. Information comes from all around you. Once a client and I were having lunch at a pricey downtown restaurant when we overheard two people at the next table loudly debating the prospects of tax policy changes for U.S. firms manufacturing in Puerto Rico. It was a critical issue for drug companies because most had major plants operating there. The two diners discussing this turned out to be a lobbyist and a Puerto Rican government official. We soon joined their discussion.

The portfolio managers I dealt with were not pressured for immediate investment decisions. They had time for lengthy discussions. They wanted to know not only the new regulations government policy makers planned but also their long-term impact. We discussed changing medical practices. Would hospitals close because of the growing number of outpatient procedures? Would new drug treatments mean fewer surgeries?

These investors were just as interested in how a company handled itself at FDA meetings as they were in the specific clinical trial data presented. Information I gleaned from the meetings helped them form an investment thesis based on an assessment of the firm's leadership, culture, quality of clinical research staff, and long-term plans.

Merck, for example, was at the time nicknamed the "Golden Company" by FDAers, praised for well-executed clinical trials and comprehensive data. It was easy to see why whenever I attended an FDA review meeting on a Merck product. The company would pack the conference room with dozens of senior executives, academics, and physician consultants flown in from around the world. With briefing books three inches thick, they answered any questions thrown at them. Merck's presentations contrasted markedly with the sloppy data or confused and disorganized presentations of other firms.

Not only were mutual funds and many money managers longer-term investors, but they primarily made money when stocks went up in price. They didn't engage in shorting stocks, a strategy that earns money when prices collapse. To short, an investor borrows shares of stock to sell and later buys it to repay the lender. If the price has gone down by the time he buys it, he profits.

Rules created in the wake of the Depression to protect investors against risky trading limited mutual fund shorting. Called the "short-short" rule, it imposed significant tax penalties if a mutual fund derived more than one-third its income from holdings of less than three months or short sales. Even when the law was changed in 1997, two-thirds of all mutual funds still operated under self-imposed rules prohibiting shorting. And of those allowed to short stocks, only a tiny number actually did so. Because of this, mutual fund investors wanted stock prices to rise and were not happy to hear negative news.

Corporate executives also wanted their stock prices to climb, especially after tax changes in the mid-1990s spurred companies to compensate executives with hefty stock options as well as cash. Companies such as WorldCom, Rite Aid, Waste Management, Cendant, and a host of others engaged in a myriad of financing schemes to prop up their stock prices. None was more adept than Enron, which pioneered new accounting practices that immediately booked as income expected future profits on power plants and international projects. When those projects fell apart, Enron resorted to shell companies to manipulate earnings.

Some research analysts at investment banks and brokerage houses helped the good times roll by writing glowing reports on companies, even while privately panning them. They wanted to curry favor with the company to foster banking deals, as investigations by New York attorney general Eliot Spitzer later revealed. Companies were unlikely to work with a broker whose analysts slammed them.

Generally this wasn't an issue at my firm because we rarely had major banking business. In fact, some well-known analysts sought jobs there when they ran afoul of bankers at their old firm or wanted to do research without pressure from bankers.

I worked closely with our drug, device, hospital, and insurance company analysts. It was challenging work and particularly satisfying when I could expose hypocrisy, distortions, or misinformation coming from some of the corporations or interest groups.

There were times I was shocked to learn a company had not revealed to its investors information that was widely circulating in Washington. One time our analyst covering W. R. Grace, which had a significant subsidiary involved with dialysis, asked me to check on whether there were any new Medicare payment policies in that area. When I called various government offices I soon learned that weeks earlier the FDA had shut down the firm's production of dialyzers after uncovering serious manufacturing issues. Dialysis centers and the FDA were scrambling to find other producers and there was fear of serious shortages.

Yet the firm had not put out a press release on this and investors knew nothing about it. Our analyst was shocked by the news. By chance, firm officials were coming to her office that day for a general discussion. I faxed her FDA releases on the issue as company executives walked in her door. Before showing them the papers, she asked if they knew of any developments regarding dialysis that could impact the firm. When they looked surprised and said no, she went to her fax machine to find the documents I sent. Within an hour there was a conference call set up between the firm and investors to discuss the issue.

The economy was humming along in the 1990s, and it was a good time to be bullish about the stock market. The wave of mergers, acquisitions, and public offerings helped it along, as did glowing reports from analysts. The S&P 500 index was 500 in 1995 and doubled by 1998; two years later it was 1,500. The Dow Jones Industrial Average topped 3,000 in 1991 for the first time and then kept rising. Five years later it was 4,000, and over 6,000 the next year. By January 1999 it was over 9,500. In another six months it was at 11,200.

During the 1980s and early 1990s I had occasionally received calls from another type of client, a hedge fund. Hedge funds managed money for rich clients in investment pools. Because these firms catered to the wealthy, Congress allowed them to operate unregulated. The assumption was that rich clients knew enough about finance to make sure their money managers treated them fairly and didn't take excessive investment risks. And if something did go wrong, well, these investors probably could afford some losses.

Hedge funds didn't have the same restrictions on shorting stocks that mutual funds did. And many hedge funds were rapid traders, getting in and out of holdings the same day.

When I started out there were only a few dozen hedge funds. The industry was in the hands of a few large firms, created and dominated by dynamic, highly skilled traders, including Julian Robertson, George Soros, and Paul Tudor Jones. Most did extensive research on companies, industries, and economic trends, and keenly observed market psychology. They searched for unique opportunities and found them, not only because they were smart but also because there were so few hedge funds. They bet big, took big risks, and made enormous fortunes.

In the early 1990s I watched as the number of hedge funds grew. Some of our clients left mutual funds and other firms to create their own hedge fund. A number of well-known investment bank research analysts did so too. Firms that later tracked the growth in hedge funds estimated there were about two thousand by 1995.[1]

Many of these new firms heavily invested in health care and I found hedge fund managers taking up an increasing share of my time. To a greater extent than at mutual funds, those investing in health care at hedge funds seemed to be experts in the field—physicians, highly trained medical researchers, former drug company executives. They were shrewd and very detail oriented. Many focused on investing in smaller companies than mutual funds did.

They drilled down more deeply than the average mutual fund portfolio manager into how a particular drug or device worked and what the FDA thought about a new technology.

Because they both shorted and bought stock, they were just as eager for insight into FDA concerns about a new technology or snags in clinical trials as they were about new product approvals. They investigated reports of nursing home abuses and also which companies won quality awards. Because of the research they did and the medical background of many, they didn't easily buy a company's hype about a new drug or device. They formed their own views about the evolution of medical technology and hospital delivery systems.

By the start of the new millennium the stock market was still soaring, companies were manipulating earnings to keep up stock prices, and the technology bubble was at its height. The number of hedge funds had reached four thousand, double what it had been five years before.[2] Their assets were just over $300 billion, up from $76 billion.[3]

Then the stock market bubble burst in March 2000 and stocks went into free fall. For the first time since World War II the S&P 500 had a three-year losing streak, plummeting more than 40 percent. More than half of all mutual funds, investing in similar large companies, did worse.[4]

Although some hedge funds lost significantly, as a group they did better than mutual funds. The HFR index of two thousand hedge funds of varying investment styles was up almost 5 percent in 2001 and down only 1 percent in 2002. Like magicians, hedge funds promised to make money regardless of how stocks behaved because they could bet on prices going up or down. Some were multistrategy funds and moved money into whatever industry or type of investment was hot at the moment. Mutual funds only promised investors they'd beat the returns of stock market indexes—not an enticing offer when markets collapsed.

Before the crash of 2000, hedge funds were seen as risky, a playground for the superwealthy, who could afford to gamble and lose big in search of a payout. But after the crash, things changed. Suddenly investors who'd watched in alarm as markets tumbled saw hedge funds in a new light. They seemed to promise the impossible: invest with us, their salesmen said, and we'll make you money even if the markets fall. As indices plunged, more and more people who'd enjoyed double-digit gains in the 1990s started turning to hedge funds, first in a trickle and then in a wave.

Money began to pour into hedge funds, not just from wealthy individuals but also from university, hospital, and other charitable endowments. Soon pension plans wanted in too. Hedge funds sprouted everywhere. Some were set up by seasoned analysts or spun out of existing hedge funds. But portfolio managers at mutual funds and money management firms were also eager to get into the hedge fund bonanza, despite their lack of experience in trading rapidly or shorting. At mutual funds their pay was based on the value of assets they managed, which collapsed along with the stock market. But hedge fund managers were paid a fee based on assets and on top of that took 20 percent of any profits they earned for clients.

For a time, whenever I visited mutual funds or pension managers on a marketing trip, our discussions quickly focused on the latest hedge fund being set up in town. They asked whether their competitors, also my clients, were discussing spinning out a hedge fund.

By 2003 the number of hedge funds had jumped to over six thousand, up from four thousand only three years earlier. The assets they managed doubled in that period, to more than $600 billion.[5]

Individual hedge funds grew large. For the first time several hedge funds made my firm's list of top twenty-five clients, people we called the most often with news. Mutual funds controlled ten times more assets than hedge funds, so they were still important. But my firm was paid commissions for buying and selling investments, and hedge funds traded fast and furiously.

Hedge funds seemed dominated by young guys, many with financial engineering, math, or physics degrees. Indeed, quants (short for *quantitative analysts*) appeared to materialize at virtually every hedge fund, using complex algorithms and high-powered computers to forecast stock price movements.

Hedge funds had always seemed focused on short-term investing, unlike the longer-term investment orientation of mutual funds, but increasingly that short-term time frame seemed to go from weeks to days to hours.

Hedge fund portfolio managers and analysts called much more often now. They wanted breaking, actionable news. They were interested in news tidbits, rumors that might move stock prices, negative rumblings about a product. They didn't want long discussions about changing medical practices or regulations. "What are you hearing about upcoming congressional hearings?" hedge fund portfolio managers asked. "What is the latest scuttlebutt from FDA?" Details weren't very important.

A friend who worked at one hedge fund told me she was urged to date investment bank analysts in order to find out when they were issuing reports. Even news that a report was coming would make the stock bounce.

Unlike mutual fund investors, hedge fund managers didn't just ask questions. I suspected some tried to plant stories that would help their investments. They phoned to report a manufacturing problem the FDA had found during an inspection of a drug company or to tell me about an upcoming congressional hearing. Sometimes I was able to confirm these stories, but often I couldn't.

Hedge fund managers were frenzied. Often when I visited their office they would run into a meeting with me, fidget in their chair, and dash out a few minutes later. Or they would stare at flashing price charts, listening with half an ear.

Several times I spoke on the phone with one well-known and tense hedge fund manager while he was in the middle of a massage in an effort to calm down. Too stressed to leave his office, even for a short time, he had a table and masseuse brought in. While his muscles were pummeled, the hedge fund manager telephoned analysts, told his assistant how to handle incoming calls, and shouted out buy and sell orders to his traders.

Hedge funds were huge. By 2004 the top five hedge funds together managed $58 billion.[6] The two largest each managed over $17 billion. With such enormous pots of money to invest, it was hard to keep up the outsize returns hedge funds promised. There were only so many really good trading ideas. They scrambled to get some edge over other investors.

Always stressful, my job became more so as hedge fund managers demanded a constant stream of information and gossip. Few seemed to care much about the companies they invested in, the products produced, or the direction of health care. It didn't matter if a nursing home was abusing patients, only whether news of this was already out in the investment community.

The hedge fund culture seemed to impact mutual funds too. If portfolio managers weren't looking to jump to a hedge fund, they were pressing executives to create investment portfolios with similar characteristics.

I had been at the job for two decades and decided it was time to leave. I started writing investigative articles on corporate lobbying, Medicare, insurance, and other issues for magazines, including the *American Prospect*, *Washington Monthly*, and *Mother Jones*.

As I started my new career in 2004, hedge funds were managing more than $600 billion. The traders investing this money started to amass wealth that would have turned Gordon Gekko green. The top twenty-five hedge fund managers raked in an average $250 million each in 2004, reported Institutional Investor's *Alpha* magazine.[7] That year hedge fund manager Eddie Lampert pocketed $1 billion, and made the cover of *BusinessWeek*.

Hedge funds were a powerful force on Wall Street, playing an outsize role because they traded often and big. Banks catered to them, earning hefty fees, and even set up their own.

And, as one of my former hedge fund clients described publicly, they were not above manipulating news to move prices to their benefit. Jim Cramer, who ran his own firm for many years, explained in an interview I watched how easy it was for that to happen. Appearing on his Internet show, *Wall Street Confidential*, on December 22, 2006 (the show was part of the broad financial news, commentary, and video conglomerate he then owned), Cramer was blunt. Suppose someone could profit if Apple's stock tanked, he said, but instead it was rising. In such a case, Cramer said, he would call six trading desks and claim he had heard that Verizon executives were panning Apple. "That's a very effective way to keep a stock down," he chuckled. "I might also buy January puts"—stock options that anticipate a stock going down. That would create an image that bad news is coming. Then he would call investors and tell them the same. "The way the market really works is you hit the nexus of the brokerage houses with a series of orders that can be leaked to the press, and you get it on CNBC, and then you have a vicious cycle down."

By the time of Cramer's public admission, some of my Wall Street friends who had moved into hedge funds were telling me that an increasing part of their assets came from pension plans. Indeed, by that point there was already $100 billion of pension money invested through hedge funds. Endowments—money that was supposed to keep schools, hospitals, and other institutions running—were just as eager to join the hedge fund bandwagon.

My friends were as concerned as I was. The whole point of a pension fund was to provide a stable, secure pot of money to pay for retirement. But few hedge funds actually tried to reduce risk. Instead they poured money into all types of complex risky derivatives. And nobody was setting any rules for them or watching what they were doing. Firms borrowed heavily to hike profits, further increasing risk. If wealthy investors wanted to take this type of gamble, that was one thing. But pension and endowment money was supposed to be well protected. A major blowout by a hedge fund could wipe out significant chunks of retiree savings.

Not many people seemed to be concerned about this in 2006, however. The buzz was about how much money hedge funds made for their investors. Pensions and endowments didn't want to be left out.

Late that year I researched and wrote an article about the need to regulate hedge funds. While still at Prudential I had had cursory contact with one of our clients, a complex hedge fund structure of entities known as Amaranth. In the course of researching the hedge fund story, I learned more about what had happened to Amaranth, which at its height in September 2006 managed assets of almost $10 billion and then imploded virtually overnight. Between the end of August and the end of September, more than $6 billion of its funds effectively disappeared.

When Amaranth went under, it was the largest hedge fund collapse ever. A firm that for several years had been besieged by pension funds, universities, hospitals, and wealthy individuals begging to enter its elite circle of investors had gone belly up. A company that was up 15 percent one year, paying out hundreds of millions of dollars in bonuses, suddenly closed its doors the next. Why?

Amaranth, marketed as a diversified hedge fund employing a myriad of investment strategies, became totally dependent on its natural gas bets and its star commodities trader, Brian Hunter. He was one of two traders who in the summer of 2006 ruled the world of natural gas investing.

The other was John Arnold, who had been Enron's chief financial gas trader and then set up his own hedge fund. His enormous trades continued to dominate the commodity exchange after Enron's collapse. During 2006 these two young traders sized each other up, gauging the bets each made and how they affected gas prices. They probed for weaknesses in the other's trading strategies. For months they waged a high stakes battle. Their contest ended when one collapsed a multibillion-dollar firm and the other became a billionaire.

The story of Amaranth's demise was a cautionary tale of two reckless traders. In researching it, I realized that telling the story was a way to shine a light on a dark corner of Wall Street where unregulated traders, playing in unregulated financial markets, take enormous risks with investors' money. It was a way to understand Wall Street's transformation over the past two decades from long-term investing into rapid-fire, hectic speculative trading. At each step of the way the breakdown of regulation raised the stakes for ordinary people. Lack of regulation of electronic and over-the-counter trading allowed the cowboys to take charge. Deregulation of the energy industry allowed wild fluctuations in the price of a vital commodity. No regulation of hedge funds encouraged them to take massive risks with money individuals were counting on for retirement.

Amaranth was opened in May 2000 by Nick Maounis, who had

built a Wall Street reputation as a careful, highly competent, and risk-averse trader. It was supposed to invest in multiple arenas as a way to reduce the risk of a blowout. But as Amaranth mushroomed in size, it was harder and harder to keep up outsize returns. Within a few years Maounis had turned billions of dollars over to Hunter, a reckless young natural gas trader with a penchant for huge, concentrated bets.

Hedge funds are carefully structured to legally avoid oversight. Its traders and owners want no restrictions or prying eyes on their freewheeling, consequences-be-damned investing. With their huge payouts and adrenaline-rush trading, hedge funds attract big risk takers. Bet big, win big—or, as Amaranth showed, lose big.

If it were just the traders or hedge fund owners who lose money when a firm goes belly up, that would be one thing. But the headlong rush into hedge funds by pension funds and endowments exposes ordinary Americans to their reckless activity. When Amaranth collapsed, these institutional investors lost hundreds of millions of dollars.

While Amaranth may have been the largest hedge fund to go under, many smaller ones have folded too. In the three months following Amaranth's demise in September 2006, a record 267 hedge funds closed shop.

While hedge funds escaped government oversight, so did many of their investments, thanks to years of deregulatory fervor. As Amaranth showed, that made for an explosive mix. The firm concluded billions of dollars in natural gas trades on electronic exchanges or in backroom deals free and clear of regulations thanks to earlier lobbying by Enron and big banks. The trades Hunter and his erstwhile opponent Arnold conducted roiled energy markets. Amaranth's massive bets on rising prices spiked energy prices, costing utilities, small companies, schools, hospitals, and homes millions of dollars.

Losing other people's money with impunity and playing games with commodity prices is serious enough. But Amaranth's massive bet on natural gas reflects an even more fundamental problem with Wall Street today. The speculative trading dominating financial markets is siphoning off an enormous swath of the country's wealth, taking it out of the productive economy. Money that should be going to expand and develop the country, create new technology, build manufacturing plants, modernize farms, expand infrastructure, and advance education instead fuels nonproductive betting.

One sector of the economy that is benefiting, however, is financial services, which by 2010 accounted for nearly one-third of all the profits generated in the United States.

Individual hedge fund managers are also amassing huge fortunes, which instead of expanding their collections of Ferraris and new luxury homes could build schools and hospitals. In 2011, even with the average hedge fund losing 5 percent, the top five fund managers took home a total of more than $8 billion.[8]

Some countries have designed financial systems geared to productive investments. The United States has a financial system that has become the world's largest casino.

When Brian Hunter and John Arnold faced off, dominating the buying and selling of natural gas, they were playing a game to enrich themselves. They wanted to profit from changes in gas prices, and the more wildly prices fluctuated, the more the two could earn. They didn't care about the effect of gyrating prices on consumers.

For years Congress and federal officials ignored pleas from small companies, utilities, and gas distributors to rein in energy speculation. Free market advocates maintained that speculators provided a critical function for buyers and sellers, even when producers and users argued otherwise.

Energy trading was part of the speculative mania—in commodities, securitized mortgages, credit default swaps, and a host of other derivatives—dominating Wall Street. By 2008 many major banks such as Lehman Brothers and Goldman Sachs earned more than half their profits from their own speculative trading.

Some argued that investment vehicles such as credit default swaps were not speculation but protection for investors in corporate bonds in case of defaults. But the value of all credit default swaps by 2009 was three times the entire amount of all bonds issued by

U.S. corporations and many more times the debt of the specific companies they were written against.[9] They were simply bets by speculators trying to earn a buck.

Tens of billions in new money poured into commodity speculation after Amaranth's collapse, helping jack oil prices to nearly $150 a barrel in the summer of 2008 and raise food prices so high even senior economists at the World Bank admitted that "financial investors" had a lot to do with the surge in commodity prices.[10] A few months later commodity prices collapsed with the start of the economic crisis.

Some hedge funds, such as Paulson and Co., helped spark the crisis by working with banks to devise mortgage derivatives likely to fail. Many more hedge funds helped spur the intense speculation by investing in these securities and credit default swaps. More than 340 hedge funds went out of business in the last three months of 2008, and another 778 followed suit the next quarter.[11] Most hedge funds had double-digit losses in 2008.[12]

When the smoke cleared, traders went back to business. By early 2012 there was 40 percent more speculative money in energy commodities than when oil prices had been at their height in 2008.[13] And a new type of investing now dominates Wall Street: high-frequency trading. Computers programmed to detect minute, inconsistent price changes trigger lightning-quick trades. Trading volume has skyrocketed, as more than half of all stock trades now come from such high-frequency trading programs. They are not investments in a company, not a way to foster new products or industrial growth. They are just a way to make some fast money.[14]

But none of this has stopped pension plans from turning over even more of their assets to hedge funds. When state and local government budgets were slashed in the 2008 recession, public pension fund managers hoped hedge funds would provide a boost to their returns. Within two years of the recession, as many as 60 percent of large pension funds invested some money in hedge funds, compared with only about 10 percent at the beginning of the decade.[15] One pension fund, the Teacher Retirement System of Texas, broke new ground recently by actually buying a direct stake in the largest hedge fund.

The economic crisis was so devastating and the outrage against Wall Street so great that Congress and the administration finally passed legislation in 2010 to rein in bankers and traders. But financial firms spent tens of millions of dollars and sent thousands of lobbyists to Washington to water down the toughest provisions. Then they waged a similar campaign to delay, defang, and decimate what was enacted.

What remained were half measures, loopholes, and regulatory agencies that lacked sufficient funding and staff. There will be a crackdown on the worst behavior only if there is strong political pressure to do so, and politicians will have the backbone to take on the industry only if there is an enraged population demanding action. Until then, Wall Street will continue its wild speculation with pension and endowment money until another bust puts a stop to it.

HEDGE
HOGS

GOING ALL IN

D ay after day and month after month during the spring and summer of 2006, a brash young commodity trader named Brian Hunter invested hundreds of millions of his clients' dollars—money that not all of them could afford to lose—in high-risk bets on the price of natural gas.

Every day Hunter, tall and athletic, sat facing a bank of flickering monitors. Over and over again he'd juggled the complicated mathematical formulas in his head, called on his trading associates, and consulted the charts, graphs, and weather forecasts that filled the screens in front of him, calculating the odds. An unexpected cold winter that would cause a spike in gas prices? It had seemed likely. Stronger than expected demand, at least stronger than other traders were counting on? He thought it possible. A hurricane-induced supply disruption? There was a good chance.

So he'd bet big. Throughout the year, he'd singlehandedly dominated the trading of natural gas. At times he'd held 50 percent or more of all the contracts for the huge natural gas market in the months ahead, betting that winter prices would rise.

But speculating on natural gas prices was risky business, and by August Brian Hunter knew he was in trouble. And billions of dollars of other people's money were on the line.

Although it was still hot and sticky in Connecticut, where his firm was headquartered, Hunter was feverishly thinking ahead to the first chill of winter, when he had expected demand for gas to pick up, sparking price hikes and letting him make a killing.

He'd already spent large sums propping up his positions while waiting for something, anything—a hurricane, a pipeline disruption, a delivery bottleneck—that would push winter prices up. But there had been nothing. Indeed, if anything caused prices of gas contracts to go his way at times, it was likely Hunter's own trading. So powerful was he that he'd created his own wave, all by himself. Now what?

Lots of other people smelled the scent of gas in the air and feared an explosion. The executives at his hedge fund, Amaranth, were getting worried, since too much of the company's assets were tangled up in Hunter's precarious portfolio. They were pressing him to unload a big chunk of his holdings. Usually Hunter and the handful of traders he oversaw operated out of an office in Calgary, Alberta. But for several months, wary Amaranth executives repeatedly ordered Hunter and his team of traders to fly east to Greenwich, Connecticut, so that they could more easily scrutinize their trading.

Brokers at J. P. Morgan, which handled Hunter's trades and collected the collateral he needed for them, were alarmed at the size of his holdings too. Already in mid-August they'd demanded that his firm post as much as $2 billion to guarantee his bets.

And down at the New York Mercantile Exchange (NYMEX) they could smell gas too. The officials at the world's largest energy commodity exchange, not unused to watching high-stakes gambles unfold, warned Hunter to cut back.

Although he didn't know it at the time, Hunter had yet another problem. About fifteen hundred miles away to the southwest, his main rival, John Arnold, didn't see things the way Hunter did. And he was ready to pounce.

Arnold was widely considered the top energy trader in the world. A wily Enron veteran, Arnold was exactly the same age as Hunter, but perhaps a bit more experienced in the high-stakes energy trading game. He too ran and reran the numbers and analyzed the fundamentals of the natural gas market, and he didn't believe that gas prices were likely to rise significantly with the approach of winter's icy blast. The previous winter had been mild, Arnold knew. Natural gas supplies during the spring and summer were relatively plentiful.

And the quantities of gas in storage were higher than at any time in the past half decade. So as Hunter placed bets on rising prices, Arnold was putting money behind his confident belief that winter prices would decline.

Not that either Hunter or Arnold came anywhere near an actual gas container. Nor did they come close to the network of buried pipelines, collecting stations, and pumping facilities that pushed gas from Texas, Louisiana, and the Gulf north to the energy-hungry Midwest and Northeast. They were speculators, buying and selling paper, placing bets with brokers and on computerized exchanges, hoping to earn a profit from shifts in the price of gas. The contracts and other investments they traded represented—somewhere in the future—millions of cubic feet of natural gas. But they made money not when actual gas changed hands but when contracts for that gas changed hands. And make—and lose—money they did.

It wasn't the first time that Hunter and Arnold clashed. They'd disagreed before on where gas prices were headed. Several times in the past twelve months, particularly on the final, crucial day of trading expiring monthly gas contracts, Hunter and Arnold faced off, with one or the other coming out ahead.

Most people think that the price of a resource such as natural gas is determined by old-fashioned supply and demand, and to some degree it is. But more and more in the kind of speculative trading that Hunter and Arnold engaged in, other factors—market psychology and the stratagems of traders who dominated any given day's trading—had a powerful impact on prices, at least over the short term. And Hunter and Arnold dominated trading that year.

In late August, there was also intense pressure on Hunter to figure out how to handle his pile of summer contracts. Just as Hunter expected winter prices to rise sharply, he also counted on summer prices to fall. Many of his investments were arranged so that he would make money if either happened. He not only bet on the price in various months but on the difference in price between summer and winter months.

But that summer prices did not go down. In fact, a heat wave that hit in the last week of July, increasing demand for electricity for air-conditioning, along with the threat of supply disruptions from a passing tropical storm, combined to cause prices to jump 17 percent.

Even tiny changes in gas prices can have enormous impact on a trader's profits or losses. Because of the way gas contracts are priced, if a trader holds ten thousand contracts, then just a measly 1-cent price shift translates into a change of $1 million in the value of his holdings. And Hunter controlled much more than that. In fact, he was invested in hundreds of thousands of contracts.

All summer long Hunter had waited for prices to fall, and as each month drew to a close, he rolled his holdings forward into the next month. By the end of August he was running out of months, and his portfolio was short 56,000 September contracts. It was an enormous position.

But Hunter took a gamble. Rather than get out of his contracts at fire-sale prices, he decided to double down on his bet. He added to his position and by August 28 had shorted 96,000 September contracts. The amount of gas they represented was about one-quarter of all the gas used by residential consumers that entire year.

The next day, August 29, was the last trading day for September contracts. With his bosses, his bank, and NYMEX breathing down his neck, Hunter desperately planned two strategies to bail himself out.

First, he would do some more trading in September contracts, shorting even more. Perhaps he hoped that would depress prices further. He planned to let September holdings expire at the end of the day. Maybe he would do all right.

Second, he decided to place another bet—that the difference between the September and October contract prices would widen. Usually these months traded within 7 or 8 cents of each other. But thanks in part to Hunter's huge trading, which had helped depress September prices, the difference between the two months was now about 34 cents. He hoped the difference would widen even more the next day and he would make some money.

John Arnold, who was watching supply and demand fundamentals, sensed something else. He looked at the wide price difference that suddenly occurred between September and October gas prices on August 28 and became suspicious. There didn't seem to be any fundamentals to justify it.

Not only that, but Arnold expected September prices to rise.

So as the final seconds ticked down before the 10:00 a.m. Eastern time start of trading on August 29, the battle lines were drawn. Hunter, from his desk in Greenwich, with vast sums at stake, wanted September prices to go down. Arnold, at his perch in Houston, was counting on them going up.

As trading kicked off, Hunter sat amidst other commodity traders who were busy buying and selling electricity, grain, metals, and oil. Behind him, looking over his shoulder, sat one of his firm's senior managers, Rob Jones, who normally stayed in his office. He was carefully watching Hunter's trades.

In Houston, Texas, on the eighth floor of a glass-walled office building in the fashionable Galleria mall area, John Arnold too began trading.

At first they seemed to be testing the marketplace, trading in small amounts. Within the first ten minutes Hunter shorted just over five hundred September contracts. John Arnold bought slightly less than half that amount. Between 10:10 a.m. and 10:20 a.m. Hunter sold close to four hundred contracts; Arnold bought an almost equal number. Over the next forty minutes they made smaller trades, but Hunter always shorted, Arnold always bought.[1]

As the morning wore on, the size of their trades increased. Right before noon Hunter sold just over 2,500 contracts. Arnold only bought about half that number. Especially during the first couple of hours of trading, Hunter seemed to get the edge. September prices tipped down in Hunter's favor by 10 or 20 cents. The difference between the September and October contracts widened to as much as 50 cents. For Hunter this was good news.

By early afternoon, with less than an hour to go before the end of trading, Hunter had shorted just over 15,000 September contracts. Arnold's buying had not quite kept up with Hunter's trading.

Although commodity investing was supposed to be anonymous, the brokers who placed many of the trades tended to talk, especially when Brian Hunter and John Arnold were facing off. "It's the Brian and John show," some quipped to other traders, asking which side they were on. "Can you believe how much money these guys are throwing around?" they marveled.

But then, at about 1:45 p.m., with forty-five minutes left to the trading day, events took an ominous turn for Hunter: September contract prices began to tick up, and the price difference between September and October narrowed.

Brian Hunter had already stopped trading. He was under orders from government regulators not to trade heavily in the final half hour of exchange activity.

So he was done for the day. But not John Arnold. He was suddenly buying thousands of September contracts. As the clock ticked inexorably toward the end of the trading day, the price of September natural gas contracts moved in only one direction.

In the balance hung Hunter's investments—along with Amaranth's very solvency and the fortunes of its myriad investors.

THE MAN FROM CALGARY

Brian Hunter first put his prodigious math skills to work playing basketball. He and his high school coach, a math teacher, saw basketball as a game of applied math or engineering dynamics. If you could master the ever-changing angles, estimate the arc for a three-pointer, calculate the angle of a bounce pass, know where to position yourself for a rebound, then you could perfect your game.

This wasn't how basketball was usually played in Hunter's hometown on the outskirts of Calgary, Canada. There it was a contact sport, physical and rough. The Canadians were mocked by American teams they competed against for playing an ice-hockey-like basketball. Along with body contact went a lot of trash talk. Some players who lacked ability tried intimidation. But not Hunter. Teammates say he used skill and finesse.

Still, Hunter didn't shy away from physical contact. He concentrated on the most dangerous part of the court, just under the hoop—where you can catch an elbow to the chops or an arm to the nose, but where games are won and lost. Already close to his full height of six feet four inches, on defense he played with his back to the basket, pressing the other team. And on offense he was always ready to attack the rim or pull up for a shot, regardless of who was defending him. He was so aggressive and determined to win that once in practice he broke a friend's nose with his elbow.

Because of his smarts, lack of fear, and skill he was a standout player. In his senior year he was voted the most valuable player on the Lakers, the local high school team in Chestermere, Alberta.

From Chestermere you could see the glowing lights and the growing skyline of Calgary. They beckoned on the evening horizon, seemingly only a stone's throw away. But as close as the small town was to Canada's fifth-largest city, Chestermere's real identity was shaped more by the Alberta farm country surrounding it than by any urban landscape. It was an area of fields, cattle farms, and scattered dwellings. The village only became a town in 1993 after its permanent population grew to just over one thousand.

Streets flowed into the wide-open prairie. Kids still biked to school, pedaling past acres of wheat and canola fields. Cattle farms hugged the horizon, and real cowboys loped through town in tight jeans with big belt buckles. Here were guys who knew how to rope calves, ride bulls, and take apart tractors. Only a few miles from Hunter's high school was the pig slaughterhouse, where neighbors on nearby farms could hear the hogs scream.

The Canadian Pacific Railway owned millions of acres of land throughout the area. It built dams and head gates and created a shallow lake as part of a major irrigation system. During the summer, Hunter and friends water-skied on the lake or used a boat to pull one another on inner tubes. In the winter they skated and tobogganed.

Hunter's family labored hard for a weekly paycheck. His grandfather Robert worked for the railroad for fifty years.

His father, also named Brian, a construction worker when Hunter was a boy, struggled to make ends meet. He went bankrupt, and the family lived in a trailer until Hunter was about ten.[1] They moved to Chestermere in 1976, when Brian, born in 1974, was a toddler. A few years later his younger sister was born.

Hunter was a gifted student who pulled the best grades and was valedictorian of his high school graduating class. He sported boyish good looks, with light brown hair, blue eyes, and a turned-up nose. To his classmates Hunter was a friendly, regular guy, despite being the star athlete and the smartest kid in his grade. "The cool thing about Brian was he had an above ninety average and he'd show up at the house parties and the victory parties. He wasn't above the rest of us. There are cliques, obviously, at high schools—the jocks, head bangers, preps. He mingled well within all those circles," remembers high school friend Gordon Rothnie.

Basketball also gave Hunter his first taste of hard work and discipline. Unlike many area schools whose basketball program was limited to an open gym after school for pickup games, Chestermere offered a rigorous, organized athletic program. The coaches had played basketball or football at college, were serious about their sports, and made sure the players were too, with daily practice and summer activities.

They also encouraged team spirit, organizing group dinners and fund-raising events, which in rural Alberta weren't the usual car washes and bake sales. In autumn, the basketball team helped nearby farmers roll hay into bales for livestock feed. And they hauled turkeys, going into a Quonset hut, grabbing a squawking bird, and dragging it out to a waiting truck.

The coaches and players developed close bonds. More than a dozen years later, when he was worth tens of millions, Hunter continued to return for annual alumni games hosted by his high school coach, Rob Wilson, though he now drove up to school in his Bentley. Looking nearly as young as he did in high school, he displayed the same smooth, aggressive skills.

A committee inducted him into the school's Hall of Fame, placing his picture alongside others in a high-profile area to inspire students. In 2008 he donated $20,000 for a new weight room, along with other state-of-the-art equipment.

In his junior year in high school Hunter was overshadowed on the basketball court by a senior, Shane Hooker, a bulldog of a point guard who scored the highest number of points in the team's history. "Shane Hooker was like a mad dog," remembers Rothnie, who was also on the team. "It was almost frightening how intense he could get. He wanted to win, but he had heart." The team came in second in the province that year, Hooker's last on the team.

Hooker's playing was several levels above that of his teammates, and so the coaches didn't expect many wins the following year. But the other players wanted to prove they didn't need Hooker to win games. To the coaches' surprise, Hunter in particular stepped up, not only playing well but pushing and exhorting his teammates to give their all, without putting anyone down or losing his cool. The Chestermere Lakers again made it to the provincial finals and won a silver medal in the championships.

Hunter also made the provincial all-star team that year. The hotheads on his team admired not only his basketball skills but his cool competitiveness as well. During a tournament in Spokane, Washington, the team met up with a squad they'd beaten previously by twenty points. But this time the refs appeared determined to keep the other team in the game, calling a series of questionable fouls against the Alberta all-stars. As the clock wound down and the other team took an insurmountable lead, passions ran high on the Alberta bench. The angry players wanted to grab the refs, curse them. Hunter, who maintained a calm façade until the final second had ticked off, made a beeline for the refs as soon as the buzzer sounded. His voice not rising above its usual level, he bluntly told them, "You desecrated the game of basketball."

Calm under pressure, thirsting for wins, not intimidated by the rough play, cleverly using his knack for math—Hunter displayed on the basketball court all the skills that would later make him a supremely talented young trader in the highly competitive world of natural gas trading.

Mark Hogan, a coach from Mount Royal College, heard about Hunter from Chestermere's coach, who was a friend, and came to watch the young man play. He wanted a player who worked hard and wasn't afraid to battle the other team to score. He also was looking for a team leader, one who challenged his teammates not to be lazy but didn't yell and scream. He liked what he saw and recruited Hunter for the Mount Royal team.

With his grades, Hunter could have easily gone on to a four-year university, but he wanted to play college basketball, and he wasn't quite good enough for a university team. Although tall, he was thin, a bit young for his grade, and not physically strong enough to go up

THE MAN FROM CALGARY | 13

against university players. So he accepted Hogan's offer. He enrolled at Mount Royal, a two-year college in Calgary, to get a chance at college basketball. He won academic/athletic scholarships and lived at home.

Nobody had to push Brian Hunter to try his best on the college team and aim for stardom. "When he walked into the gym he was focused on what we had to do in practice," says Hogan. "And he moved as fast as he could, he worked as hard as he could, he supported his other teammates as often as he could. You never saw him walking or dawdling when he should be sprinting and running."

Attending a two-year school didn't dim his career ambitions. He knew he was headed to a four-year university. He talked about becoming a geophysicist or a doctor.

On long bus rides to games in Medicine Hat, Red Deer, and Edmonton, he dove into his books and also tutored other players who needed help in computer science or Canadian politics. Everybody liked Brian. He was friendly, laughed easily. He spoke fast, with a low voice that often faded at the end of his thoughts, as if he had already moved on to the next thought, the next action, the next thing.

Even then he had a trader's instincts: if a good opportunity came along, he was quick to sell assets he'd planned to hold.

Once he drove up to practice in an old truck he'd purchased.

"I got it for a pretty good deal," Hunter told Hogan. "I'll drive it for a long as I can."

Less than two weeks later, Hogan saw him in a different vehicle.

"What happened to your truck?" he asked.

Hunter told him he'd sold it. "I made a thousand bucks on that truck," he said.

Practicing every day, traveling out of town for games, team members became friends. They went out to eat, saw movies. They often went for chicken wings at their favorite hangout in Calgary, Coconut Joe's, along a street of college bars known as Electric Avenue. Hunter, younger than most and still living at home, didn't socialize quite as much as the others.

Once again, however, he was overshadowed on his team by a star player, Pete Knechtel, who scored a whopping 186 points that season to Hunter's 29. Knechtel transferred the next year to the University of Alberta in Edmonton, having been recommended by his college coach for the university basketball team. That season, 1993–94, Knechtel and several other star players brought the national championship title home to Edmonton.

That same year Hunter also transferred to the University of Alberta in Edmonton, to earn a four-year university degree. Unlike Knechtel, he wasn't recruited by the university basketball coaches. But Hunter still harbored some hope of playing. He tried out but, competing against Knechtel and several other high level athletes, didn't make the team.

So Hunter concentrated on his studies, earning top grades. He majored in physics. He spent time with a close friend, another physics major named Matthew Donohoe. Later, when he went to work at Amaranth, Hunter hired Donohoe to help him implement the energy trades he designed.

Paying for university was not easy and Hunter relied on scholarships and summer jobs. His dad set up a company that did concrete restoration projects, and Hunter worked for him in the summers. He also worked on rigs in the oilfields up north.

By his senior year Hunter knew what he wanted to do with his life. He certainly wasn't going to toil in the oilfields, and he dropped his talk of medicine. He decided instead to head to Wall Street. There his ease with numbers could bring him the kind of money his struggling family had only dreamed about.

He enrolled in a graduate program in mathematics at the University of Alberta. In earlier times mathematics would not have been the road to Wall Street. But as Hunter was finishing school in the mid-1990s, the world was changing for math majors.

Until the 1970s, job options for mathematicians were limited and low-paying. They could always teach or work as corporate accountants or statisticians. They could find places in government economic offices, the census bureau, the military. But that changed dramatically with a breakthrough in the pricing of financial products. Suddenly there were new opportunities.

It began in 1973 when Myron Scholes, trained in finance and a self-taught computer whiz, along with his colleague, mathematician Fischer Black, devised a formula to price stock options. When an investor bought a stock option, he was buying the right, but not the obligation, to buy or sell the stock. There were two primary types: puts (giving investors the right to sell stock at set prices within a certain period of time) and calls (the right to buy the stock at set prices). The option seller was paid a premium by the buyer, which he hoped would be his profit. The seller was betting that the buyer would not actually take advantage of, or exercise, his option.

Until that time few options were traded. Congress had banned options on agricultural commodities back in the Great Depression, unwilling to leave the country's food supply in the hands of money men. Options on stocks were allowed, but investors didn't know how to price them. Since they were tied to future stock prices, investors needed to estimate what those might be. But stock price movements seemed random, volatile, and impossible to predict. Only a few traders in a small ad hoc market in New York bought and sold options.

The basis of Scholes and Black's formula was an assumption based on physical sciences. Large numbers of random events fall into a typical pattern, and Scholes and Black determined that a stock price would do the same over a long period of time. Random events distribute themselves in a bell curve shape, with most clustered around the mean of whatever is being measured, such as speed or size. While some events fall into the extremes at both ends of the curve, higher and lower than the mean, these are rare. They occur with less and less frequency the farther away from the center of the curve you go.

Another economist, Robert Merton, gave the model a more rigorous mathematical underpinning using stochastic calculus, which is used to model random processes.

At the time, economists at the University of Chicago, led by Milton Friedman, were trying to start a stock options exchange in the city, and the mathematical formula now gave it legitimacy. "It wasn't speculation or gambling," said a lawyer for the options exchange, "it was efficient pricing."[2] Trading standard options on the exchange grew quickly. And investors started trading many more complex and varied options (known as exotic options) directly with one another in the over-the-counter market.

These efforts were aided by a handheld calculator developed by Texas Instruments that came preprogrammed with the Black-Scholes formula. But it was soon overtaken by the first IBM computer, then breakthroughs in computer hardware and software.

Salomon Brothers and Bankers Trust were the first firms to realize that successfully trading complicated financial option products and using sophisticated computer technology was indeed rocket science, requiring mathematicians and scientists. In 1977 Salomon Brothers launched a small proprietary trading unit under John Meriwether, a math teacher with an MBA. Meriwether hired mathematically oriented economists with degrees from top schools such as MIT and Harvard. He placed the geeky nerds in the middle of the firm's otherwise raucous, brash trading floor. He even brought Myron Scholes and Robert Merton on as consultants. His trading group took off in the 1980s, generating 87 percent of the company's annual profits by the early 1990s.[3]

Salomon Brothers' efforts were mimicked by Bankers Trust. In the 1980s, Bankers Trust's CEO, Charles Sanford, also hired several hundred physics and math PhDs, trained them in finance, and then sat them in front of stacks of computer terminals.[4]

Suddenly a whole new world opened to math majors—finance. Quants were increasingly sought out by Wall Street companies to oversee their burgeoning and ever more complex trading operations.

On college campuses students were buzzing about the money that could be made on Wall Street. In 1988 Bankers Trust paid Andy Krieger, a currency options trader, a $3 million bonus, double what it paid its chairman, Charlie Sanford.[5] "Every smart young mathematician and physicist said, 'I don't want to be a civil engineer, a mechanical engineer, I'm a smart guy. I want to go to Wall Street,'" former Federal Reserve chairman Paul Volcker lamented.[6]

Two years later when Salomon Brothers' quants had a phenomenal year, they worked out sweet pay deals. Bonuses ranged from $3 million to $23 million for thirtysomething math whiz kids. These payouts also overshadowed the salary of Salomon's chairman, John Gutfreund, who netted a mere $2.3 million that year.[7]

As this was happening on Wall Street, mathematicians at universities were turning their attention more and more to finance. Increasingly they were interested in how the Black-Scholes concept of pricing could be applied to other investments, such as bonds and insurance.

One pioneer in this field was a University of Alberta professor, Robert Elliott, a mathematician trained at Oxford and Cambridge, who wrote two books and numerous articles exploring this area. "In the middle of the 1980s mathematicians, particularly those working in probability theory and random processes, realized that there were interesting questions in finance," he says. "Previous to that time, I'd been looking at random processes and stochastic calculus motivated by engineering application, modeling random signals from satellites or aircraft when they are corrupted by noise. Some of the same mathematical tools can be used both in engineering applications, particularly electrical engineering, and in finance."[8]

Elliott participated in the first meeting of academics exploring these issues, held at Cornell in 1989. He kept in close contact with many of his fellow trailblazers. They began to realize that business schools were not providing their students adequate training in this new approach. Also, mathematics programs that sent graduates into finance did not offer business courses. In 1994, Carnegie Mellon set up the first U.S. program integrating business, quantitative finance, and computer technology.

Elliott decided to do the same in Alberta. As an adjunct professor in finance as well as a mathematician, he already bridged the two departments. He knew that graduates of his program would find ready employment. "Financial houses, banks, and in Alberta the energy companies, oil companies, gas companies were interested in how to price commodities contracts," he says.

Elliott's program began just as Brian Hunter was finishing up his undergraduate honors degree in physics and planned on earning a master's degree in mathematics. Elliott, looking for students with solid undergraduate courses and good grades in math among these candidates, offered Hunter a coveted slot in the new program.

Hunter met periodically with Elliott and impressed him. "He was very enthusiastic and determined. He worked hard." Students were required to write a paper to complete the course. Hunter chose commodity pricing as his topic. "He was quite enthusiastic about the project," remembers Elliott. "He wrote quite a nice little paper."

Even before he graduated, Hunter was lobbying hard for a job on Wall Street. "Mathematical finance was his entrée into the world of trading," says Elliott. "I'm sure it was really the financial rewards that attracted him. He was very enthusiastic and anxious to go to New York. From the second semester onwards he was very focused on trying to find a position, making applications to New York. He was in touch with headhunters and people who would hire in New York."

New York was where traders working for major investment banks such as Salomon Brothers earned the big bucks. Even the major Canadian banks ran much of their trading from New York.

But Hunter didn't land a job in New York at the time. Instead he settled for one in Calgary, joining the options trading desk at a major Canadian natural gas pipeline company, TransCanada Pipelines Ltd.

If the rise of quants on Wall Street played a large role in shaping the direction of Brian Hunter's life, so too did the deregulation of natural gas in North America. Legislation enacted in the 1930s to protect consumers from price gouging on a critical commodity, along with a 1954 Supreme Court decision, created a system of tight government control over the pricing, marketing, storage, and transport of natural gas. The federal government controlled what interstate pipelines paid for gas, as well as what they charged end users. Customers bought from the pipelines that transported and stored their gas, not producers.

But years of aggressive lobbying by industry and free-market advocates succeeded in gradually dismantling that oversight throughout the 1980s. In 1985 Canada lifted the regulation of the wellhead price of gas by the Canadian government and the province of Alberta. In the United States the entire regulated system was gone by the early 1990s. Producers, users, and pipeline companies were free to arrange and negotiate prices on the sale and transport of gas. Utilities could negotiate directly with producers and then pay pipeline companies to transport the gas. But pipeline companies were also free to search for cheap gas, market it to customers, and ship it.

As one of the largest natural gas pipeline systems in North America, connecting eastern Canadian cities with western Canadian gas, TransCanada saw the enormous potential of marketing gas. The more sales they could lock up, the better the prices they could negotiate with producers and the more profit that would roll in. TransCanada became the largest marketer of Canadian natural gas.

But gas prices move quickly and marketing natural gas to users can be a tricky business, especially over the course of contracts, which at TransCanada ran out to five years in the future. Prices could turn against the marketers by the time they went to buy the gas they needed to deliver. So, to protect against losses, TransCanada bought a firm that ran a trading floor, buying and selling contracts, options, and other products. TransCanada's CEO hoped it would not only limit the risks of long-term gas contracts but bring in money too.

Part of the trading involved options that were designed to reduce risk, not increase it. They helped companies such as TransCanada moderate their exposure in a number of ways.

One was to mitigate the risk of long-term sales agreements at set prices. Let's say you were worried about prices going up in several years, when you needed to deliver gas. In that case you could protect yourself by options that for a small fee allowed you, at your discretion, to buy gas contracts in the future, but at today's prices. If prices rose, the options' holder would activate them and buy paper gas contracts at the cheaper price and sell them at the higher price.

Options traders could structure their deals so the delivery dates and volumes of gas they held in paper contracts coincided with the physical gas that needed to be delivered to customers. There were many ways to trade options and they could be quite complex, with options on options. But the main idea was that the money earned from the financial options would offset any losses to marketers from actually buying and selling the physical gas.

TransCanada also allocated some money to the options traders to make a profit, without regard to what marketers were doing. Hunter's primary job was trading options, particularly a complex derivative known as swaptions. These are options to buy or sell swaps. Swaps are bets between two traders on the price of gas. At the time the most common swap involved betting on the price of gas at the main gas delivery point in the United States, the Henry Hub in Louisiana, where a dozen pipelines converged, versus the price of gas sold at another location.

TransCanada's trading floor didn't measure up to New York firms in size, freewheeling atmosphere, or huge payouts. But for Hunter, then only twenty-four and fresh out of school, it was a chance to put into play the strategies and formulas he'd learned as one of the first financial engineering graduates in Canada. Trading paper related to gas prices was still a relatively new business and there was room to create all sorts of derivatives.

He worked alongside some half dozen traders, some boisterous and loud, compared to the rather reserved Hunter. Although confident, Hunter wasn't cocky; he didn't "exude an aura that I'm smarter than all of you people by any stretch," says a former colleague. The options traders socialized after work and were a close-knit group. Away from the office, Hunter played pickup basketball with his colleagues. He was friendly with Shane Lee, then a physical gas trader. Hunter later brought Lee into his energy group at Amaranth, and Lee became a close confidant.

Hunter quickly became the go-to man, along with only one or two others, for structuring innovative derivatives sought by some of the firm's clients—primarily large users of natural gas.

At informal group meetings on the trading floor, Hunter won

praise for the design of his trades. His boss, Greg Shea, the head of the options group, lauded Hunter as one of the smartest guys in the industry, an innovative thinker. Fellow traders say Shea told them that the young Hunter possessed the potential to one day become the firm's CEO.

With deregulation transforming the gas industry, it was a heady time to be in the business. Natural gas prices moved rapidly, often dramatically. One day the options traders would be up a million, the next down two. Earnings whipsawed. "Some months they made money, some months they lost money. That could even translate into some quarters they made money, some quarters they lost money," says a former senior trading executive. But "if you added it all up, they were always ahead, they made more than they lost." He estimated they earned the firm tens of millions of dollars.[9]

The options group negotiated many trades with the two largest gas trading firms at the time: Enron, the largest U.S. pipeline company, and El Paso Corporation, another major pipeline firm. In comparison, TransCanada's trading was relatively small-scale. Its traders were somewhat wary of the power wielded by the big firms and their lead traders, Enron's John Arnold and El Paso's Bo Collins, who traded hundreds of millions of dollars. "John Arnold and Bo Collins were good traders," acknowledges a former TransCanada executive, "but they certainly were willing to take massive positions and both of them could really run the NYMEX around a bit."

TransCanada was no Enron—it always made most of its money as a utility and a transporter of natural gas. It never relied on its trading operations for profit, as Enron later did. But it did find marketing and trading natural gas lucrative in the mid-1990s.

This became more difficult as the number of merchant energy companies competing grew. In a good year, its trading operation earned TransCanada $50 million—but for that it needed to buy and sell $10 billion worth of natural gas.[10]

Hal Kvisle was hired by the firm in 1999 to run the nonpipeline side of the company, including trading and marketing, and to divest certain assets to reduce the firm's debt.

Kvisle grew increasingly wary of trading and marketing. Large producers were squeezing the firm on contract prices, hurting its marketing revenues. A marketer mispriced a huge deal; another suffered large losses, say former employees.

And the options group, which bet heavily that gas prices would fall that winter, lost millions of dollars in December when an unexpected cold spell shot gas prices up. Although the firm made back much of these losses the following month when warmer weather lowered prices, the volatility showed just how risky energy trading was.

"We were exposing ourselves to a lot of risky business," Kvisle later explained. "There was just no money to be made. We were buying and selling $10 billion a year worth of natural gas and other products and in a good year we might make $50 million. And in a bad year, the losses were unlimited."[11] After Enron's demise he admitted that "we were always baffled by how some people like Enron were able to make such highly profitable margins on a business that we found painfully unattractive."[12]

Kvisle was promoted to CEO of TransCanada in May 2001, but had already convinced the board to sell the trading and marketing business. The firm's shareholders wanted steady, consistent earnings with attractive dividends, not volatile profits and losses. "They were trying to build credibility back with the investors," says a former TransCanada executive. "They closed the trading shop down because of the volatility in earnings."[13]

It took some months to make it happen. Ironically, TransCanada's marketing and trading units were sold to Mirant Corporation the day before Enron filed for bankruptcy in December.

But even before TransCanada's board had made the decision to leave the business, Hunter had decided to leave the firm. With its small-time trading operation, TransCanada was merely a way station for him to bigger and better things. He never gave up plans to join a major trading firm in New York and had been looking for openings.

Few others from TransCanada contemplated such a radical change in lifestyle, preferring to remain in Alberta. "I don't think anyone else there had an appetite for going to the big city, to be honest with you," says a former TransCanada trader, who like many traders still in the business did not want to speak on the record for fear of offending someone in the relatively small world of commodity trading.

In early 2001 Hunter flew down to New York for an interview with Deutsche Bank, which had a large trading operation in lower Manhattan. Soon after, he was offered a job as vice president in the bank's global commodities markets division trading natural gas. His TransCanada buddies "remember him being pretty excited and stoked to go."

Despite his eagerness to get to New York, the move from Calgary was a dramatic change for Hunter and especially his new wife, Carrie Wivcharuk, a pretty, smart, blond Canadian who had grown up in the farming country of Saskatchewan, far enough north to sometimes see the aurora borealis. Her father was a surveyor of the remote forests, lakes, towns, and Indian lands there. She was close with her parents, who still lived there, and her two siblings, who lived elsewhere in Canada.

Calgary was still a relatively small city, with just over a million people. The snowcapped Canadian Rockies peeked out behind its few skyscrapers. Its quiet, slow pace was a far cry from the noise, grit, and frenetic tempo of Manhattan. The city fathers perpetuated its rugged frontier image. The city flag featured a cowboy hat, and politicians gave the hats out to visiting dignitaries. The fifty-two-story twin Bankers Hall office towers downtown sported distinctive crowns in the shape of cowboy hats. And every July the entire city shut down for more than a week of rodeos, chuck wagon races, and other events that were part of the Calgary Stampede.

Hunter and his wife never really adjusted to life in New York. Over the two and a half years he worked at Deutsche Bank they never grew comfortable with the city. "We didn't like the culture," Hunter told a reporter.[14] They planned on returning to Calgary as soon as feasible. Even while living in the New York area they bought land on the outskirts of Calgary, high on a ridge where a cluster of new mansions were going up on land recently carved from ranches and farms. Moose, deer, coyotes, and foxes still roamed freely. They planned to build a stone-and-wood home with majestic views of the massive mountains.

Undoubtedly the Hunters' move to New York was made even more wrenching because it coincided with the most traumatic time in the city's history. Four months after they arrived, the World Trade Center was hit by planes and collapsed. Deutsche Bank was located across the street from the twin towers and the bank's building was badly damaged. The employees abandoned the building and never went back to it.

It was a difficult move to a city in turmoil, but Deutsche Bank itself was a tremendous career opportunity for an ambitious, eager trader such as Hunter. It was in the process of a major transformation and its aggressive culture, hunger for profit, and tolerance for risk were a far cry from the stodgy gas pipeline company where he had worked.

Commercial banks, with Deutsche Bank in the lead, were rushing to expand trading, sell securities, and engage in other activities that had been reserved for Wall Street investment banks. Congress had recently repealed the Depression-era Glass-Steagall Act of 1933, which had separated investment banks from commercial institutions. Under that law commercial banks had provided a safe haven for depositors and facilitated corporate growth and business by generating loans. Investment banks were the Wall Street players, underwriting corporate securities, facilitating mergers and takeovers, trading derivatives.

But staid commercial banks increasingly wanted in on the more lucrative action of their investment banking colleagues. Building companies and providing security for depositors did not generate huge profits. So commercial banks exploited loopholes in the law to get in on the securities business. They also pressed for Glass-Steagall's repeal, succeeding in 1999.

Deutsche Bank inked a deal that year to buy Bankers Trust, creating the world's largest financial services company, with $850 billion in assets, giving the German bank a major U.S. presence. Bankers

Trust, with its quant-dominated trading floor, had been aggressive in finding ways around Glass-Steagall, trading bonds, currencies, and securitized loans. A few years before the deal with Deutsche Bank, Bankers Trust was forced to settle lawsuits after tapes of executives boasting they made money off clients who didn't understand these complex trades were made public. They bragged that a key aspect of their success was the "R.O.F.," or "rip-off factor."

The following year, as commercial banks began legally trading financial derivatives, Congress passed a law exempting these derivatives from oversight. Trading mushroomed. Deutsche Bank's aggressive traders were in the vanguard.

One was Boaz Weinstein, who helped jump-start credit default swap trading. When Hunter arrived at Deutsche Bank in 2001, Weinstein, then just twenty-seven, was promoted to managing director, the youngest in the bank's history. Weinstein loved to gamble, and he joined members of MIT's secretive blackjack team (made famous by the book *Bringing Down the House*) on a number of their trips to Las Vegas. The traders who worked for him ran a weekly poker game off Deutsche Bank's trading floor.[15] Weinstein incessantly promoted credit default swaps throughout Wall Street but lost $1.8 billion in 2008 when his swaps couldn't protect him from losses on his corporate bonds.[16]

Deutsche Bank was also a major player on both sides of the mortgage securities business. By 2007 it owned mortgage derivatives with a face value of $128 billion. At the same time it was shorting billions of dollars' worth of other mortgage securities.[17]

Hunter's arrival coincided with Deutsche Bank's push to become a major force in commodity trading. At the time there were about fifty people working on its commodities trading floor, a handful in natural gas. In 2001 the bank's worldwide commodities business generated $86 million in revenue.

The following year it grew to $140 million. In early 2002 Deutsche Bank brought in a new global head of commodities, Kerim Derhalli, who embarked on a hiring spree. The bank was very creative in devising new hybrid investment vehicles. These included combining bonds and commodities, connecting gold with credit derivatives. One innovative product for clients connected gold prices, oil prices, the three-month European interbank rate, and the three-month Eurodollar rate.[18]

Derhalli quickly saw an opportunity to further expand the bank's derivatives trading when Enron and the other merchant energy companies collapsed. These companies had provided options and swaps that helped firms, such as airline and trucking companies, protect themselves from wide fuel price swings. They had also helped small businesses, hospitals, and schools manage their heating expenses. Deutsche Bank sought to fill this void. It created new commodity investments and expanded its client base. And it did so aggressively.[19]

"It was basically a second-tier bank energy trading group, and the first tier was Goldman Sachs and Morgan Stanley," explains a former employee. "It was a second-tier bank trying to emulate the first tier. They had a heavy desire to win business at all costs."

Over his first seven months on the job, Hunter took credit for $17 million in profits, one-fifth of the total earned that year by the bank's worldwide commodities business. His bonus for the seven and a half months he was at the bank in 2001 was $330,000. With deferred compensation and salary included, he earned $800,000.[20]

But Hunter was dissatisfied by this payout. He believed he had been promised a bonus of 5 to 10 percent of whatever profits he generated, and therefore Deutsche Bank owed him between $850,000 and $1.7 million. His Deutsche Bank bosses tried to assuage his concerns. They assured him he was "part of a small group of 'star' employees at his level who are paid between $3 million and $5 million per year because they are 'really, really good,'" Hunter later said.[21]

Throughout 2002, Deutsche Bank's commodity business grew dramatically. And the more it grew, the more pressure was placed on Hunter to keep performing. "He was told to take more risk, rather than reduce his risk," says a former colleague.[22]

He was becoming a top performer on the trading floor. The natural gas desk earned $76 million, more than half the total Deutsche

Bank earned from commodity trading. Hunter generated the vast majority of that—$52 million. He was showered with accolades. In his year-end evaluation executives praised him for his "ability to generate customer business through original trade ideas." His boss extolled him for having "a standout year" and lauded him as "our standout performer in commodities."

But again, although the natural gas traders earned more than half the total revenue generated by commodities trading, Hunter was told he would receive only $1.6 million. He was angry. Based on promises he said were made to him, he believed the bank owed him between $2.5 million and $4.5 million. He complained vociferously in a telephone call with the head of over-the-counter derivatives trading.

He didn't win any increase in that payout. But just before he was given the money in February, the head of commodities told Hunter that he had indeed been lowballed on his bonus, given his outstanding performance. He was told this would be corrected in future years when his profits weren't so good.[23]

That same month Hunter was promoted. He became director of global markets—commodities, officially taking charge of the natural gas trading desk. Two natural gas traders now reported to him.

From time to time he returned to Calgary to visit family and friends and for the annual Stampede. Brokers were starting to throw money at him to get his business, and he was enjoying it. Traders from his TransCanada days would bump into him and noticed he "now had more of a taste for $400 bottles of wine than $40 bottles," according to one.[24]

Hunter continued his aggressive trading. That month, February, 2003, he was on the winning side. His trades earned $50 million when prices suddenly spiked dramatically. He was lucky that time. He would soon learn that things could easily go the other way for him.

"Were there signs then that he was an aggressive risk taker? Yes," asks a trader who knew him at Deutsche Bank. "Were there signs that he was pushing the envelope? Yes."

As his trading success grew, so did his confidence. "Hunter's a supremely confident person with a great grasp of natural gas pipelines and mathematics," explains a former bank colleague. "He can easily talk circles around a lot of people when it comes to derivative pricing. But people that have this master-of-the-universe mentality, they really lose commonsense grounding."

A few months later, a new boss at Deutsche Bank came into the picture: Kevin Rogers, a British banker based in Deutsche Bank's London office. About ten years older than Hunter, he was newly elevated to global head of energy trading and became Hunter's supervisor. From the beginning there was a clash.

It was more than just a difference in personalities. While Hunter was all too eager to trade aggressively, Rogers was more cautious. Hunter was willing to double losing bets in hopes of recouping losses. Rogers quickly pulled the plug on trades to contain losses. And while Hunter couldn't be bothered with exacting detailed records of his fast and furious trading, Rogers wanted a careful accounting of what his traders were doing.

Kevin Rogers "is very structured, very rigorous" about trading, says a former colleague who knew them both. "He's a simple quant trader-slash-manager. But he can be very academic and rigorous. When he has a theory, a view, he's outspoken. He's the kind of guy that would say something and cite a passage from the *Economist* or *Barron's* or the *Financial Times* to back it up. That would contrast with Brian's disposition, which is more laid-back and cerebral. He kind of feigns indifference."

Rogers wanted rigorous and careful reporting of trades. But he was not getting that type of accounting from Hunter. Hunter was "not being as careful about trade reconciliation, the operational side of the business," says a former colleague.

Shortly after taking over energy trading, Rogers paid a visit to New York. He took his team to dinner. When he came to the office the next day he asked Hunter to come into a corner office off the trading room. The company was pleased with the profits Hunter was bringing in, he said. But he also expressed concern about reports of "careless behavior" by Hunter that had made their way across the

Atlantic. Deutsche Bank back-office administrative staff complained to Rogers that Hunter was often late with many procedural tasks. Staff also reported that record keeping for many trades needed revision because Hunter's reports were incorrect.

He was troubled, Rogers said, about the "perception of sloppiness," about Hunter's lack of care detailing his trades. He warned Hunter he "wanted that perception to go away."[25]

Hunter indicated things would change. But, he said, he needed help; he was short-staffed. Rogers agreed and within a few weeks hired a support staffer to book trades for Hunter and to do other administrative work.

Despite these concerns, however, Deutsche Bank executives wanted Hunter "to continue to make as much money as he had been doing because it was good for their bonuses as well as Brian's," explains another former Deutsche Bank trader.[26] And Brian delivered. From January to November 2003, his team earned $76 million.[27]

In late November, however, Kevin Rogers again found himself with reason for concern about Hunter. Rogers didn't receive timely assessments of Hunter's October trading results. Usually these numbers were available a week after the end of the month. He asked the division that monitored trader performance and risk taking to give him the October trading report as soon as possible.[28]

Back then at Deutsche Bank, traders compiled monthly reports on the value of their holdings in the marketplace, and the reports were reviewed internally.

It was easy to determine the value of products traded on the New York Mercantile Exchange, since the prices were public. But for the trades negotiated directly between traders, that was not the case. Those products were lightly traded and, because not many people wanted to buy or sell them, it was more difficult to determine their worth. Deutsche Bank, like other firms at the time, relied on its own traders' calculations. For complex or long-term arrangements, traders called their counterparts to determine current market pricing. Holdings were generally put near the middle of what sellers were asking and buyers were offering to pay. Sometimes it was difficult to get several prices if there weren't many interested traders. It wasn't an exact science. But one thing was clear: traders were expected to approach the job honestly and not skew the value of their holdings in their favor. The point of all this was to allow banks to discern how much they lost or gained. Since having a trader estimate the worth of his own holdings invites abuse, most firms have since changed that.

Rogers finally received the October assessment on December 2. As he leafed through it, he realized Hunter's estimation of his profits was $7 million more than the reviewers figured them to be. Then on December 4 he was also told that Hunter's November trading results were $18 million higher than the reviewers' estimate.

Realizing there was a problem, Rogers called Hunter from his London office. The discrepancies, he told him, were "very serious . . . $7 million was bad, $18 million is clearly a lot worse." He demanded evidence from Hunter to support his numbers. Hunter responded, Rogers said, by telling him that his own trading assessment was "bang on market." Hunter delivered some data to support his price assessment and Rogers recalculated the November trading. Rogers believed Hunter's numbers were still at least $10 million off.

These favorable trade marks were not an accident, concluded Rogers. In the case of one type of option, Hunter valued his trades at the most favorable level in thirty-two out of thirty-six months for which he had purchased or sold positions. The odds of that happening randomly were several million to one, Rogers later said.[29]

Then an even more critical problem erupted. On Friday, December 5, an early winter storm ripped through the East Coast. Fierce winds gusting to fifty miles per hour and heavy snow hit the Northeast. Temperatures plunged well below normal, and New England meteorologists termed the storm a "once-in-50-years" event.[30]

Hunter was in a vulnerable position. Early November had been warm and natural gas supplies in storage were higher than the previous year. Hunter, along with many other traders, was shorting contracts on the New York Mercantile Exchange. Each contract they sold represented 10,000 MMBtu of natural gas (*MMBtu* stands for 1 million British thermal units). The contracts were an agreement to deliver this gas at the agreed price at a certain location on a certain day. Traders either delivered the gas on that date or closed out their positions by buying equivalent contracts. Hunter also traded on the other main commodity exchange, the electronic IntercontinentalExchange (ICE), which was similar to NYMEX except that there was never the obligation to actually deliver gas with ICE holdings, as positions always closed out with cash only.

As a bank trader, Hunter never intended to take possession of the gas, he didn't need to use it, couldn't store it. So no matter which exchange he traded on, he always closed his positions financially. That fall he was hoping prices would be lower by the time he was ready to do so.

But by Thanksgiving only the temperature was falling, and it was sending gas contract prices up. That week they were up as much as 28 percent. Many traders viewed the price rise as an anomaly and believed prices would soon drop.[31] They added to their short positions.[32]

But the weather worsened significantly, and when the December 5 storm hit, the price of natural gas soared further. Hunter was seriously hurt.

Friday morning, December 5, Kevin Rogers made an urgent call to Hunter. He insisted that "the positions had to be reduced, to stop any further bleeding." It was untenable to hope that prices would swing back in his favor, Rogers told his young trader.

Hunter laughed off Rogers' insistence that he sell, Rogers said later, and talked about increasing his investments rather than liquidating them.

"We're going to double up and make all the money back," Rogers recalls Hunter saying.

Rogers was horrified.

"Absolutely not," he replied.[33]

Hunter didn't double up. But Rogers, who was in London, wasn't sure what Hunter, who was in New York, was up to. He insisted Hunter provide a detailed rundown on the value of his holdings that evening.

Hunter didn't deliver. Instead, he left the office about 3:30 p.m., after the NYMEX closed, and headed to Calgary. It was a grand-parent's ninety-second birthday and he had already delayed his departure a day.

Rogers wasn't told in advance about the planned trip. When he found out Hunter had left the country in the middle of a major market disruption, he was stunned.

Hunter could technically trade and work out of Deutsche Bank's Calgary office on Monday, Rogers knew, but no one would be monitoring his activities. And Rogers worried that Hunter could not, from Calgary, interact easily and quickly with Deutsche Bank salespeople or clients demanding to know what was happening. He believed Hunter would be much better able to deal with his portfolio problems from New York.

On Monday, December 8, as natural gas prices continued to soar, Deutsche Bank's energy holdings lost $21 million.

There didn't seem to be an end in sight. By then several private weather forecasting services were warning, in contrast to predictions by the National Weather Service, that some regions of the country were likely to be colder than normal for the rest of the month.

As prices climbed, other traders who were similarly positioned were also in trouble. That included John Arnold, then running his own energy hedge fund, Centaurus Advisors LLC. He was one of the largest traders on NYMEX.[34] Hunter was hearing that Arnold was actually contributing to the gas price hike because he had shorted heavily and needed to buy significant amounts of gas to close out his losing positions.

An angry Rogers demanded that Hunter fly to London for a "serious conversation." Most immediately, they had to curb losses. But Rogers also accused Hunter of deliberately misrepresenting the value of his investments. He made clear they would discuss why Hunter hadn't corrected this despite orders to do so. And he wanted to get answers as to why Hunter, in the middle of the crisis, had left New York to head home to Calgary, and why he was still there.

Worried by Rogers' tone, Hunter asked his boss if he was being asked to "pack his bags." Rogers said he wasn't, but Hunter would be expected to explain his actions.[35]

Hunter reduced his holdings a bit that Monday. But not enough.

With losses continuing, Rogers decided it would take too long for Hunter to fly from Calgary to London. Instead, the next day, Rogers flew to New York, where he told Hunter to meet him.

During the four trading days, between December 4 and December 9, the bank's natural gas desk lost $60 million, said Rogers.[36] Deutsche Bank executives believed Hunter had been too slow to unwind his positions when prices started climbing, and they wanted Rogers in his face.

By December 10, Rogers was sitting four or five seats to Hunter's right on the New York trading desk. They talked throughout the day about what was happening in the market. Rogers watched what Hunter was buying and selling and discussed strategy to stem losses.

By the next day, Thursday, December 11, Deutsche Bank's holdings had been significantly repositioned. On Friday, when gas prices went up another 12 percent, the bank actually made money. Rogers stayed in New York until just before Christmas to untangle the mess.

In the end the bank's losses were significant—$53 million between the end of November and December 12—because of natural gas price hikes in December and the revaluation of Brian's November gains.[37] Hunter argued his unit had still eked out a profit in gas trading for the year, in the range of $26 million, but to no avail.[38]

The bank came down hard on its trader. At the end of January, Hunter was told that "due to his lack of integrity and immaturity," as Rogers put it, he was not getting any bonus. Jim Turley, then in charge of the bank's foreign exchange trading, told him the zero bonus decision was the result of "his lack of professionalism, attitude and lack of maturity."[39]

Hunter was demoted from head of natural gas trading to research analyst. Suddenly he no longer reported to the head of global energy trading. Rather, his boss was a newly hired trader. Even more demeaning, Hunter was stripped of his trading authority. Senior executives feared he couldn't be trusted to "do the right thing for the bank" and would not "act in a mature and professional manner," according to Rogers.[40]

Hunter was physically moved off the trading desk, isolated from its activities, and kept out of discussions with clients he previously had dealt with daily. He was mortified. "It was one of the low points in my life," he later testified in a lawsuit against Deutsche Bank he filed soon after leaving. In it he argued the bank had profited that year from his trading and therefore he deserved a bonus. He claimed Deutsche Bank owed him for his inadequate compensation the year before. Hunter also blamed his inability to quickly trade out of his positions on problems with the bank's electronic system for monitoring and analyzing risk. He faulted accounting errors made by a backlogged back office. During depositions by bank officials, his lawyer implied that Hunter had been pressured to mismark trades in order to please clients.[41]

Hunter told the court, "I was humiliated, it was embarrassing. My wife and I were very distressed over the situation and were very worried about my career in the future. You lose a little bit of self-confidence any time you go through a situation where you feel like you are forced out of a business that you created and built and which was one of the best in the world."[42]

Hunter again started looking for a job, giving his resume to headhunters to circulate. Although he may have been embarrassed and angry over what had happened at the bank, it was a good time for Hunter to be back in the job market. The hedge fund industry was burgeoning, and firms saw an opportunity to expand into energy trading.

Hunter had worked for a gas company that was starting to speculate on energy prices and at a major bank that was dramatically expanding its trading operations. Now he was quickly scooped up by a hedge fund eager to grow its commodity trading, Amaranth.

But executives at Deutsche Bank did not quickly forget him. On the day news of Amaranth's demise became public some two and a half years later, they looked at one another knowingly. Using a reference to cricket players practicing before a game, London-based commodities head Kerim Derhalli voiced what they were all thinking: "He was merely playing in the nets when he was here."[43]

LONE STAR GAMBLER

Back in Enron's heyday, when its natural gas traders could make—
and lose—half a billion dollars a day for the company, an important visitor might find himself directed to pay attention to
one man in particular on the floor of Enron's vast Houston trading
room. The object of this attention was a slightly built, pleasant-
looking young guy with brown hair, a rectangular face, and deep-set
eyes, dressed in blue jeans and bearing a faint resemblance to a
young Tom Hanks. He sat inconspicuously in a long row of other
young traders in front of an equally long array of computer monitors. He might not at first glance have seemed worthy of special attention.

But this was John Arnold, who daily traded well over $1 billion
worth of natural gas futures contracts.[1] And in 2001 he earned his
company more than half a billion dollars.

By 1998, when Brian Hunter was still in school working on his
thesis on options trading, John Arnold—although only three months
older—was already established as one of the most successful natural
gas traders at Enron, the company that virtually invented natural gas
trading.

Arnold, like Hunter, was born in 1974, but grew up in a middle-
class household in Dallas. His father, who died when John Arnold
was a teenager, was a lawyer and his mother an accountant. He had a
brother, two years older, who followed him to Enron and worked on
coal projects. A precocious teenager, Arnold read the *Wall Street Journal* and was fascinated by the quants on Salomon Brothers' trading

floor led by John Meriwether, particularly the amount of money they traded and earned.[2]

He set his sights on a business career and, after graduating from high school in 1992, enrolled at Vanderbilt University in Tennessee. He decided on a dual course of study, mathematics and economics.

Admiring Salomon's traders and aware of the growing importance of math in finance, Arnold wanted a grounding in mathematics. The Vanderbilt program offered basic courses in calculus and differential equations. Like Brian Hunter, Arnold could do complicated equations in his head.

But he was not as focused on math and science as Hunter. His real interest was in understanding how markets work, how supply and demand and other economic inputs affect an industry. The economics curriculum at Vanderbilt provided that type of fundamental education. While there were courses in business, the economics program focused on how economies and industries function. It was designed to stimulate broad thinking, not provide specific professional training.

He impressed his professors as smart and independent, standing out from his peers. In his junior year he was offered a coveted slot in the economics honors program. Out of the two hundred or so economics majors, the faculty chose only a handful of students, focusing on those considered best able to complete a high-quality research project on their own.

Vanderbilt also encouraged collaborative projects between students and teachers. The summer before his senior year Arnold hoped to complete a project with his honors thesis advisor, Professor James Foster. He was intrigued by Foster's freshman seminar, a class focusing on market fundamentals in business. He wanted to do more in-depth research on several industries, including airlines, automobiles, and oil, analyzing key buyers and sellers and the factors that affected prices.

Arnold was preparing for a business career. Understanding what drives an industry would help him in that, he told Foster. So too would the master's in business administration he intended to earn, he said.

But the summer project never happened because the university didn't come through with funding. Arnold soon turned his attention to his senior thesis. Professor John Siegfried, who oversaw the honors program, encouraged research into real-world phenomena and suggested a project in one of his own specialties, sports economics. Payroll caps on sports teams was a controversial issue at the time. What about analyzing how pay caps affect players and owners? Was there a point at which salaries stabilized, where both players and owners were satisfied?

Arnold's paper "was a very good one," Siegfried remembers. An economics journal might even have published it if it had incorporated more sophisticated mathematical analysis. "What he used was graphical analysis that is typical of an undergraduate, what we call an intermediate microeconomics course, as opposed to the mathematics that you would use if it were a graduate course."

His professors recall his smarts a decade and a half later. He stood out even among the select half dozen or so students in the honors program. Professor Foster, his thesis advisor, remarked on Arnold's ability to independently go off and complete the paper. "He was the type of student you just love to have, who can understand things quickly, gets the job done, and really understands what he's talking about."

While many students took a parochial view of U.S. economic developments, Professor Stephen Buckles remembers Arnold's interest in how they affected the rest of the world. It was Buckles' first year teaching at Vanderbilt, and Arnold, a senior, was one of about a dozen students in his spring seminar. The class explored economic issues in the news. Should taxes be raised or lowered? What were the priorities for federal spending? Arnold tried to take a broader view, says Buckles. "He was very aware of international kinds of issues and how economies interacted with one another. He would ask questions like, 'How does this particular policy affect China or Europe?'"

His innate abilities were not the only reason Arnold seemed different from his peers. Vanderbilt attracted many smart, competitive undergraduates to its economics program, students professors remember as forceful and assertive. But Arnold was quiet and mild-mannered, thoughtful and reserved. Neither his personality nor his physique—he was a few inches shy of six feet—was imposing. He did not fit the image of the hard-driving Wall Street trader he would become. "This doesn't sound the way I intend it," says Siegfried, "but I never would have guessed that he would have been so successful. He's too nice a guy. He didn't seem pushy, aggressive."

Arnold was in a hurry to complete his undergraduate work and sped through the Vanderbilt curriculum, completing coursework and thesis in three years and graduating with honors. It was time to move on. He told people he intended to get a business degree. But he soon changed his mind when Enron came to town.

Working for Enron was an attractive prospect for ambitious students. By 1995 its reputation as an innovative company was growing. It was hugely profitable, raking in hundreds of millions of dollars annually. Its pay scale was so lavish that on bonus day, luxury car dealers promoted their Mercedes, BMWs, Aston Martins, and Alfa Romeos around Enron headquarters.[3]

It was quick to take advantage of gas and electricity deregulation, aggressively marketing to users and searching out deals for cheap supplies. It was jump-starting a whole new area of financial trading—natural gas. Perhaps most enticing to young college graduates, Enron had a reputation for letting them oversee huge portfolios and operate major projects. Its trading activity was growing and young hires took on a lot of responsibility.

Enron recruiters came to the Vanderbilt campus. They were focusing at the time on leading southern schools; their Ivy League push came a few years later. Enron interviewers sought out the top-tier students—that was a given. But they weren't only looking for smarts. "Of course everyone had to have the type of personality that they felt would fit well with the Enron culture," says Kristin Gandy-Horn, a former Enron recruiter at Vanderbilt's graduate school. And what was that? "Someone who was very ambitious, a fast learner, a go-getter. Able to speak in public forums. Enron was a very cut-throat organization and they didn't want to hire people that wouldn't be able to hold their own."[4]

Arnold's low-key demeanor didn't fit what the recruiters sought. Still, his grades, intelligence, and determination won him a spot in the interview rounds. The firm flew him to Houston, where, after a series of interviews, he was hired into the associates and analysts program. Years later, when Arnold was the standout trader at Enron, Greg Whalley, who oversaw the trading operation, would laugh and tell people that Arnold had struggled to get hired by Enron.[5]

Getting into Enron was only half the battle. Once on the job, there was stiff competition among the new hires to stay there. The associates and analysts program involved six-month job rotations for two years. Every six months employees needed to find, interview for, and be hired for another job internally. If they didn't find one after a couple of months, they were ousted. Finding a job usually involved socializing, meeting people, and selling oneself. There were happy hours for the associates, where senior-level people came and informally interviewed candidates for open positions in their group. There was a directory that listed everyone in the program, their background, and their current position. "It was truly a networking type of organization," says Gandy-Horn. "It was what you knew and who you knew that got you a job."

In addition to fostering a tough competitive environment, this process also gave new hires a feel for different parts of the company. Despite their lack of experience, they plunged right into trading, analysis, or marketing, because Enron taught its young recruits on the job.[6] New employees learned the business as they went, and their mentors were only slightly more seasoned, just a few years older.

Arnold cut his teeth working on Enron's crude oil trading desk, building option-pricing models for oil and gasoline. It was the first time he was exposed to options trading. Using his math skills, he learned how to write models for the options. He also conducted studies, such as one that looked at whether price volatility over a weekend was equivalent to price volatility over one, two, or three weekdays.

When it was time to rotate jobs, Arnold found one as an assistant basis trader on the Texas natural gas desk. It meant actually trading physical gas and playing off price differences between gas delivered at the Houston ship channel and that at the Henry Hub in Louisiana, which was the pricing point for NYMEX futures contracts. As he would later tell it, he was "pretty much" thrown onto the desk and told to trade. "I think I had the benefit of sitting around a lot of smart people, and you ask questions," he recalled.[7]

As his impressive gifts as a trader became apparent, though, Arnold climbed rapidly up Enron's trading hierarchy. In less than a year, at age twenty-two, he headed the Texas natural gas desk.

In February or March 1997 he moved into the area he would come to dominate, natural gas financial trading. It's where he would be for the remainder of his Enron career. And it would become a major revenue source for the company.

It was a propitious place for Arnold to find himself. Enron was writing the book on natural gas trading, helping to create a business that didn't exist before. Arnold arrived as the size and type of financial gas trading Enron did grew dramatically. And soon after he became a financial gas trader, Enron pioneered the first significant computer-based commodity trading operation.

Enron was created in 1985 when two smaller pipeline companies merged. Soon after, it was operating coast to coast, border to border. Today it is primarily remembered as the emblem of corporate greed and accounting fraud, and for its electricity traders who laughed and joked as they shut down California power supplies. But less well known is its role in creating the highly speculative world of natural gas derivatives trading.

For decades producers sold gas to pipelines at government-set rates, and pipelines in turn sold gas, also at government-controlled prices, to their customers, largely utilities, businesses, factories, and local distribution companies (often utilities) who delivered to homes. Deregulation of wellhead gas prices began in 1978, and gas producers started negotiating long-term contracts with pipelines for much of their product. In the early 1980s a marketplace for sale of excess gas began. This was known as the spot market. Every month, during what was termed bid week, producers and pipelines sold monthly supplies of available gas to wholesale buyers. Traders screamed their deals over the phone to buyers and gas flowed through pipelines.

Ken Lay, then heading a company that supplied most of the gas to the New York–New Jersey area, helped develop the spot market. Lay, who in 1984 took over Houston Natural Gas, teamed up with five other pipeline companies and an investment bank to lay the basis for a national spot market. By the next year, after more than doubling his firm's pipeline network, he merged it with an even bigger company, forming Enron.[8]

Lay, soon Enron's CEO, was one of the most vociferous proponents of deregulation, which was moving forward rapidly by the mid-1980s as agency rules and legislation unshackled the industry.[9] Pipelines negotiated with customers to transport gas. They sold gas to utilities and businesses.

Initially, Enron sold a month's or several months' supply of gas to utilities and other customers. It purchased most of the gas it needed in the spot market. By the late 1980s Enron considered negotiating longer-term deals, two- to ten-year contracts. Enron executives decided to test customer interest, offering its first longer-term contracts over a three-week period in 1989. Interest was high.[10]

But there were problems. Longer-term contracts weren't always possible for both sides of a transaction. When a producer had gas available, there weren't always buyers. And when there were buyers interested, there wasn't always gas available. Coordinating this was difficult. Market prices could also fluctuate wildly. If Enron had contracts to sell gas at low prices and then needed to go into the spot market when gas prices were high, it could be hurt.

The driving force behind Enron's creation of gas trading was Jeff Skilling. As a McKinsey consultant to Enron, Skilling created its "gas bank." Enron would contract to get gas from producers and deposit it in the bank. Customers would contract to buy the gas they needed from this bank. But there were snafus and Lay pressed Skilling to go to work directly for Enron in 1990 to run the bank.

Skilling worked out the kinks in getting producers and consumers to sign long-term arrangements for gas. It was a complex business. There were many places to deliver the gas and prices varied in each. Power plants wanted to be assured of long-term supplies. Needs of industrial users varied; utilities wanted seasonal gas. There were many pricing and supply risks. Skilling wanted the financial trading tools used in the oil industry and other commodities that could mitigate these risks.

Under Skilling's direction, Enron traders started using options and other derivatives to reduce the risk of gas sales and transportation. Financial trading was a means to reduce the risk in the physical business.

By the spring of 1990 there was enough interest in trading gas contracts among other energy companies and financial firms to prompt the New York Mercantile Exchange to start trading natural gas contracts. They were simple contracts, representing a certain amount of gas, priced for delivery in the future at the central pipeline nexus in Louisiana, the Henry Hub.

But Enron's budding trading desk was already ahead of the exchange. That year it offered contracts priced for delivery at four other hubs along Enron's pipeline system. Enron traders devised other types of contracts too, such as one reserving space on pipelines. They traded options on the NYMEX futures contracts.

Enron wrote the first major gas swap in 1989, a deal with a Louisiana aluminum producer that wanted to pay a fixed price for gas. The firm and Enron agreed on a set price but the Louisiana firm actually bought its gas locally at market prices. Enron reimbursed the company if market prices were higher than the agreed price. In effect Enron functioned as an insurer for the aluminum company, providing protection against sudden huge price hikes.

These early swaps often took weeks to negotiate. And there were any number of ways they could be structured. Over time they got quite complex. Enron also traded options on the swaps.

Enron traders were the key link between marketers (those who negotiated gas sales to distributors, utilities, and industrial users) and the deal makers (those who paid producers for long-term supplies). What really jump-started Enron's trading to new levels was an enormous sale Enron concluded in 1992 to supply gas to a power plant in upstate New York over twenty years, a deal worth about $4 billion. To make it actually work, Enron traders had to round up gas supply contracts for two decades at the right price.[11]

As Enron concluded more and more sales, its trading activity grew. By 1992 it was the largest marketer of gas in North America. Its trading and finance operations grew from 144 people in 1990 to 548 only two years later, and it generated 12 percent of the company's earnings.[12]

One issue the traders had to resolve was how to calculate gas prices several years out. For deals shorter than eighteen months, Enron traders could rely on NYMEX futures contracts, where pricing was determined in an open arena. But for longer-term deals, its traders operated without price precedents to guide them. Nobody knew what pricing ten or fifteen years out should be because prices had so recently been set by the government. So traders argued with the marketers and producers about estimates of future pricing and made their best guesses. "It was definitely loosey-goosey," says a former Enron trader.

"In an environment that was really at the frontier, there were no precedents, no rules or regulations," says a former Enron energy analyst. "Everyone was miles behind the people that were creating this new industry. There was so much money to be had and it was all fair game."[13]

While Enron began trading to hedge the price risks of its physical natural gas deals, its executives quickly realized that trading could be hugely profitable on its own. As the largest U.S. pipeline company, with massive information on who was buying and selling gas, Enron could use that insider knowledge to bet on gas prices. Trading gas became an end in itself.

As Enron embarked on its speculative ventures, Ken Lay wanted government interference kept at bay. In November 1992 he petitioned the chairman of the Commodity Futures Trading Commission (CFTC), Wendy Gramm, to remove the swaps Enron was creating from CFTC oversight. Banks, including J. P. Morgan and Chase Manhattan, along with major oil companies, sent letters to the CFTC supporting Enron's position.

A week before she resigned from the CFTC, Gramm rammed through a vote by the commission exempting Enron's energy swaps from regulation. Six weeks later she joined the company's board of directors.[14]

Other pipeline companies, such as Texas-based El Paso Energy Corporation and Oklahoma-based Williams, eager for new sources of income, followed Enron into trading. On a much smaller scale, TransCanada did too. But Enron dominated the business. It was known in the industry by the moniker "the evil empire," reflecting the wariness and perhaps envy it generated because of its size and power.

Enron transformed into something akin to a Wall Street firm— employing traders, setting up trading floors, and engaging in complicated financial transactions. While its executives publicly promoted it as a pipeline or power company or emphasized its international projects in energy and water, Enron grew to rely on its financial trading for revenue. But Enron executives never admitted its key source of earnings was trading because that would have sent its stock value tumbling. Investors wanted stable, relatively safe earnings, not profits based on risky and volatile speculation.

Enron traders were aggressive. They used Enron's massive trading power to their advantage. They took huge risks, bet big. They won or lost enormous sums of money.

As its other businesses collapsed, Enron relied more and more on trading for its profits. "Our market grew so big because we were making huge amounts of money and being looked at to support the entire company because of the failures of Enron in India, [the] water business, and broadband," explains a former trader.[15]

Executives used the trading profits to hide losses in other parts of the firm. When earnings projections overall fell short of Wall Street expectations, company officials massaged them with trading profits stored in what was called a "prudency reserve."

Some Enron traders went wild, such as the West Coast traders who joked as they created energy shortages in California, costing consumers and businesses hundreds of millions of dollars.

But there was another side to Enron's trading: extensive and in-depth research to plan trades. Some information was gleaned from Enron's large pipeline business; Enron also spent lavishly on re-search analysts who could monitor supply and demand, weather pat-terns, and whatever else might affect investments.

When, for example, Enron inherited some agricultural business and decided to set up trading operations around it, it hired a con-sulting firm to analyze North American agriculture and identify trading competitors. They hired a lobbying firm, a trading team, and researchers. "We went to Tyson Foods, started to buy a grain company, talked to West Texas cattle and feedlot owners," explains Gary Hickerson, who was asked to start the trading division. "We spent a year and a half and millions of dollars before we traded one contract."[16]

That emphasis on fundamental research appealed to Arnold when he went to work on Enron's key natural gas financial trading desk in 1997. Around that time Jeff Skilling became the firm's presi-dent; under him, Enron's appetite for risk grew, and so did the amount of money allocated to trading.

Arnold beat out several other competitors when Jeff Shankman, head of the financial gas trading desk, hired him. Shankman, only about a half dozen years older than Arnold, was already a star on Enron's trading floor. His team, called the "fixed price desk," traded all the NYMEX gas contracts and options, as well as all the swaps and swaptions tied to NYMEX futures prices. The other natural gas financial traders focused on gas in Canada or gas delivered in various parts of the country other than the Henry Hub. There were maybe four dozen others who traded physical gas. Shankman did trades both for Enron's physical gas traders and its customers and with money Enron allocated directly to his desk.

Shankman knew Arnold because of his work on the Texas physi-cal natural gas desk. They sat only about fifteen feet apart. Arnold placed a lot of orders through Shankman, who was impressed by the inquisitiveness of the younger trader. Whenever the market moved unexpectedly, Arnold was one of the first people over to his desk to discuss why. More than others, Arnold seemed eager to get to the bottom of surprise price shifts, especially when they contradicted supply-and-demand fundamentals. Arnold wasn't like the other guys, who asked why prices went down 15 cents as opposed to 20 cents. He wanted to understand why it moved in the first place. He and Shankman talked about unusual events—an unexpected sale from a producer, problems that forced a company to sell its holdings—that might have sparked the price moves.

When it was slow or after the market closed, Arnold often went over to Shankman, grabbed an empty chair, and sat down to talk. Shankman was blown away by the quiet young trader. "He came across as the most thoughtful, deliberate, and inquisitive person of anyone I had worked with on the gas floor," he recalls.[17]

Shankman hired Arnold to work under him as the options trader while Shankman dealt with the rest of the portfolio. And they backed each other up when too many phones rang, multiple orders came in, or prices changed unexpectedly.

It got very hectic. Arnold might be on the phone trading through a broker when a call came from a customer interested in buying some options. Other Enron traders shouted across the room, telling him they wanted to buy or sell something. At first Arnold was overwhelmed on the financial desk.[18] There was so much to keep track of, and he needed to be right all the time. Positions had to be recorded correctly; customer trades could not be missed. It was sensory overload.

Arnold, who had traded Texas gas, was the first person on the financial desk with experience in the physical natural gas market. When interruptions on pipelines occurred, Shankman turned to him for advice on how long the problems would persist. Arnold possessed a keen sense of the relationship between the physical market and futures prices.

Always hungry for data, Arnold was able to call upon a dedicated research staff. They looked at market trends, which fuels were substituted for one another, and the new pipelines and power generators coming online. The research team would call up people at other pipeline companies and attend industry association meetings to pick up information. Arnold also drew on Enron's own team of meteorologists. Their job wasn't only to predict weather but also to analyze how other meteorologists generated their forecasts. They might survey a number of meteorologists on their ten-day forecasts and do a composite forecast. Or they might analyze which meteorologist had the best prediction results or which was better on cold-weather forecasts versus hot-weather ones.

Arnold was demanding about the quality of the data he got. "He was pretty exacting," says a former Enron energy analyst. "People I knew that worked for him would say he looked closely at what they did and they knew they had better do it right. Casual analysis wouldn't fly with him. He'd yell if he had to, to get the right information."[19]

Unlike Hunter, who loved designing his trades, Arnold often relied on the experts at Enron for that. There was a quantitative analysis group under Vincent Kaminski, a PhD economist, which built complex options pricing models for him. They would compute how the supply and demand of options affected prices, or the impact of interest rate changes. They assessed how the closure of a pipeline would impact demand on others.

But Shankman warned that relying on models, even with massive research, wasn't enough. The guys at Long Term Capital Management (LTCM) had "let math be their trading god," he cautioned colleagues when that hedge fund collapsed in 1998. Founded by John Meriwether, the man behind Salomon's first trading floor, LTCM was the epitome of a quant shop. Nobel Prize winners Robert Merton and Myron Scholes, who developed the option pricing formula, had worked there.[20]

Later, when financial journalist Roger Lowenstein published his book on LTCM, Shankman bought copies of it. He gave the book, *When Genius Failed,* to every Enron gas trader.

"The market had evolved to a point where a lot more people understood the math involved in option pricing but a lot fewer people understood emotion and psychology," Shankman explains.[21] "I think the best traders are the smart ones that understand the emotions of the market." And John Arnold, he says, "put both of those pieces together better than anybody."

On the financial trading desk, Arnold quickly became one of the most profitable Enron traders. That year he earned between $10 million and $20 million for the company.

Arnold and Shankman got along well, but there was a key difference between them. Arnold was much more of a gambler. He was willing to bet big and take massive risks, even if he didn't have all his information in place. "I was less risk averse than Jeff was," Arnold said later.[22] Shankman wanted the moon and stars to align before taking a big position on, say, gas prices rising in March, explains a former Enron trader. Arnold was comfortable placing the trade even if one of the stars was out of whack.

Arnold's appetite for risky and huge trades only fully emerged later, after he came out from under Shankman's wing. In 1999 Shankman moved up in the firm, leaving Arnold in charge of the desk, a position he held until he left Enron. There were four traders and a half dozen back-office employees reporting to him. At the time, Brian Hunter was only in his first year or so of trading at TransCanada.

Most days Arnold came onto the Enron trading floor about 7:00 a.m., checked weather reports and overnight trading, looked at headlines, and formed an opinion on where prices were headed. He met with his team and then went to a morning meeting where other traders discussed events in their geographic regions. Then he went back to his desk and checked to see that his monitors were up and his holdings from the day before were correctly posted. Dozens of other gas traders were on the floor, most of them buying and selling physical natural gas. If there was time, Arnold did some reading or over-the-counter trading before the NYMEX opened at 10:00 a.m. Eastern time.

Then Arnold swung into action, conducting a frenetic billion-dollar dance with a recalcitrant, moody market that tolerated no mistakes. While other traders used a desk phone, Arnold usually used a headset. It took too long to pick up and put down a phone receiver.

He wasn't conspicuous. He sat at the bottom of a U-shaped trading room, in the middle of three or four rows of desks built around an elevator bank. His desk faced a wall with a twelve-foot-wide whiteboard, used by nearby gas marketers to note their deals— maybe a utility wanting a long-term contract or a fertilizer plant needing gas. Above it was a row of clocks, set to the time zones where they did business.

Arnold was too busy to notice much of what was happening on other parts of the floor. Traders constantly signaled him to place their trades, standing up to yell over to him when it got busy and noisy. They called him on the internal intercom system or typed messages on their old-fashioned internal communication system devices, which resembled oversized calculators with screens. They used shorthand codes, numbers and letters indicating the traders, the products they wanted, and how much to buy and sell. Arnold kept track of all his internal customer orders on trading pads on his desk.

Before him were six to eight computer screens. One showed his holdings, and every time he traded he noted it on the screen. Another sported technical charts with prices or volumes over time. There was a screen for news and another showing various weather service reports. Another projected Enron's own internal marketing analysis. Still another was for emails. Next to Arnold was one of the coveted Bloomberg terminals that other traders joked was a mark of success. He used it to follow the Federal Reserve's latest actions and currency trading.

Usually there was no time to break for lunch, so they ordered in. In between buying and selling for Enron traders, Arnold called brokers, arranged swaps, and traded for his Enron account.

It all required a cool head, split-second timing, and the ability to store enormous amounts of data in his head. Although trading slowed after NYMEX closed at 2:30 p.m. Eastern time, Arnold continued other trading until 3:00 p.m. After that he talked with fellow Enron traders and did market research or read reports.

After work, he and a group of traders went out to bars or restaurants, often at the expense of a broker eager for their business. He took advantage of broker invites to the Super Bowl, watched the Houston Rockets in playoff games, and attended concerts by U2 and other big names.

Even when suffering trading losses, Arnold showed little outward emotion; in fact, he grew more introspective. He never threw tantrums, screamed across the desk, or belittled his assistants, as some managers were apt to do when the going got rough.

On a floor of loud, aggressive traders Arnold never lost his shy, unassuming manner. "He looked like the quiet little MIT guy who sat in the corner, more like somebody's kid brother than a tough trader," says a competitor. In fact, he was so shy and soft-spoken that at dinners with other traders they couldn't hear him unless they sat right next to him. But when you listened closely, you knew why Enron had hired him. "When you started talking to him you realized the guy's a frickin' genius," says a former trader. "He didn't have big airs; he was a regular guy, very reserved," says another who worked on the Enron energy trading floor.[23]

But beneath Arnold's quiet demeanor was a ferocious competitor. In one email to a colleague in August 2001, he responded fiercely to a question about his market strategy, saying he would love to hurt a slew of traders he believed were vulnerable because they had bet prices would drop. "I think there are so many shorts that some of the weak guys are squeezable here . . . everybody wants the market to go down," he wrote. "I'm relatively flat and would love to squeeze all the fuckers out, so I can sell them 20 cents higher."[24]

Soon after Arnold took over the natural gas financial trading desk, his trading volume soared. Skilling was completing Enron's transformation into a Wall Street speculator, and he grew increasingly desperate to keep up the firm's profit stream and stock price. Profits from other operations were flat in 1999 and down in 2000, so trading revenue was critical to the firm.

Arnold's trading levels also jumped when Enron launched its stunningly successful Web-based trading division, EnronOnline, late in 1999. A few years earlier online stock investing had been sparked by brokerage firms such as Charles Schwab and TD Ameritrade, but there were only a few tentative tries at commodity trading. When Enron powered up its system, it soon became the major player.

Enron's online business traded hundreds of financial and physical products—everything from telecom bandwidth to paper, metals, and even financial weather instruments that let snowmobile makers hedge against mild winters—but the bulk of its trading was natural gas and electricity products. In its first year of operation EnronOnline doubled the company's natural gas sales and Enron dominated the natural gas marketplace.

By 2001, almost 38 percent of all natural gas trading was done online, predominantly on EnronOnline.[25] Enron's trading ballooned from about $50 billion in the first part of 2000 to more than $555 billion a year later. It was commonly thought that Enron was on the other side of one-fourth of all the over-the-counter trades, although some said it was more than half.[26] One researcher who did extensive investigation of Enron concluded that EnronOnline was partner to about one-third of all natural gas trades.[27] Arnold was responsible for key natural gas swaps traded on EnronOnline. His team eventually traded ten different swaps tied to the closing price of various NYMEX futures contracts.

Arnold was a market maker, providing customers with a willing partner for a trade. He was always ready to do a deal, but at his price. He posted his prices for buying or selling swaps on EnronOnline. A trader who liked Arnold's price could agree to the trade with just a click. Arnold could reap huge profits if he was savvy about handling the contracts he had bought or sold. Should he, for example, keep these positions or trade them to someone else?

Some of the people he traded with worked at other pipeline companies, such as El Paso, while others were at gas producers or utilities. Some were at banks. He also concluded swaps with other Enron traders, and these amounted to between 25 and 40 percent of his trading volume.[28] Between 1999 and 2001, his swaps trading increased by 25 to 50 times.[29] He conducted energy trades worth well over $1 billion daily.[30]

Until EnronOnline, traders had to call other traders to do a deal, or they arranged it through a broker. Either way, it took time. But EnronOnline—where trading could be done with the touch of a mouse—dramatically simplified and sped up trading.

Everyone who traded on EnronOnline was transacting a deal with Enron. For smaller firms this relieved their worry about trading with someone with credit problems. Enron seemed to be making money hand over fist. So not too many companies worried that their trading partner would go out of business or not be able to pay up.

Enron's online trading was also completely unregulated thanks to Wendy Gramm's husband, Senator Phil Gramm, a political powerhouse (and recipient of generous Enron campaign contributions). In December 2000 he pushed through legislation guaranteeing this. The legislation also put the force of law behind the CFTC regulations Wendy Gramm had steered through, so all Enron's over-the-counter trading flourished unimpeded.

EnronOnline's huge volume and the fact that it was partner to every trade gave it enormous power. Customers, including the traders at TransCanada working with Hunter, were wary because Enron knew so much about what they were up to. "Their electronic platform gave them a window into seeing the world and they knew what everyone was doing. They could make money," says a former trader who worked at TransCanada when Hunter was there. "I never got told, 'Don't trade with Enron because they get to see everyone's trades,' but I thought about it, and used some discretion in trading with them."

The Federal Energy Regulatory Commission (FERC), which later investigated EnronOnline, charged it was worse than a casino, where the house held the advantage. At least at a casino there were set rules and everyone sees who they are competing against, said the FERC. Not so with EnronOnline, where Enron was the only one with this information. "Enron had access to trading histories, limit orders and volumes of trades and therefore understood the liquidity of the market." It could post any price it wanted on the screen, the FERC stated.[31] EnronOnline was "a key enabler" of gas price manipulation, it concluded.[32]

Arnold acknowledged the startling informational advantage EnronOnline gave him. EnronOnline let him see "the flow of business," he later said—the direction of trading and whether there were predominantly buyers or sellers, who was trading, and why. This helped him predict price moves—and to place his own trades, buying in an area where momentum was building or selling when he knew his clients were selling. And it explained to him what was happening on the commodity exchanges. "I could tell what a customer was doing over-the-counter. If I saw similar actions on the [NYMEX trading] floor, I could assume that it was the same client doing the transaction," he explained later.[33]

He also admitted that the enormous trades he placed could move prices. "If Enron were to start buying a particular product, the price would move—more so than if a competitor started buying it, simply for the sheer fact that Enron's positions were bigger," he said.[34]

In an evaluation of one trader he supervised at Enron, Arnold wrote approvingly that he was learning how to use "the Enron bat" to "push around" the market. He later explained he meant that "if Enron thought the market was undervalued or overvalued . . . there were times when you could take a large position, and the result of that, taking that position would be to, that the market would move to a different pricing level."[35] But as Arnold correctly argued, taking large positions by itself was not market manipulation. For that, regulatory agencies had the difficult task of proving price moves were deliberate, benefited a trader's positions, and were not in line with supply and demand.

Beyond placing trades for customers and other Enron traders, Arnold maintained his own book of business. These were the trades he placed on behalf of Enron to earn profit for the company. As Enron grew to rely on trading to prop up its stock price, Arnold was given more room to trade.

Enron conducted complex analyses to gauge the amount of risk a trader's activity exposed it to. These tools were developed by Dr. Vincent Kaminski, who headed quantitative analysis. The energy risk assessment he pioneered for Enron analyzed the volatility of current trades along with historical price trends and other variables. Based on how markets had acted in the past, his analysts determined how much the traders might lose today if things went south. This potential loss was known as the value-at-risk, or VAR. As Kaminski's group calculated it, VAR represented how much Enron, or a trader, could expect to lose once every twenty days. These were minimum estimates, however, although people tended to forget that there was no real limit to loss.

Other firms used somewhat different parameters but also assessed how much risk their traders were taking. The aggressive companies were the ones with higher risk limits. Enron's VAR ranged between $100 million and $150 million—one of the largest risk limits in the business, Arnold later admitted.

Kaminski was almost fired for developing the risk models because his assessments threatened to limit Enron's freewheeling trading operations. "I would get my memos back from my bosses with invectives written on them," Kaminski recalls. "My bosses said that what I was doing was necessary for outside consumption, but that Enron wouldn't change what it was doing."[36]

Arnold's own limits were huge. In 2001 he was allowed a VAR of $30 to $35 million. When Shankman ran the desk it was only about $10 or $15 million. Arnold's VAR was one-fifth to one-third of Enron's entire limit.

When traders exceeded their VAR caps, they were supposed to reduce their exposure and take offsetting positions. But at times Arnold traded at twice his VAR limit. Usually his bosses didn't care. But once he was fined for exceeding limits—no small achievement at risk-tolerant Enron.

Like Hunter, Arnold believed huge profits only came from huge bets, and Arnold always had the stomach for it. "The greater the value-at-risk," he said later, "the greater the possibility of having higher gross trading revenues."[37]

Arnold and Hunter agreed on another trading perspective: their own ability to understand the market. And because of that, each felt he should hold on to his positions—including huge ones—even while losing heavily.

At the end of 2000, Arnold refused entreaties at Enron that he shift out of his positions. He shocked Enron executives when he lost heavily, although he recouped most of it by clinging to his investment view. It was the same period during which Hunter's options group at TransCanada lost heavily.

At first the year went well for Arnold, and by early December he was up about $200 million. He was heavily shorting natural gas prices, anticipating prices falling that winter. But the opposite happened. In December, the January contract price skyrocketed to $10 per MMBtu. Just a month earlier the December contract had traded at half that.

The price hike was attributed to a sudden spell of extreme cold, combined with low storage supplies. Indeed, it turned out to be the coldest November-December in the country on record. In December, Chicago was hit with a whole season's worth of snow in just one month, and the snow piled so deep in Wisconsin that the Green Bay Packers put out a call for two hundred people to help shovel out Lambeau Field in time for its Christmas Eve game against the Tampa Bay Buccaneers. Record low temperatures—into the teens— hit Mississippi and central Florida as well.

Arnold later argued that he was short because of his role as market maker for other Enron traders. They were buying gas and he was required to do the trades that his customers wanted, so he needed to sell to them. "Each day, the weather came in colder, and the market ran up more," he later recalled. His losses mounted. He acknowledged that he should have more aggressively hedged his holdings or gotten out of them if he'd been able to find a buyer.[38] But others at the firm told a different story. They say Arnold rejected advice from other senior traders to cut his losses. Instead, he clung stubbornly to his holdings.[39] Whatever the reason, in a sickening nosedive Arnold lost his $200 million profit and then gave up an additional $200 million as gas futures prices continued to move against him.

When his name came up at the performance review meeting that month—the rancorous "rank and yank" meeting, as it was called, because employees at the bottom of the rankings could be fired—managers were given a background profit-and-loss report that indicated Arnold had earned $200 million for the year. "That was a few days ago," corrected his boss at the time, John Lavorato. "Now it's minus $200 [million]."[40] People started complaining about his stubbornness, recalled an attendee at the rank and yank. He was criticized for refusing the advice of most on the trading floor to close his positions when he was still up.

Luckily for Arnold, and for Hunter's group at TransCanada, the weather saved them. After the December cold spell, warmer-than-normal weather in January and February rolled through the nation, sending prices down dramatically.[41] Arnold's positions came roaring back. He managed to recoup most of his losses, ending that ugly stretch down by about $50 million.

But even this near mishap failed to dim Arnold's star. As his losses mounted Jeff Skilling signaled his support by going to the trading floor to put his arm around Arnold. Although Skilling sometimes went to the trading floor to give traders a pat on the head or a hug, it was usually when they were making money.[42]

But as 2001 wore on, Enron overall was in crisis, despite huge profits by the energy traders. There were enormous losses in other parts of the firm. For one, Enron Energy Services (EES; the retail side of Enron, providing electricity, gas, and energy management services to businesses) was $1 billion in the hole, a loss Enron executives tried to cover up by folding it into Arnold's trading division. EES traders were not supposed to engage in speculative trading to make money for the company. They were only supposed to buy or sell contracts to protect customer needs. Arnold warned his bosses EES traders were speculating. When EES was bailed out by his division, he was incensed, and worried that his bonus might be affected.[43]

EES was not Enron's only problem at that point. Other Enron losses were being hidden in all sorts of illegal financial entities. By September, Enron started unraveling. Skilling suddenly quit. Within a month whistleblowers accused executives of financial mismanagement. In October, Enron announced its first quarterly loss in four years. The SEC launched a probe into the company's financial frauds. Its stock price sank to its lowest level in nine years.

Enron was going down.

Arnold's trading results in 2001, however, were spectacular. In the spring he made an aggressive bet that prices would fall later that year. And now it was starting to pay off. His profits were between $600 and $750 million for 2001.[44]

As Enron's troubles mounted other traders grew restive. They too were having a very good year and were expecting huge bonuses, now threatened by the company's precarious financial situation.

Many traders demanded assurances they would be paid bonuses. And Enron management, weighing options to keep the company afloat, was desperate to keep them happy. Traders were promised huge retention bonuses, and Arnold, the key guy company executives wanted to retain, was promised $5 million.

Enron started talks with Dynergy, a power and natural gas marketer, in early November, but they collapsed on November 27. Bankruptcy appeared imminent. Some executives hoped to keep the trading franchise intact and maneuvered to immediately pay bonuses as long as traders remained with the firm for three months. Some traders were leery about accepting the bonus with Enron's bankruptcy on the horizon. They consulted lawyers, who assured them the worst that could happen was they'd have to pay it back. Enron filed for bankruptcy on Monday, December 3. The previous week, executives had handed out cashier's checks to traders.[45] The largest bonus by far went to John Arnold. Two months before he was promised $5 million and now he actually received $8 million.

Executives agreed to keep the bonuses quiet, but Arnold was concerned about a backlash from Enron employees if news leaked out. He shot off an email to a company official, saying he had an "important favor to ask. I am worried about the reaction should the names and numbers of the trading retention pool be made public. If you get notice of it and when that is to happen, advanced warning would be very helpful."

Indeed, Enron employees who didn't get bonuses but instead

lost retirement savings and health benefits, along with their jobs, were outraged. A lawsuit was filed, and years later bankruptcy court judges ruled that bonus money had to be returned. But Arnold had long since settled with the employees filing the suit, repaying an undisclosed amount of his bonus.

Enron's collapse sent its energy trading business into disarray. There was no bidding war for its trading operations, as many had expected, because no one wanted it. UBS Warburg eventually agreed to take over the trading but wouldn't pay Enron anything for it up front.

After speaking with UBS executives, Arnold decided against going to the firm. He did not want the restrictions of a conservative Swiss bank. He wanted to make money—more than he guessed he could at the bank. UBS wanted to cap the entire trading group at the same risk limit he personally had while at Enron.

"The lower value-at-risk would bring in lower trading revenues," he later said. "I thought compensation would be low."[46]

He also didn't want to go to another merchant energy company. He had already worked for the largest, helped it create and shape natural gas trading, but there was always someone he had to report to.

He opted instead to create his own hedge fund. He would determine trading strategy, plan investments, and reap the rewards if he was successful.

Hedge funds were opening everywhere. Pensions and endowments were eager to invest with them. But at the time most were focused on stocks and bonds. Arnold planned to open one of the first hedge funds devoted to natural gas trading.

In March 2002, shortly after his three-month-stay agreement with the company expired, he left Enron.

Enron's implosion and the California power crisis soon triggered federal and state investigations and hearings. Enron paid more than $1.5 billion in fines related to electricity price and supply manipulation. The FERC investigated EnronOnline's practices and charged a handful of the firm's traders with manipulating gas and power markets.

But much of its trading activities were outside the scope of regulators, thanks to Enron's congressional friends. University of San
Diego finance professor Frank Partnoy, who studied Enron's trading
practices, terms it "alegal." "It wasn't legal in the traditional sense
and it wasn't illegal in that it would be pretty hard to go in after the
fact and prosecute a lot of this because some of it was made legal by
regulations, some of it was in an unregulated area, and some of it was
just ambiguous as to whether it was legal or illegal."[47]

John Arnold, as Enron's lead financial gas trader, was questioned
extensively by federal investigators. He was never charged with any
wrongdoing.

Still, questions about Enron continued to dog him. On May 6,
2005, he was deposed by Antara Resources, a small oil and gas producer that was sued by Enron over a long-term gas contract the two
had negotiated. Enron claimed it was owed a substantial amount of
money, based on calculations of future gas prices done by Arnold
when he was at Enron.

By then numerous energy companies had been accused of and
paid millions to settle charges they had manipulated and falsified
information used for published gas price indices. If Arnold had been
involved in any of this, it would help Antara's position in the case. At
Arnold's deposition, Antara's lawyer, George Lugrin, went down a
list of abusive activities other merchant energy companies either admitted to or were accused of. These included wash trading (simultaneously buying and selling trades of the same size and type to create
the illusion of volume or otherwise affect prices), reporting false
prices to firms that collected and disseminated price information,
inflating revenue figures, and issuing misleading price forecasts. He
questioned Arnold about each type of activity and asked if Arnold
ever engaged in them.

Arnold's lawyer, Cynthia Rerko, was hooked in via phone from
another city. For every question she advised Arnold not to answer.
In response to every question Arnold asserted his rights under the
Fifth Amendment.[48]

Rerko declined an interview request for this book. Perhaps
Arnold's decision to not answer questions was an attempt to avoid

being drawn into additional Enron lawsuits, a tactic other Enron employees used. If he wasn't going to say anything at all, lawyers wouldn't involve him. Antara's lawyer, Lugrin, sees it differently. "I'm not sure I see any other reason why he would have taken the Fifth, unless his lawyers believed there was a real concern that he could be the target of some criminal prosecution at that time."[49]

By the summer of 2002 Arnold was ready to set up his hedge fund, using $5 million from investment bank Smith Barney, $1 million from a Chicago investor, and $2 million of his bonus money. He named it Centaurus, a constellation whose stars are said to represent a mythical creature combining a human head with a horse's torso.

At Centaurus Arnold replicated key elements of Enron's operation. First he set up his own research department, hiring several of Enron's top research analysts. He employed his own meteorologist. A number of Enron's traders joined him, as did Enron's final president, Greg Whalley. Later he brought his mother in as his accountant.

Arnold also found a way to duplicate the intelligence he had garnered from EnronOnline by becoming a market maker for clients. It was a startlingly ambitious role, especially for a new hedge fund. Few others had the capital or the specific skill set required to take on such a responsibility. Providing this service gave Arnold important information about order flow, who was active in the market, supply and demand, and general market psychology.

He was closemouthed about his specific trading approach, though later on he allowed a brief glimpse into his overall strategy at an energy conference in early 2006. It mirrored what Shankman had taught him about market psychology years before. "We ask ourselves," he said, "can we identify what is forcing a market to price a product at an unfair value, and then, what will push it back to fair value?"[50]

It was a rare public appearance by Arnold, who almost never gave interviews after leaving Enron. One attendee in the audience that day described him as "shy, not at all dynamic."[51] That demeanor did not change over time. Even as he became more and more wealthy and was at the top of his game, Arnold still came off in public more like a nerdy science professor than a high pressure trader. Testifying in 2009 before a meeting of the Commodity Futures Trading Commission, Arnold, dressed in a rumpled suit, awkwardly twisted his hands, and raised his eyebrows as he softly spoke to the panel.[52]

Along with building his hedge fund, Arnold married a high-powered New York attorney, Laura Elena Munoz, who had degrees from Harvard, Yale, and Cambridge. She had worked on corporate mergers and acquisitions in New York and co-founded an energy exploration firm.

They moved to Houston's wealthiest enclave, prestigious River Oaks, founded by flamboyant oilmen. The area's showy, opulent homes were now coveted by Houston's nouveau riche: land developers, attorneys, and financiers. Top executives at Enron, including Lay and Skilling, had also bought homes there.

River Oaks is not just the city's geographic center but the social hub of the richest residents as well. They are regulars at gala charity balls, where Arnold and his wife have been spotted. Today they are two of the city's leading donors to various causes. Avid art collectors, owning works by Picasso and de Kooning, the two have been long-time contributors to the Houston Fine Arts Museum. Laura Arnold serves as a museum trustee.

As their wealth grew astronomically over the years, the Arnolds created a foundation. In 2010 they took a pledge initiated by Warren Buffett and Bill Gates to donate at least half their fortune to charity.[53]

Their money would be used, they said, to "effect positive and transformative change." They poured millions into education programs, including charter schools and Teach for America, along with criminal justice reform programs. They supported a group campaigning to replace public pensions with 401(k) plans, a proposal that would pour more pension money into Wall Street firms. Arnold also contributed tens of thousands of dollars to political campaigns, primarily for Democrats, and hosted fund-raisers for Barack Obama.

Arnold could afford lavish giving because year after year Centaurus made money. Lots of it. It never had a losing year until well after Amaranth's demise. True, there were some months, such as December 2003, when Arnold lost heavily. That month a surprise, massive cold spell hiked gas prices, hurting both Arnold and Hunter, then at Deutsche Bank. But Arnold had the capital and enough willing investors to hang on until prices went his way. His track record was so good, another trader says enviously, that his investors "would die for him."

Arnold believes in his convictions, says a trader who knows him. "When he decides on something, whether in the gas market or oil market, he sticks to his guns. And his guns are really big."[54]

In his first or second year as a hedge fund manager, his profits were about $200 million. His assets quickly grew to $600 million.[55] People clamored to invest in his firm. "By his second or third year he could have raised much more money because his performance was so exceptional," remembers a friend. "He probably could have raised $5 billion if he had wanted to."[56]

But Arnold didn't want to. He didn't want his firm too big. He believed there were a limited number of good investment ideas, ones that could earn huge returns, especially in energy. And there were dangers for a big player in an arena with only a small number of huge investors. His own money could move prices. Or if things went south he might not be able to exit holdings quickly. So Arnold returned profits to his investors, trying to limit the size of his firm. And within three years of starting his hedge fund, he closed it to new investors.

Arnold spent most of his time developing his energy hedge fund. But in his downtime he turned his competitiveness to another passion, soccer. He joined a Houston area league, playing in a high-level competitive division. The quiet, soft-spoken Arnold was replaced by a much more openly aggressive version when games got under way. He yelled to teammates, instructing them on maneuvers and where they should be positioned. When someone messed up he'd make his disgust known: "Get your head in the game." And he wasn't shy about letting the referees know if he disagreed with a call, frequently picking up yellow cards.

Arnold was a defender, a position that required stamina, strength, and aggressiveness. But to be successful in that role he had to do more than just be in an opponent's face or fight him for the ball. He needed to observe and watch the field, to stand back and try to anticipate other players' moves. Was the guy coming down the field with the ball likely to pass or try to kick into the goal? He had to get inside his opponent's head. And Arnold, a very good player, was able to do just that.

A FUND FOR EVERYONE

The unlikely inventor of the hedge fund, A. W. Jones, was not a finance specialist but a sociologist with a doctorate from Columbia University. He worked with the Foreign Service in Berlin in the 1930s, raised money for Quaker-run relief activities during the Spanish Civil War, and later funded research into the causes of poverty. In his forties he started writing for Time, Inc., and it was only when working on an article for *Fortune* about technical approaches to the market that he decided he could make money investing.

In 1949 he set up A. W. Jones & Co., primarily to invest his money and that of his friends, who were doctors, artists, and writers. His aim was not to become rich but to earn enough for himself and his friends so they could pursue their real interests—science, medicine, art, and in his case social services.

Jones decided to borrow as much money as he could from brokers, leveraging his investors' cash as much as possible. He could buy more stocks that way and potentially earn more profits. But it was a dangerous strategy. In a crisis he might end up losing more money than his investors had actually handed over to him.

So Jones tried to hedge his bets. His primary investment approach was to buy stocks he believed would go up in price. But he also did some shorting of companies he thought weren't doing well, betting that their price would drop. This reduced his risk by broadening his investments. He wasn't relying on only a few companies doing well. More important, however, it gave him some protection against broad market swings. If the market overall turned bearish and most stock prices fell, then at least some of his investments would likely profit. On the other hand, if there was a broad bull market, with most stocks going up in price, he wouldn't make as much money with this mixed investing style. Jones recognized this. But what he was most concerned about was having "a hedge against the vagaries of the market."[1] Taking too much risk was wrong, Jones explained, because "we are handling other people's money." Without having some protection, "I would not have been able to sleep so well at night."[2]

As it turned out, Jones' returns were astounding. From 1960 to 1965 he was up 325 percent. By contrast, the best mutual funds over the same period had a return of 225 percent. Over ten years, Jones had returns of 670 percent. With this kind of record, Jones felt he was owed significant compensation. And so he took 20 percent of profits—a compensation benchmark that became the standard for hedge funds.[3]

But it wasn't just smart stock picking or hedging bets that made Jones money. He had figured out how to get an inside track on stocks likely to go up.[4] Jones knew that well-regarded brokerage house research analysts with a Wall Street following moved stocks when they recommended one and issued a report. Jones wanted these analysts to pick stocks for him too.

He would invite certain analysts to lunch and propose they run a paper portfolio for him. He agreed to pay the analyst and his firm commissions. If the stock picks worked out, Jones then set up a real portfolio at his firm. The more money these investments earned, the higher the commissions Jones paid out. This gave analysts a strong incentive to front-run their own firm's clients. If they tipped off Jones first about stocks they were going to recommend, he could buy them. Then when the analyst issued his report and clients bought the stock, Jones would benefit.

"Jones never implicitly suggested the analyst front-run his recommendation or his firm's clients, but he made it clear that analysts got paid strictly for investment ideas that worked and that A. W. Jones & Company couldn't care less about long, scholarly research reports," recalled hedge fund manager Barton Biggs, who ran one of these portfolios early on.[5]

At the time there were no rules in place preventing this type of conflict of interest. "Basically Jones used commissions to develop an informational advantage and hired smart, young guys to exploit it. Fortunately Eliot Spitzer was still in diapers," quipped Biggs.[6]

Jones' strategies were soon copied by other investors. A 1966 *Fortune* article, "The Jones Nobody Keeps Up With," reported Jones' spectacular returns and brought hedge funds to wider attention.[7] By 1968, the Securities and Exchange Commission counted 140 investment partnerships that it considered hedge funds.[8]

From the beginning, hedge funds found loopholes in regulations passed in the wake of the Great Depression to protect investors, rules that governed mutual funds. Provided hedge funds catered to the rich and didn't market to a broader public, Congress exempted them from most oversight. The rich could take care of themselves, according to legislators. A 1996 Senate report termed the wealthy sophisticated enough to "evaluate on their own behalf matters such as the level of a fund's management fees, governance provisions, transactions with affiliates, investment risk, leverage and redemption rights."[9]

Hedge funds avoided the restrictions of the Securities Act of 1933 if they focused on "accredited investors": individuals with incomes of at least $200,000 or a net worth of $1 million, or institutions (charities, trusts, and certain companies) with $5 million in assets. They weren't subject to the regulations of the Investment Company Act of 1940 if their clients were "qualified purchasers": individuals, couples, or companies with $5 million in investments, or institutions with investments over $25 million.[10]

Because mutual funds were subject to various rules and regulations that hedge funds were allowed to ignore, the operations and investments of each were very different. From the start hedge funds invested in complex, highly leveraged, and risky transactions, along with more traditional stocks and bonds.

Mutual funds, on the other hand, were limited in their ability to leverage investments and the degree to which they could invest in risky strategies. Hedge funds moved freely in and out of investments and charged investors what the market would bear. But mutual funds' purchase and sale of investments were controlled, and fees, which were regulated, had to be disclosed.

Many hedge funds were secretive about sharing information on investments and strategies with investors, while mutual funds were required to publish this. Hedge fund investors were forced to rely on the fund managers to value their investments and to tell them periodically how the fund was doing. Mutual funds were required to be more transparent—they posted the fund's value daily.

Investors could buy into or sell out of mutual funds daily. But hedge funds limited when investors could withdraw money to protect against mass defections if a hedge fund ran into trouble. Amaranth's initial withdrawal schedule—like that of other hedge funds—was complicated and restrictive. Initially investors were subject to a thirteen-month lockup, which turned into a two-year lockup on new investments made after January 2006.[11] After that, investors could only cash in their funds on the anniversary of their investment, with ninety days' notice. They could take out their profits annually, but with forty-five days' notice. They could cash out quarterly too, but had to provide forty-five days' notice and pay a 2.5 percent fee.[12]

Mutual fund fees were generally between 1 and 2 percent of the amount under management. But under the hedge fund compensation system pioneered by Jones, hedge funds customarily pocketed a fee of 2 percent of the cash under management and 20 percent of any profit they achieved—the "two and 20." This meant that when bets went well, the hedge fund manager collected a bundle. And when things went badly, the worst that could happen was the fund owner didn't get the 20 percent bonus. He still got his 2 percent management fee, however, which on a $1 billion fund was a hefty $20 million. And he had no financial penalties. Only the investors suffered the losses.

Hedge fund payouts attracted people willing and eager to take huge risks in the hope of receiving huge bonuses. "The bonus structure in the financial industry encourages traders to take a lot of risk because there is very little downside and a big upside," says options trader Espen Haug, who has authored numerous articles and books on derivatives and trading.[13] "Only traders with very high morals, who are thinking about their reputations, will think long term and take risks in line with what best serves investors. On top of good morals, you naturally also need very good knowledge about the markets you trade. Often, though, we see a lack of morals and lack of knowledge."

From the late 1960s onward, hedge funds branched out considerably as currency and commodity markets generated new opportunities. The 1970s breakdown of the Bretton Woods system, which had pegged exchange rates to gold, created volatile currencies, making them profitable to trade.

With the development of the Black-Scholes formula, options trading exploded. Futures markets expanded as opportunities came in commodity trading. Computers increased the volume, complexity, and speed of all the markets.

A number of hedge funds that grew up in this environment used the basics of the A. W. Jones approach—leveraging and hedging. But in the early 1970s a number of funds that were highly leveraged without hedging collapsed when a bear market took hold.[14]

In the 1980s, a group of highly skilled commodity and currency traders became successful hedge fund managers—legendary names, including George Soros, Bruce Kovner, Paul Tudor Jones, Louis Bacon, and Julian Robertson. They started funds with a few hundred million dollars and returned 50 percent, 100 percent, even 200 percent to investors. In the next decade, the largest hedge funds were managing billions of dollars each. Investors clamored to buy into the funds. And as fund assets and profits grew, some fund managers cleared $100 million a year.

Many of the leading funds emphasized strong economic analysis, political evaluation, and market dissection. Some were more cautious than others, less willing to take excessive risk. Some avoided extreme leveraging and quickly jettisoned losing trades, abhorring the idea of doubling up. Some, such as Paul Tudor Jones, understood that market psychology was sometimes more important than economic facts in determining price moves.[15] Jones, whose flagship hedge fund, BVI Global, has had a 24 percent average annualized return since its 1986 inception, also said he saw no reason to take a lot of risk.

Marc Chamberlin, who has traded commodities for twenty-five years, learned the business working under Paul Tudor Jones. "The perspective I got, the way those guys—Tudor and Soros and Louis Bacon and Julian Robertson—grew up, was that they played the game professionally," says Chamberlin. "They were largely humble, they did a lot of homework and they knew how and when to apply the accelerator and the brakes, much like a successful Formula 1 driver. Their long-term track records were established and built during the industry's infancy. They stayed true to their trading process over time and evolved as required. That's a recipe for long-term success no matter how the industry as a whole is ebbing and flowing."[16]

Through the 1980s and 1990s, hedge funds generally were created by experienced portfolio managers, traders, and top-rated analysts.

"Hedge funds used to be the best people," recalls a trader who worked at several hedge funds. "Hedge funds used to be Wall Street traders that had worked ten years on the Street and were tired of working for big banks and wanted to set up their own hedge funds. They got some seed money and hired experienced people."

With skilled traders and relatively little competition from other such funds, these pioneers found specific niches in the market and many profited.

"When we were first starting in the fund industry, there weren't crowded trades because Julian [Robertson] would have an idea and Michael [Steinhardt] would have a different idea and Jordan [Schreiber] another," said Richard Medley, who ran his own money management firm, along with overseeing the A. W. Jones hedge fund until his death in late 2011. "It came from their own work, own research, and intelligence. You had a limited number of hedge funds, and they were doing their own work."[17]

"What we started to see was that more and more people had the same trades on. When we delved into why, they said it was 'because everyone was doing it, and it was working.' You had a lot more people into trend following."

Throughout the 1990s quants started to play a greater role on Wall Street. As they did, investment time horizons narrowed and trading sped up. The quality of a corporation's product and the abilities of its management became less important for many investors than a host of data points such as how cheap a stock was and its volatility. Hedge funds, aided by eager banks and yield-hungry investors, increased leveraging and decreased hedging.

Fundamental research on companies and products lost its cachet, while young math wizards became the new superstars. Investors were enticed by complex algorithms that could seemingly predict price moves and find profitable arbitrage transactions. As the years went on, the quants became more and more important at investment firms. Medley, who also was partner and political strategist for George Soros, and ran a company providing policy analysis to hundreds of hedge funds, explained that basic research was considered "so unsophisticated . . . That quant thing sounds so much more sophisticated than somebody who comes in and says 'No, we generate our own research, we do it ourselves.' "

When Long Term Capital Management, whose principals pioneered quant trading, crashed spectacularly in 1998, it should have been a wake-up call to Wall Street. Leveraging was dangerous. Risk comes from unexpected places. Predicting worst-case scenarios based on what has happened before doesn't work well when markets are in turmoil and you can't unwind holdings.

Underlying LTCM's pricing calculations and trading was the idea that even though random events exist, markets are ultimately efficient. Random price jumps over time distribute themselves into a predictable pattern, with most congregating around the average. That means that if some prices got out of sync with historical norms, they would probably come back eventually.

LTCM's principals carefully calculated their trades, monitored their risks, and assumed that markets would follow past patterns. But they misjudged the causes and impact of unexpected events. Firms base risk management on "flawed theoretical models or on some years of historical data that don't necessarily reflect the worst case for the future," warns trader Espen Haug.[18]

Russia's decision in mid-August 1998 to devalue its currency and default on $40 billion of its bonds had catastrophic ramifications for the firm. That was the case even though LTCM held only a modest amount of the bonds and could have weathered those losses. But the event triggered a cascade of other activity. There was a general sell-off of holdings by investors who needed cash to cover their own Russian bond losses. Others wanted to transfer money to safer investments. A wide array of LTCM's holdings lost money. The massive short bet it had against Treasury bonds got killed. Other holdings it expected would rise collapsed instead.[19]

LTCM's mathematicians had underestimated market volatility and overestimated the firm's ability to liquidate its holdings at acceptable prices. They had predicted that over a month's time the firm could not lose more than $339 million.[20] But on August 21, 1998, LTCM lost a devastating $550 million. By September, it was bleeding $100 million to $200 million daily.

It was also hurt because other investors, in awe of the brilliant traders at LTCM, had mimicked their trades. Still more traders plowed into them because the firm's huge positions affected prices. When the crisis hit, all the traders lined up behind the firm were also forced to bail out of positions, driving prices further against LTCM.

LTCM had borrowed heavily from banks to trade. It had a leverage ratio of more than 25 to 1 at a time when most hedge funds were leveraged 2 to 1 and only a few dared leverage ten times their capital.[21]

LTCM had an epic loss of $4.5 billion.[22] Fearing its collapse would trigger a wider financial crisis, Federal Reserve chairman Alan Greenspan corralled leading banks and pressured them to take it over. By early 2000, the fund had been liquidated.

It should have led to a significant change in how Wall Street does business. It should have led to regulations for hedge funds. It didn't. The hedge fund industry was on the brink of a major expansion, and within a few years Amaranth too would underestimate its risk and ability to unwind positions.

By the time LTCM collapsed, the long-running bull market was heading toward a nasty ending. The technology stock bubble burst. The economy soured. The September 11 attacks further weakened it. Exposés of companies that had rigged earnings reports and investigations into analysts who had engineered research to win banking deals hit the news. The stock market toppled. The S&P 500 lost 42 percent of its value between 2000 and 2002.

Investors, stunned at their losses and searching for better returns, turned to hedge funds, the dangers of LTCM forgotten. Hedge funds were supposed to earn money when markets went down as well as up. Their track record at least appeared better than those of other investment vehicles. In contrast to mutual funds, hedge funds—as measured by the CSFB/Tremont Fund Index—made money every year between 1993 and 2003, except 1994.

Wall Street fell in love. Investors wanted to put money in them. Mutual fund managers wanted to run them. Brokers wanted their commissions.

The number of hedge funds grew. But there were just so many Paul Tudor Joneses and Julian Robertsons. There was a dearth of standout traders, those who did their own research and developed innovative ideas that could make money. "In 2000 or 2001, the quality of management declined and people were allowed to run funds that should not have been," recalls hedge fund manager Selena Chaisson. "They had no experience."[23]

"As these hedge funds exploded, you ran out of creativity and intelligence and things like that," as Medley described it. "So everyone is sitting in front of their Bloomberg terminals, coming up with financial models and watching trends and the same charts, and you have them investing in the same thing."

By 2003, when money was pouring into Amaranth, hedge funds were on their way to becoming a dominant trading force on Wall Street. One 2003 report calculated that hedge funds then represented 10 percent to 20 percent of equity trading volume in the

United States.[24] By 2006, one estimate was that they made up as much as half the volume of the New York Stock Exchange.[25]

They were an even larger factor in more speculative markets: one study in 2004 estimated that hedge funds accounted for 80 percent of trading in distressed debt and 20 to 30 percent of trading in collateralized debt obligations, credit derivatives, emerging market bonds.[26]

While wealthy investors moved more money into hedge funds, institutional investors really turned on the tap. By 2003 it was estimated that about one-third of hedge fund investment capital was coming directly from institutional investors—including public and private pension funds, endowments, and foundations.[27] The actual percentage, however, was probably higher because many institutional investors didn't put money directly in hedge funds. They used a fund of funds, companies that invest in a portfolio of hedge funds. About one-quarter of hedge fund investment money came through them.

Mutual fund managers chafed at the restrictions that limited their investment strategies and watched their investors go elsewhere. A number of them convinced their executives to figure out ways to create investment portfolios with some of the qualities of hedge funds. Well-known mutual fund companies, such as Invesco Funds Group, had already moved in this direction, and others wanted to set up aggressive hedge-fund-like mutual funds that would be able to short stocks, use leverage, and pursue higher-risk investments.[28]

Others, seeing their compensation drop as money flowed out of mutual funds, left to try their hand at running a hedge fund. Among the wave leaving in 2002 and 2003 were David Glancy, manager of Fidelity Investment's three top funds, a half dozen other Fidelity portfolio managers, and Janus Capital's high-yield bond fund guru Sandy Rufenacht.

Almost everyone on Wall Street looked hungrily at the hedge funds' "two and 20." Indeed, the more sought-after hedge firms commanded fees even higher than 20 percent. John Arnold, after being in business just three years, raised his management fee to 3 percent and took 30 percent of profits.

Hedge fund assets soared from an estimated $50 billion in 1993 to an estimated $600 billion in 2003—an increase of 1,093 percent. By contrast, over the same decade, mutual fund assets grew to $6.4 trillion—still totaling far more than hedge funds, but growing at a far more modest rate of 290 percent.[29]

Investors didn't look at the risks; they just looked at whether the fund had made money in the last few years. "When an asset class does well, people think it's safe," says Chaisson. "So by the time pensions were going into hedge funds, they had convinced themselves that it wasn't so risky."[30]

As the number of hedge funds mushroomed, banks saw ways to profit from them. "At this point, J. P. Morgan and the other investment banks were almost desperate for the business of the hedge funds," said former J. P Morgan banker Douglas Elliott.[31]

Banks coveted the trading commissions they earned from hedge funds' rapid-fire transactions. And they became prime brokers to hedge funds, providing, for a fee, an array of services. Most important, investment banks extended hedge funds easy credit to expand their investing. In 2003, hedge funds' use of credit from banks began to soar. One-quarter of hedge funds surveyed in one study reported that their banks were extending more credit than they had been six months previously.[32] Prime brokers also offered technical support, accounting services, and research. They even introduced hedge funds to potential investors. When hedge funds needed to borrow stocks to short, prime brokers arranged it.

Some banks facilitated trading in energy and other commodities. Known as clearing brokers, they functioned as middlemen between the commodity exchanges and traders. Clearing brokers collected the good-faith deposits the exchanges required buyers and sellers of derivatives to pay before trading. This wasn't full price, only a deposit, known as the margin requirement. For energy futures contracts this was as low as 10 percent.

Margin requirements were set by the exchanges, ICE and

NYMEX, although clearing brokers could negotiate additional money from clients. The profits and losses of a client's account were calculated daily. Profits were added to the client's account balance, and losses often triggered additional margin requirements. If a client defaulted, the clearing broker was financially responsible.

Bankers competed with one another for hedge fund business, and did so by relaxing standards for lending money.[33] For hedge funds, money became plentiful and cheap. And the bigger and more successful the hedge fund, the more the banks wanted their business. Credit Suisse estimated that by 2004, hedge fund business generated $25 billion in fees and commissions annually for investment banks.[34]

Investment banks also set up formal hedge funds. Bear Stearns had two, and the funds' heavy bet on subprime mortgages led to the bank's collapse in 2008. More and more banks came to operate as hedge funds, their revenues increasingly derived from trading their own money. By 2006 Goldman Sachs earned 63 percent of its revenue this way. In its last year in operation Lehman brought in 55 percent of income that way.[35]

In the new world of hedge funds, if a firm suffered heavy losses, fund managers often just shut it down. One study found that 30 percent didn't make it past three years.[36] They usually did not struggle to recoup losses the next year. That's because hedge fund traders and owners couldn't collect a 20 percent incentive fee until they made back the losses.

After incurring millions of dollars in losses, many fund managers just walked down the street and started another fund. John Meriwether, founder of LTCM, had another fund up and running with some of his colleagues within fifteen months of the spectacular failure of his firm. Many investors were willing to give failed hedge fund managers the cash to restart, especially if at some point they had been successful; the logic was that they had learned their lesson and would be hungrier than ever to make some money.

Indeed, hedge funds became increasingly apt to shut down. Between 1994 and the early to mid-2000s, the closure rate of hedge funds almost tripled, to 11 percent.[37] Hundreds closed every year.

Up until the economic crisis of 2008, the record for hedge fund closures was 848 in 2005.[38]

"The modern, highly leveraged derivative hedge fund is not structured for longevity," says a manager. His fund collapsed. He too soon opened another.

AMARANTH

One of the largest clusters of hedge funds in the country lies about fifty minutes north of New York City in Greenwich, Connecticut, nestled between the rolling hills and farms of rural Connecticut and the blue waters of Long Island Sound. Here the signs of wealth are everywhere. Greenwich Avenue, the main shopping promenade, resembles Palm Beach's Worth Avenue, with its expensive boutiques and branches of Tiffany, Brooks Brothers, and Kate Spade. Car dealers on Putnam Avenue sell Ferraris, Porsches, Bugattis, and Bentleys.

Set amidst acres of some of the East Coast's most expensive residential real estate are enormous mansions of brick, wood, and hand-hewn stone. Manors of 20,000 and 30,000 square feet are not unknown. There was even one effort to replace a 20,000-square-foot mansion with a 54,000-square-foot palace, until community opposition nixed it.

Greenwich has long been home to wealth. Major firms, including American Tobacco, IBM, and Xerox, were headquartered in the area, and many of their executives lived in Greenwich. The heirs to old corporate money settled there too. Charles A. Moore, an early twentieth-century industrialist who manufactured railroad machine tools, owned a 168-acre estate. The Gimbel family, of the department store, and the Havemeyers, who dominated sugar refining throughout the early 1900s, built mansions in town. Two sons of Standard Oil founder John D. Rockefeller lived there, along with an heir to the Carnegie steel fortune. Political leaders were residents as well, including Senator Prescott Bush, father and grandfather to two presidents.

But by 2000, when Amaranth was founded, Wall Street money dominated the town. Greenwich was a mecca for firms and executives connected with investing.

It started with the stock market boom of the 1990s. Investment giants—including GE Capital, with its two thousand employees, and Swiss Bank Corporation, with the largest trading floor in the United States—moved to nearby Stamford. Smaller buyout firms, branches of major brokerage houses, investment bankers, trust companies, bond traders, and institutional money managers all settled in Greenwich. Firms already there expanded further, such as Greenwich Capital Markets, which opened as a two-man firm in 1981 trading government bonds and in 1993 built a one-hundred-person trading floor.

Then the hedge funds moved to town. First it was a trickle. Long-Term Capital Management, Ardsley Partners, and Paloma Partners opened offices in Greenwich. Others, such as SAC Capital, moved close by.

Three of the wealthiest hedge fund managers—Paul Tudor Jones of Tudor Capital, SAC Capital's Steven Cohen, and Edward Lampert, founder of ESL Investments—lived in Greenwich, where their lavish lifestyles included epic-size mansions. Cohen, for example—an extravagant art collector who paid $8 million in 2005 for a British artist's preserved shark in a tank of formaldehyde—lived in a 32,000-square-foot house equipped with a 6,700-square-foot ice-skating rink, an indoor basketball court, a hairdressing salon, two putting greens, and gardens reminiscent of the Tuileries in Paris.

Paul Tudor Jones paid about $11 million in 1994 for a waterfront house that he tore down and replaced with an enormous mansion that recalled Monticello—except for its twenty-five-car underground garage.

Hedge fund managers were drawn by the lifestyle, the beauty of the area, and, more pragmatically, the financial benefits—including lower taxes than in New York City or nearby areas. The burgeoning Internet made it easy to conduct business away from Manhattan.

More hedge funds clustered in Greenwich, and the business advantages grew. Hedge fund managers in Greenwich met for lunch, saw one another at their kids' soccer games, and played golf together on weekends, where they passed along market chatter, gossip, and their analyses.

They made an enormous amount of money and enjoyed spending it. Yet they generally avoided media scrutiny and didn't flaunt their wealth on the pages of *People* magazine. But within their circles in Greenwich, it was a different story. Charity events, where people arrived in Bentleys and Ferraris, were often held in someone's mansion or in lavishly decorated tents on their lawns. At one fund-raiser guests took home gift bags containing a Tiffany key, one of which opened a box at Saks Fifth Avenue with expensive jewelry.[1]

A well-connected Greenwich resident remembers an investment manager who hired two airplanes for his wife's birthday, ferrying fifty of their friends to a resort in the Dominican Republic. In between rounds of golf and tanning, they constructed a school in the area.[2]

Greenwich attracted even more hedge funds after the 2000 stock market collapse. As investors shifted into hedge funds, many new managers opened their firms in Greenwich. Others moved up from New York City, unnerved by the destruction of the financial district during the September 11 attacks. Some hedge funds clustered in a building on Steamboat Road, overlooking Long Island Sound. Others moved into offices next to the train station, which provided easy access to New York City. Still others scattered throughout town and along the country roads.

While hedge funds crowded into Greenwich, people doing business with them came too. A constant parade of limos and town cars met the Metro-North train from New York as corporate CEOs, brokers, institutional salesmen, and analysts flocked to Greenwich seeking hedge fund business. Pension funds, endowments, and the wealthy also came looking for investment managers.

As hedge funds swelled in size, they started to spin out others, many of which set up shop in Greenwich. Often a newly spawned fund maintained the same investment style as its parent or was funded by it, because the hedge fund didn't want to completely lose the skills of its most talented employees. Some of the "Tiger cubs," portfolio managers who started out with Tiger Management's legendary founder, Julian Robertson, landed in Greenwich.

That was how Amaranth was born—spun off from a parent investment firm.

Nicholas Maounis, founder of Amaranth, was a local guy. He grew up in neighboring Stamford and went to the local public high school, spending a lot of time on the wrestling team. He worked hard, was a good wrestler, and was well liked by his teammates, recalls his former coach Nick Giancola.[3] Giancola also remembers Maounis' playful side, the fact that he liked to joke around. "He was a character, a clown in a lot of respects," laughs Giancola.

After graduating in 1981, Maounis didn't venture far from home for college, getting a degree in finance from the University of Connecticut. And then he began his Wall Street career.

Finance was a family tradition. His father was a trader and his brother is a financial advisor. His mother had worked in the back office of an investment firm and enjoyed telling people she helped her husband and her son Nick get their start on Wall Street.

In the 1960s, Maounis' father worked at a firm alongside George Soros. When Soros left to start his own hedge fund, soon to be enormously successful, the senior Maounis passed on an offer to join it. Nick Maounis often chuckled about the fact that his dad turned down Soros' offer, and probably the chance to be extremely rich, all because his firm offered him an all-expenses-paid cruise if he stayed.

Maounis found his niche on Wall Street right out of college, developing models for convertible bond arbitrage trading. Convertibles are bonds that can, at the holder's discretion, be exchanged for a set number of shares of stock of the company at a specified time. Traders seek out bonds they believe are mispriced compared to their value. Often they short the underlying stock, so they can profit if stock prices go down instead. Convertible bond structures can be quite complex and traders rely on sophisticated quantitative models to identify bargains.

Maounis spent five years, from 1985 to 1990, at two firms trading convertible bonds before landing at Paloma Partners. Paloma, set up in 1981, was the brainchild of S. Donald Sussman, a Manhattan lawyer turned money manager. Sussman was a very cautious investor and insisted on protecting investments through various strategies. He also wanted his managers to maintain the flexibility to rapidly exit trades should they go wrong.

Under Sussman, Paloma pioneered a concept of spreading out risk by dividing assets among independent investment professionals and demanding absolute transparency of their holdings. The firm also reserved the right to quickly withdraw money from managers. The system was called "managed accounts." In this manner, Paloma could take advantage of different managers' skills, diversify its investment strategies, and keep portfolios relatively small. But it could also move quickly if it thought there was a problem with a manager. Sussman believed that as funds grew larger and moved away from their core strategies, their risk increased—an anathema to him. He also didn't accept volatility. Even swings of a few percentage points up or down over a short period of time drew his ire.

The system seemed to work. Paloma lost money in only three of its first eighteen years.

One of Paloma's money managers when Maounis worked there was Nassim Taleb. Taleb later drew a wide following for bestselling books debunking Wall Street's reliance on risk analysis and warning that extreme, unpredictable, and improbable events do occur, with massive consequences. In his book *The Black Swan*, Taleb lambasted the "geniuses" of LTCM for "using phony, bell curve–style mathematics" that turned the "entire financial establishment into suckers."[4]

Paloma was housed in a concrete office building among grassy knolls on a meandering shaded road in backcountry Greenwich. Outside a four-story building, ducks and geese bobbed on a pond. Despite the buildings' austere external appearance, floor-to-ceiling glass windows made the interiors light and airy, with striking views of undulating hills, trees, and sky.

Maounis became one of Paloma's star traders. Eventually he oversaw its convertible bond arbitrage desk with a team of about twenty-five traders and analysts. His prowess was widely acknowledged on Wall Street. According to an admiring manager at another hedge fund, he would have been on anyone's list of best traders.

Maounis fit in well with Paloma's risk-averse culture. A trademark of his team was its caution, especially its concern about the effect of outside events on its investments, and they used shorting and options to protect themselves from heavy losses.

Maounis' reluctance to take significant risks didn't dampen his group's results.

In the ten years he was at Paloma, he generated annual returns of 22 percent—losing money only ten months out of the entire decade. He substantially outperformed the S&P 500 stock index. Even during the 1998 financial meltdown, when many funds had a rough time and Paloma's overall investments plunged 30 percent, the performance of Maounis' trading group didn't budge much, losing only 2 percent.[5] Investors began flocking to Maounis' team. Eventually it was investing about $200 million.[6]

As a manager, Maounis employed a hands-on, collaborative style. He liked to get out of his office and sit on the trading desk, following the action and talking with the traders. The atmosphere was congenial. The traders felt he was one of them—somebody who understood the pressure they were under. As a result, they opened up and asked him specific questions about the job at hand. There wasn't much of a pecking order. Later, as Maounis got ready to run his own shop, he even opened up the hiring process to traders' input. Incumbent traders would interview a prospective employee to make sure he or she would fit in with the team. They asked tough questions to ensure that the new trader wouldn't take huge risks.

As his success at Paloma increased, Maounis settled into Greenwich, buying a 10,000-square-foot Georgian-style mansion in 1993 for $850,000—a value that rose quickly into the millions as hedge fund managers crowded into town, sending the cost of already pricey Greenwich real estate soaring.

By 2000, Maounis was itching to do more than just oversee trading operations. He wanted to own and run a hedge fund, to determine his own fate—and to have the chance to become fabulously wealthy. His decision was prompted by a frustrating episode in 1998. His group at Paloma was holding its own in the midst of the market meltdown. But he was forced to sell off much of his group's holdings to bail out the rest of Paloma, which—uncharacteristically—had lost heavily and needed cash.[7] That was the year when stock markets melted down, global currency markets went haywire, especially in Asia, and hedge fund LTCM went bankrupt, alerting many for the first time to the markets' vulnerability to the unwinding of hedge funds and their excessive leverage.

Maounis, who had anticipated ending the year with a profit, told Sussman he was going out on his own. He wasn't going to have to bail out someone else's mistakes again. Sussman gave his blessing. He provided the initial seed money for the new firm, giving Maounis $200 million to manage—one-third of Amaranth's initial investment fund.[8] Sussman also became a minority owner in Amaranth Advisors, which was the management firm that technically employed the traders, analysts, risk managers, and other staff.

In May 2000, Maounis launched his hedge fund, Amaranth LLC. He was taking his team of Paloma traders with him. They were friends and fiercely loyal to him. The word was that Maounis reached into his own pocket to pay them during Paloma's meltdown. Maounis' goal: to build a firm that would ultimately manage about $1 billion.[9]

While 30 percent of the firm's money was initially invested in convertible bond arbitrage, the new fund was designed to go beyond Maounis' expertise and embrace a broader investment approach.[10] Two other initial investment areas were merger arbitrage, which focused investments in stocks of firms involved in a merger, and utilities arbitrage, which played one group of utilities stocks against another. The firm dabbled a bit in other areas as well.

Amaranth didn't venture too far afield from Paloma. Its offices were in the same building, just below Paloma's. Maounis used Paloma's support staff to process trades and for other back office work. The risk management staff, which daily assessed Paloma's holdings, also evaluated Amaranth's investments.

The new firm needed to be christened. Maounis had seen and admired an ornate antique pool table dubbed "the Amaranth" because it incorporated a purplish decorative wood veneer of that name. A good name for a hedge fund, he decided.

Colleagues weren't so keen on it, though. Name a hedge fund after a pool table? It could send entirely the wrong signal to investors. But when Maounis discovered that to the poet Milton and the ancient Greeks the amaranth flower, which did not fade quickly, was a symbol of immortality, his mind was made up.

And so the Amaranth hedge fund was born.

Maounis was busy traveling and raising money, so in mid-2001 he hired as his second in command Charles Winkler, a lawyer, who was the chief operating officer at a large Chicago-based hedge fund, Citadel Investment Group.

Maounis oversaw trading, determined investment strategy, and allocated investor money to traders. Winkler supervised all non-trading-related matters, including legal, accounting, human resources, and tax issues.

Winkler had management experience, but like many other chief operating officers, he had never traded. That didn't sit too well with some of the initial cadre of Amaranth traders, who felt he didn't always understand their concerns about such issues as allocating resources.

It also fell to Winkler to be the tough administrator because Maounis wasn't one for confrontation. He wanted to be liked by his employees. But Winkler was brutally honest with people. He got along well with those he felt were doing a good job, but he was tough on those he thought were not.

Even some staffers who rarely had contact with Winkler fretted about him, since senior portfolio managers threatened to raise Winkler's ire against them if they didn't shape up. "Charlie was generally feared by everyone," says a former trader, who like most former Amaranth employees still working in the hedge fund industry would not speak on the record for fear of angering former Amaranth executives also still in the business. "If you were on his good side, you did great, but if not, then there were problems. You would have tough questions from Charlie."

Early on, Winkler created controversy when he imposed employment contracts with noncompete clauses that barred employees who quit from immediately going to work for a competitor. Such contracts were not too common at the time. Under its terms, traders would have to wait a year after leaving Amaranth before accepting a job with another hedge fund. In the meantime Amaranth would pay them varying amounts that could in some cases be several times their base salary. Of course, there was room for negotiation regarding the agreement if someone was really unhappy and determined to leave; Amaranth executives wouldn't risk problems by forcing them to stay. But the hope was the contract would stem defections from the firm, prevent other hedge funds from poaching successful traders and portfolio managers, and protect proprietary trading information. It was also a selling point to investors, with Amaranth executives arguing that it led to a more stable staff and longer-term investment strategies.

But it was a hard sell to the employees of the new firm. It didn't help that a buzz arose that Winkler employed hardball tactics to enforce such contracts when he was at Citadel. This wasn't so; while Citadel had called in the FBI to investigate the theft of proprietary computer programs by an employee, this had occured before Winkler even arrived there. But the incident morphed into a myth about the noncompete clause, and a number of people balked at signing the contract, though most did. There were other disagreements over which people would trade which products, and several traders, including some who were close friends with Maounis, opted not to work at Amaranth.[11] Still the firm was soon up and running.

As at most hedge funds, when Amaranth netted a profit for its investors, the company took 20 percent of it. This was the firm's incentive fee. Amaranth awarded traders a firm-wide bonus, allocated from the company's overall profits. And some traders were given a discretionary bonus by supervisors. But mostly a trader's compensation was tied to what he himself earned for the firm. If he lost money, he didn't receive a trading bonus. And traders would have to earn back the loss the next year before receiving a bonus. A requirement that traders put about one-third of their bonus back into the company and leave it there for several years was aimed at tying traders to the firm and the firm's fortunes. If they had some skin in the game, they were less likely to take excessive risks that could collapse the firm. At least that was the theory.

On top of the 20 percent of profit, Amaranth also took 1.5 percent of assets from investors as a management fee. It went primarily to Maounis, with a small portion going to Sussman. In some years Amaranth also passed through to investors certain general expenses, such as new and sophisticated technology. This could add another fee of as much as 2 percent of a client's investment.

As the firm grew and its assets increased, the 1.5 percent management fee made Maounis extremely wealthy. He drove a silver Bentley to work and also owned a few sports cars. In 2002, he built a second home—a nine-bedroom, twelve-bath, 21,000-square-foot mansion in Jupiter, Florida—and bought a fractional ownership in a private plane to fly his family and friends down for weekends. He joined the exclusive Hudson National Golf Club in Croton-on-Hudson, New York, which had an entrance fee of more than $150,000.

Maounis enjoyed having a dozen or more guys over for poker, playing a high-stakes game. He was well known for the lavish March Madness parties at his Greenwich mansion, attended by other hedge fund top guns, such as Citadel founder Ken Griffin, whom he knew from his days trading convertible bonds. After at least one party, Griffin created a stir on his own trading desk when he returned from the party pushing new strategies he'd heard from Maounis, many considered too risky by Citadel's traders.[12]

Early in 2002 Maounis saw his chance to take his fund into an area in which he had recently dipped a toe: energy.

Enron had just collapsed. Revelations surfaced about other merchant energy companies mimicking Enron's accounting fraud and power trading manipulations. One by one, they declared bankruptcy or abandoned financial trading. This created a problem for energy producers and users who wanted to hedge prices. Companies such as Enron had been their primary trading partners. When they collapsed, energy trading slowed dramatically.

Maounis always intended to make a move into energy. Its ups and downs were not correlated with the other areas Amaranth invested in. That meant that if the rest of the portfolio tanked, energy might not, and vice versa. It diversified the book of business and seemed to offer greater safety for investors.

Now Maounis grabbed the opportunity Enron's demise presented.

"When the energy market was at its height, we had to pay a big guarantee just to get some people," says a former Amaranth trader. "But now with Enron bankrupt, Nick said, 'Why don't we try to get some good people from Enron cheaply?'"

Maounis wasn't alone. Banks and other hedge funds with little experience in energy trading had the same idea. "Hedge funds saw all those energy trading companies going under and decided this was a great market opportunity," says a former Enron executive. "Nature abhors a vacuum. So when Enron went down, hedge funds like Citadel Investment Group, D. E. Shaw, and Amaranth decided to jump into this business." Fund managers flew to Texas to interview former Enron traders. "Commodities were hot," recalls a trader. "Enron blew up, and suddenly there was an alignment of stars where there was demand for those markets and an availability of energy traders."

Even before Enron collapsed, Amaranth took a few tentative steps into energy, trading some futures contracts on the NYMEX. Some Amaranth traders wanted to go further and trade energy directly with Enron. But Paloma's lawyers and risk managers nixed deals with Enron. Enron was a risky partner. It didn't put up sufficient collateral to back its trades. For about a year, Enron and Amaranth tried to negotiate energy deals that would pass muster with the Paloma people, but before they could work something out, Enron declared bankruptcy.

Now Maounis put out feelers to energy traders. As always, he planned to move cautiously, devoting just 2 percent of his capital to energy trading. Some Paloma traders knew a few energy traders at Enron. One in particular appealed to Maounis: Harry Arora.

Arora fit the Amaranth mold—cautious, risk-averse, and exacting. Born in India, he was part of that country's burgeoning middle class but moved to the United States for graduate school and hoped to stay afterward. Ambitious and clever, with mathematics training in India, he got his MBA at the University of Texas, where his professors considered him a rising star. He was also engaging, lively, and animated. Fellow traders, both at Enron and later at Amaranth, liked him, and many respected his trading style.

Arora was "a very careful trader, very disciplined," says a former Amaranth trader. At Enron his style was the same, says a former colleague there. "He wasn't swinging for the fences. Harry is a very smart guy. He wasn't a buccaneer."

That more judicious attitude set him apart from many of his former Enron colleagues, says one of Enron's energy analysts. "He was thought of as a cross between a rocket scientist and a really good practical trader—book smart and street smart. He had a really good sense for risk. And he was a solid professional. His reputation was sterling at Enron, and that wasn't easy to do. He really was unlike a lot of the traders at that time that were basically just cowboys."

Arora was shaped in part by his religious upbringing. He believed in karma—the idea that a person determines his own destiny by his actions. Although a strong family man, he told friends he would help an honest stranger over a dishonest family member.

At Enron, Arora ended up trading electricity. But he'd started out trading currencies and interest rates. This was a way to hedge against the risks associated with Enron's enormous global projects, which Arora also helped evaluate.

He didn't have an easy job. Enron was arranging with governments around the world to build power plants, lay gas pipelines, and supply electricity and gas. The deals involved long-term contracts, some going out decades, and they exposed Enron to considerable risk. Enron wanted to hedge the risks, which ranged from a host country's currency increasing in value to shifts in interest rates and the inflation numbers on which the deals were based.

As Arora learned currency and interest rate trading on the job, he and his boss, Gary Hickerson, built the largest corporate financial hedging operation, rivaling many top U.S. banks.

"It was not cowboy trading," says Hickerson, who mentored Arora in currency and interest rate trading, which Arora helped run for about four years before moving to electricity trading. "It was driven by hard-core fundamentals . . . understanding macroeconomics, whether the Federal Reserve was going to ease or tighten, how interest rates would react to that . . . geopolitical concerns." Equally important, Arora's team monitored market psychology.

At Enron, Arora oversaw a group of traders in Houston and opened an office in London. He did trades involving tens of millions of dollars in currency and learned how to do so without alerting other traders. "History is littered with single traders taking big positions and the market finds out about it and you are dead," warns Hickerson.

Once Arora needed to convert a huge amount of U.S. dollars into Canadian currency in order to buy an asset in Canada. He and Hickerson had to move fast, before a major bank got wind of it and traded against them. "We did that process very stealthily, using the cash market, the futures market, currency market. And we distributed the trade on different days, through a variety of different brokers, trading the large position without disturbing the market or showing our hand," remembers Hickerson.

Enron International was under intense pressure at the time to churn out new deals to meet corporate earnings projections. Arora checked out the financials of the contracts before they were inked. It didn't make him overwhelmingly popular.

He engaged in a pitched battle with Enron's power plant negotiators, for example, over a deal with the Brazilian government. The deal was worth—at least on paper—tens of millions of dollars. Under Enron's rather creative accounting methods, it would be booked immediately as profits. And bonuses would rain down on its Enron deal makers. But Arora discovered that Enron International's power plant negotiators incorrectly computed the inflation costs of the deal. Instead of profiting on the project, Enron would actually lose money.

The originators were furious. They didn't really care whether the plant lost money in the long term; they wanted to book the profit now. They tried to prove Arora's calculations wrong, to convince him to allow the deal to go through anyway. When that failed, they went over his head to his boss, Hickerson, claiming Arora had incorrectly assessed their data. But Hickerson backed Arora, and the two wouldn't budge.

In the end, the angry power originators were forced to renegotiate the deal. It went through months later—profitable, but much less so than the original contract claimed. Bonuses were lower than anticipated.

In 2001, Arora, like other Enron employees, was stunned at the speed of the company's collapse. "Things did indeed move out of control sooner than anyone could have imagined," he wrote to a friend. "It's been one heck of an experience watching the situation and learning about how leadership works and how markets can make you and destroy you."[13]

With Enron's collapse, Amaranth traders contacted Arora, and Maounis talked to him about his plans to set up an energy team. Maounis was looking to trade several energy products, including gas, oil, and electricity, along with metals and agriculture. Maounis told Arora he was looking for someone who could build the firm's commodity business. Arora liked what he heard. He told UBS Warburg, the Swiss bank that acquired Enron's trading business, that he was not going to be part of the Enron team coming over. By early spring 2002 he'd packed up and moved to Connecticut to start Amaranth's energy trading operation. He brought along a colleague from the Enron floor, Hai Chen, to work as an analyst for him.

His first year on the job, Arora was buying and selling natural gas, fuel oil, coal, and electricity. His desk managed about $50 million.[14] That year the firm was going gangbusters. It ended 2002 with solid results—profits somewhere between 11 percent and 15 percent.[15] Amaranth's gains came in a terrible year for the stock market. The Dow Jones Industrial Average nosedived almost 17 percent, and the broader NASDAQ index shed almost one-third its value. Investors caught sight of Amaranth's stellar returns, and the cash started pouring in. By January 2003, the company was managing about $2 billion—twice what Maounis had envisioned earlier.[16]

The stock market had a rough start in 2003, although it finished the year rebounding significantly from its 2001–2 nosedive. Amaranth's returns continued to catch the attention of yield-hungry investors. All through 2003, earnings increased every month but one. The firm finished the year up more than 21 percent. Maounis doubled the assets of the energy trading desk to about $100 million. It brought in profits of about $20 million.[17] Arora started building his commodities group, hiring two more people to work under him. Overall, Amaranth managed a whopping $3.5 billion by the end of 2003—far beyond Maounis' original intent.[18] With so much more money under management, the firm branched out into new areas. It hired a portfolio manager to trade health care stocks, and added a financials group. Amaranth hired 120 more people that year and opened an office in Toronto.

But as Amaranth's financial firepower and varied investment strategies grew, the man who had provided the money to start the firm, Paloma's Sussman, grew increasingly concerned. Amaranth's activity was now too big for Paloma's back office to handle, which meant Sussman couldn't see all the trading Amaranth conducted. He always required transparency into the activities of managers with whom he invested. And he worried that Amaranth was managing too much money and had branched into areas that were outside Maounis's expertise.

So in October 2003, as money poured into Amaranth, Sussman told the firm he was pulling out all of Paloma's investments, although he kept a small personal ownership interest in the company.

Sussman's actions didn't upset Maounis. The relationship between the two firms was already growing strained. Maounis thought Paloma took advantage of the transparency they demanded of Amaranth's trading. He believed that whenever Amaranth traders did anything new, Paloma copied it. He even suspected Paloma traders of front-running Amaranth's trades, getting in ahead of Amaranth's investing.

Sussman explained his decision to exit from Amaranth to his investors in a December letter: "Amaranth is now simply much larger than what we believe is optimal for our capital." It would be difficult for the firm to exit positions if it ran into problems, he noted prophetically. Paloma's strategy, he reminded his investors, was to invest with "smaller trading managers, earlier in their life cycle, when they are not constrained by the illiquidity of large capital pools."

It was a maverick move. "Amaranth was an incredibly popular, trendy investment," says a former Paloma manager. "People were dying to get into Amaranth. Their returns were great."

The torrid pace of Amaranth's growth continued into 2004. Almost $1 billion was collected in the first quarter of 2004 alone.[19] Virtually overnight, Amaranth was managing more than $4.5 billion—more than four times what Maounis had originally planned—and the money still kept gushing in. And with it came enormous riches for Maounis. As the major owner of the firm, he pocketed most of the 1.5 percent management fee. Every $4 billion his firm managed for a year meant roughly $60 million for him.

Amaranth was hiring so many people so fast that salesmen from brokerage firms—who provided hedge funds with research reports and brought analysts to visit them—struggled to keep up. They scrambled to meet new employees and figure out what areas they covered and what kind of information they needed.[20]

Amaranth added four new investment strategies to its three original ones. And it overhauled its computer technology systems. Executives wanted better risk management and more advanced trading tools, as well as a system to integrate strategies and information.

It hired a chief information officer, expanding its fifty-five-person technology staff by several dozen, and bought more than three hundred computer servers, housed within a data center that could be accessed only through two fingerprint checkpoints.

But the new computer infrastructure, the research analysts, the legal staff, and the array of operational support staff the expanding firm needed were expensive. Amaranth, like other hedge funds at the time, passed some of those costs on to its investors.

Although he had once said he was aiming for a firm of $1 billion, Maounis now pushed hard to grow it ever bigger. The more money Amaranth managed, the more fees it took in and the greater the profits it could earn. Maounis traveled frequently, soliciting investments.

As the firm grew, with so many new employees and investment focuses, Maounis didn't micromanage his senior traders. They didn't need to run trades by him. Since he was not expert in many of the new investment areas it would have been difficult anyway. "Do what you want," he told traders, "but make sure the fund doesn't blow up."

He did, however, offer them some market wisdom from his father: "A trader can't be married to the model." It meant that traders could not just rely on their mathematical formulas to determine good investments. They had to understand industries and companies, not blindly follow their calculations.

When he was in Greenwich and not traveling, Maounis preferred the activity on the trading floor to being cooped up alone in his office. He wanted to follow financial markets and hang out with the traders he knew from his Paloma days. "It was kind of a joke," recalled a trader, "but people wondered what Nick did all day, because he spent two or three hours on the trading desk reading the *Wall Street Journal*."

At lunchtime he often corralled a group of traders, pressing them to go out to a restaurant. He would playfully tease them to enjoy life and cajole them into ordering fries or a high-calorie dessert.

He often picked up the tab. But sometimes he would smile and make a game out of who was going to fork over money for the bill. They'd flip a coin. He'd rib the other traders and get a kick out of watching someone else pay the check.

But despite the jokes and playfulness and the stream of new investment money pouring into the firm, all was not going well at Amaranth. During the first months of 2004 Amaranth's investments were struggling. In the first quarter, Amaranth was only up around 3 percent, about half what it had been in the same period the year before. By April, the firm's earnings were in a tailspin, down $29 million. The fund lost $21 million more in May. In June it was down another $6 million.[21] These three months of losses came close to wiping out the small profit of the first quarter, and by midyear Amaranth had a tiny gain of only 2 percent—compared to the 21 percent hike the year before. Its core strategy, bond arbitrage, made no money at all.

Maounis knew he needed to take dramatic action. He further expanded Amaranth's range of investment strategies. And he decided to expand the energy group. He increased the money allotted to it, and he and Arora looked around for another trader.

A headhunter sent Brian Hunter's resume to Maounis. Although Amaranth had traded with Deutsche Bank for some time, neither Arora nor Maounis really knew much about Hunter.[22] In the course of checking him out, they found out about a dispute Hunter had with the bank regarding his bonus. But they considered it just the usual pissing match between traders over payouts. They didn't know about the sudden December losses Hunter incurred at Deutsche Bank—only that his natural gas holdings over the year were profitable. Amaranth executives ran the usual background check on him. It turned up nothing about other issues Deutsche Bank had with Hunter. It would be August of that year before he filed a lawsuit against the bank, which would bring to public attention for the first time his heavy December losses, the zero bonus he received, and misgivings by senior Deutsche Bank executives about his maturity.

After interviewing Hunter, Maounis and Arora came away impressed. He appeared to have a good understanding of how to manage the considerable risks of energy trading. And if any Deutsche Bank officials had hinted at concerns about Hunter, well, Maounis and Arora had their own misgivings about some of the other Deutsche Bank people, so they weren't fazed by it.

Even if they had known all the details of Hunter's days at Deutsche Bank, it might not have made much difference. "There's a joke in the natural gas business that one way to get promoted to another firm is to blow up at your old firm," says an energy trader. "It seems to make no sense. But people know that if an individual can push the envelope in trading, one out of two or three times he will be right. And when he's right, the firm benefits."

Maounis also believed he had a talent for identifying gifted traders and portfolio managers. There were other energy traders he interviewed, but he really wanted Hunter. He hoped that Hunter would work under Arora as part of the energy team. But if Arora didn't like Hunter and didn't want to oversee him, then Maounis was prepared, despite his own lack of experience with energy futures, to have Hunter report directly to him. As it turned out, Arora was ready to bring him onto the commodities desk.

What complicated the move, however, were the negotiations around Hunter's pay. After his experience at Deutsche Bank, Hunter wanted to be paid a set percentage of whatever profits he generated. He wanted no part of the discretionary bonuses that the junior traders then working for Arora were allocated.

After some back-and-forth they hammered out a deal. If he made money for the firm, he would pocket part of it. But so would Arora. As in most hedge funds, Amaranth's senior portfolio managers who oversaw other traders were paid a percentage of the total net profits earned by all the traders on their desk. It was a means of compensating the senior trader for supervising and for taking a chance with new traders. After all, many new hires lost money initially. If that happened with Hunter, his losses would be netted with the revenue from the rest of the energy desk and would cut into Arora's bonus.

But Arora and Hunter were optimistic that wouldn't happen. So in the spring of 2004, one of Nick Maounis' new hires was the tall, athletic energy trader from Deutsche Bank, Brian Hunter.

WIDOW MAKER

E ven among hedge funds, which often fostered a more relaxed atmosphere than banks and usually offered their staff amenities such as free snacks, soft drinks, and sandwiches, Amaranth was considered as employee-friendly as you could get. It boasted spectacular facilities, perks, and parties.

Nick Maounis wanted his people happy. Happy people worked harder, thought more clearly, and made more money. They were less likely to skip to another firm. He wanted his firm to be such an enjoyable place to work that even when people left, they spoke glowingly of it. There would be no sniping and bitching about the firm, no negative rumors or innuendos to scare investors away.

Maounis enjoyed being able to satisfy his employees and basked in their appreciation. "Nick so much wanted to be liked," says a former colleague. He organized parties and big social events at the firm. And when he moved the company's offices up two floors to larger space in the same building, a short time after Hunter joined, he outfitted it with numerous toys and equipment.

There was a complete gym—with weights, treadmills, a movie screen, and a room devoted to Pilates—where employees could take a break from the market or work out after it closed. There was also a music room, which contained drums, high-end guitars, keyboards, and even sound equipment, so people could jam together.

At the back of the floor was an expansive game room with a giant big-screen television, pinball machines, and game tables, including Ping-Pong and, Hunter's favorite, air hockey. There was "always a kind of ongoing poker game after work," recalls a former Amaranth employee.[1] But the signature focus of the area was a stunning hand-carved pool table with amaranth stalks etched on the legs. Talk around the firm was that it cost tens of thousands of dollars.

Maounis spent lavishly to create the facilities, but believed it well worth it. If it helped generate a moneymaking idea from two portfolio managers meeting there to unwind after work, he explained to Amaranth executives, "that one idea could pay for the room ten times over."

Amaranth employees were a young crowd, in their twenties and thirties. A few were married, and some had small kids; they often hurried home after work. But many weren't. The atmosphere was fun, the facilities were great, and there was a lot of after-work socializing. There were Super Bowl parties, fantasy football leagues, and Ping-Pong tournaments. Every month employees celebrated birthdays with hors d'oeuvres, cake, and wine and beer at the bar.

"There was a fraternity house feeling. There was a keg on Friday nights in the break room in summer, every type of candy, snack, and soft drink in the kitchen," says a former employee. Hot breakfasts were served every morning. When the weather turned warm, people looked forward to seeing the ice cream cart come around. "They tried to bring in the best and the brightest and to keep them happy," says a former employee.[2] The dress code, although not quite flip-flops, was hedge fund casual—$300 jeans, polos, and T-shirts. Employees preferring a more formal look sported khakis and button-front shirts open at the collar. Sweatshirts, especially with team logos, were common in winter. Brian Hunter was often seen in a red Calgary Flames jersey. Suits and ties, if seen at all, were for meetings with clients.

When Amaranth was small, Maounis had everyone over to his Greenwich home for parties. As the firm outgrew that, the entertaining became more elaborate. In the summer, boats were rented on Long Island Sound for theme parties featuring magicians or poker, roulette, and twenty-one.

Of all the holiday celebrations and parties Amaranth sponsored, none left as big an impression on employees as Halloween. It was a way to foster employee bonding, particularly important in a firm hiring new people left and right. Halloween was Nick Maounis' favorite holiday, and at employment interviews, potential hires were asked if they liked to dress up for Halloween.

Every year just before Halloween, an office manager asked employees for any special requests. Then on the day before Halloween she and the company limo driver, who usually chauffeured guests and staff to and from the train station, drove over to Sofia's Costumes, in downtown Greenwich, for dozens of outfits. The store offered an extensive collection of antique, vintage, and new costumes. There were heavy brocades, thick velvets, metal armor, soft leathers, and satins. A rental for one costume could be as high as $300.

Some of the costumes were chosen with specific people in mind. Others might appeal to traders who were having a really good week or were locked in battle on certain trades. Those in a particularly megalomaniacal mood might like the Superman costume or the Napoleon uniform complete with hat. Others engaged in some difficult investment skirmishes might prefer Crusader, Darth Vader, or Batman outfits. There were Elizabethan dresses, lace wedding gowns, and Disney characters.[3]

The clothes were hung carefully on racks in the conference room. One by one, employees came into the room to choose their costume. Then a professional makeup artist and a hairstylist went to work. For some costumes, say a geisha, a special wig was purchased and fitted. After a few hours, virtually everyone in the office was in costume. They would stay that way throughout the day. There would be prizes for the best costume and the most outrageous getup.

One year Maounis, perhaps in a throwback to his former wrestling days, dressed as the muscular cartoon hero Popeye the Sailor Man. A couple of times he appeared in drag, complete with garish makeup. He got a kick out of teasing other guys into wearing drag too. Amaranth's costumed traders and portfolio managers would oversee millions of dollars of trades, place buy and sell orders on investments, run complex computer programs, and discuss risk analysis. One can only imagine what clients would have thought if they knew it was Batman or Tinker Bell on the other end of the phone line.

After joining Amaranth, Hunter first commuted to Greenwich from his home in New York City. Eventually he moved up to nearby Stamford with Carrie and their young son, Kaelen. Although Arora and his new hire were very different personalities and sported dissimilar trading styles, they got along. Hunter even attended Arora's wedding.

"Harry is quieter, has less need to be the center of attention than Brian," says a trader who knew them both. "Harry likes to sit down on a one-to-one basis and discuss things. He is much more intellectual than Brian. Brian is more intelligent than intellectual. Harry is the opposite. They're both way more intelligent than the average person. But sometimes Harry likes to sit back and think where Brian just moves forward."

As Hunter's manager, Arora—the slightly more seasoned and certainly more cautious trader—held Hunter's youthful exuberance in check. He oversaw Hunter's trading strategies, monitoring how he managed his investment risk and the degree to which he spread out his holdings.

Hunter and Arora discussed strategies and analyzed the market. Hunter readily shared his thoughts and ideas, telling Arora what he was buying or selling. When Arora thought Hunter was on to something, he asked him to acquire similar but much smaller positions for Arora's portfolio. Arora would "piggyback on me," recalled Hunter later.[4] It also gave Arora a good read on exactly what Hunter was doing and how his trades were performing.

But Arora, the commodities portfolio manager, was building a diversified trading desk. He strongly believed in allocating his assets among many products and different strategies, including metals, electricity, natural gas, oil, coal, and agricultural products. He didn't want to concentrate on natural gas, Hunter's specialty. Hunter was allocated only 10 to 20 percent of the money earmarked for commodities. Hunter bristled. He wanted to trade more, much more.

Despite the limits on the amount of his trading and the risks he could take, Hunter turned out to be wildly successful. Overall, Amaranth had lost money in three of the first six months of 2004. But in the last half of the year, thanks largely to the energy group—and Hunter in particular—the firm started eking out some gains each month. By the end of 2004 his part of the energy desk generated about $100 million in profit. Hunter, on the job for less than a year, brought in about $80 million of it.[5] And the firm as a whole was up between 8 and 10 percent for the year.[6] That was less than the previous year, but at least it was making money. For the last three months of the year, its net performance was more than $300 million.

All through the year money gushed in from investors, and the hedge fund continued to balloon. By the end of 2004, it managed between $6.2 billion and $6.7 billion, making it one of the largest hedge funds in the country.[7] Maounis rushed to hire enough people to manage all the money. Soon there were more than 220 people working at Amaranth. The firm opened offices in London and Singapore as well as branches in Toronto and Houston. Amaranth set up a campus recruiting program to bring in graduates from top schools such as Stanford and the University of Pennsylvania.

Brian Hunter was a standout trader at Amaranth in 2004. He had brought in tens of millions of dollars. He was eager and enthusiastic. But when Arora told him his payout for 2004 was going to be $8.5 million, he was not happy. In fact, he was visibly upset at the news. After what he had earned for the firm, he felt cheated. Although the bonus reflected the percentage of profits he had been promised when he signed on, he felt he deserved more. He had generated the bulk of the energy desk's profits, so why shouldn't he get an additional payout?

Hunter also resented the fact that Arora took home some of the profits he had generated, since Arora, as manager of the desk, was paid a percentage of the net total. That included the $80 million Hunter had racked up.

Arora and Hunter argued about it. Arora countered that he took the risk of overseeing Hunter. If Hunter had lost money instead, that would have cut into Arora's bonus. And if the loss exceeded the total profit of other traders it would mean they had a "loss carryforward." That loss would have to be earned back the next year before Hunter and Arora earned a bonus.

Arora asked Maounis what he should do about Hunter's demands. "It's your business, handle it," the confrontation-averse Maounis told him. Arora stuck to his position. But Hunter's anger didn't diminish, although he said little about it. Bonus checks arrived around late February. Then Hunter made his move.

Steven Cohen, founder of SAC Capital, was eager to have Hunter move over to his hedge fund. In April 2005 Hunter inked a contract to join SAC, sweetened with a $1 million signing bonus.[8]

SAC had about $5 billion under management and was having a phenomenally successful year. Indeed, Cohen came in second on *Trader Monthly*'s list of top earners in 2005, earning close to $1 billion. Cohen, aside from being a mega art collector, was an aggressive risk taker, known for sticking with losing investments if he believed in them. Not only would he stay in them, but he would double up his investments in hopes of recouping losses—just what Hunter had wanted to do at Deutsche Bank.[9] SAC seemed a good match for the young aggressive trader.

When Hunter handed in his resignation letter at Amaranth, Maounis panicked. Hunter was the best natural trader he had ever met, he told colleagues. He needed Hunter. Maounis wasn't going to just let him walk away. Maounis asked Hunter what it would take to keep him at Amaranth. In numerous closed-door meetings, they hammered out the lucrative terms.

Hunter issued three demands for staying at Amaranth. First, he wanted his own portfolio to trade, free from Arora's interference. Second, he wanted a higher payout than he and Arora had negotiated. Third, he wanted to move back to Calgary. On all three counts Maounis agreed. He dramatically upped Hunter's bonus allocation, agreeing to a hefty 15 percent on the profits he generated. He was no longer tied to the general energy and commodities group. In the industry it was called an "eat what you kill" bonus. If he made a lot of money for investors, he would make a lot of money for himself. It was a strong incentive to take huge risks to win big.

On top of that he got a guaranteed $10 million retention bonus.

Equally significant to Hunter—and ultimately catastrophic for Amaranth—was that Hunter was no longer under Arora's wing. He was allowed to manage his own trading fund. Hunter now reported directly to Maounis, not Arora, and was vice president and co-head of energy trading. He was on his own, planning his own strategy and making his own trades.

With the terms agreed upon, Hunter tore up his contract with SAC and opted to stay at Amaranth.[10] Maounis called SAC and worked out a deal to get him out of his contract there.[11]

Arora resented Maounis' decision to separate Hunter from the energy group. He had taken the risk of overseeing the new trader and had stood to lose money if Hunter had losses. Now that Hunter was successful, Maounis was taking him out from Arora's supervision, meaning that Arora would earn nothing from Hunter's trading. It set a bad precedent. Other traders having a good year would also want to go out on their own. The commodities group would fall apart.

Maounis' actions indicated he didn't consider Arora a partner, someone who would build up Amaranth's book of business, as Maounis had professed when hiring him. Energy products were interconnected, and Arora believed that gas, oil, coal, and electricity traders needed to be working as a team. But Maounis didn't appear interested in that. He had a trader earning enormous profits, and so that was where his focus lay.

Arora's dissatisfaction was widely known, and he considered leaving the firm. But Maounis was quick to try to mollify him. He gave Arora the same payout he'd given Hunter—Arora would take 15 percent of any profits his desk earned. Maounis also promised to consider Arora's proposal to start a separate Amaranth fund investing only in commodities.

So both Hunter and Arora remained at Amaranth, but their relationship was severely strained. Arora was angry about what had happened. Hunter knew it and recognized that Arora had lost money with the new arrangement, as well as face. But he didn't seem to care, flaunting his new independence. And he resented Arora for wanting to profit off his trading prowess.

From then on there was little interaction between the two energy traders. Hunter confined his laughing and joking to a few close pals, such as Matt Donohoe, his friend from his University of Alberta days, whom he had brought to Amaranth. He didn't discuss his trading with Arora.

Hunter had a new swagger, a new cockiness. He was supremely confident. His allocations increased. Brokers courted him, and the more money he managed, the more they fawned over him. He loved their expensive dinners and never-ending supply of high-priced tickets to sporting events. He bragged about becoming the most successful natural gas trader in the game. But to do that, he would have to upset the reigning king of natural gas.

"Everybody gets personal about it, everybody gets competitive about it," says another energy trader. "That's just part of the machismo of the industry. Everyone thinks they're the smartest guy, everybody thinks they're the best trader . . . If you're looking to make a billion dollars this year, there are only five or six guys out there you can make it from." And John Arnold was on top of that list.

As Hunter fired up his own trading operation and imagined himself as the premier natural gas trader, the man who sat atop the heap, John Arnold, was embroiled in a rare public dispute with descendants of the oil barons who'd prospected and developed the Texas oil and gas fields.

At the time, Arnold was getting ready to marry, and wanted to build his dream house. A year earlier he had purchased three acres along the bayou in the prestigious River Oaks section of Houston. On the site stood a turreted redbrick house designed by two famous Houston architects in the 1920s and built for one of the city's most politically and culturally influential families. Homes such as this, both architecturally significant and historic, were an increasingly endangered species in Houston. Adjacent to it was another house built by the same architects for the same family; it had now become part of the Museum of Fine Arts.

But Arnold had little interest in the house he'd bought, and he planned to raze it. In its place he wanted to build a 20,000-square-foot stark, angular structure of limestone, wood, and glass designed by the prestigious New York architect Alexander Gorlin, who dubbed the proposed house "cubist landscape." In the architect's renderings it looked less like a home than like a modern art museum.[12] And in some respects that was what it was going to be. With its interior courts, sides of glass, and expansive walls, it was the perfect showcase for Arnold's growing art collection.[13]

Historic preservationists in Houston were up in arms at Arnold's plans, arguing that if he wanted to build, he should have chosen a location without an important structure on it. What raised their ire too was Arnold's indifference to their concerns. He didn't return phone calls, didn't agree to meet. He rarely spoke to the preservationists. And when he did, they thought him condescending. "I remember saying to him, 'Sorry that the house couldn't be saved,'" recalls preservation activist Lynn Edmundson, director of Historic Houston, a nonprofit salvage firm. "That's when he brought up he was hiring this well-known, well-respected architect and building a one-of-a-kind masterpiece, and that would somehow justify tearing down a piece of Houston history."[14]

Ironically, the historic house known as Dogwoods had been built by the family of oilman James Hogg, who more than a century earlier had battled energy barons and financial speculators. Hogg became governor of Texas in the late 1880s. He rallied Texans against New York bankers, railroad magnates, and oil barons who were fixing prices and crippling small farmers and independent oilmen. For some Texans he remains the symbol of the independent, self-reliant entrepreneurs who founded the Houston oil industry. Many of the descendants of these entrepreneurs still live in River Oaks, which was the handiwork of the governor's son, Mike Hogg. The younger Hogg, a pioneer of urban planning, developed River Oaks as a model residential community in the 1920s. For its time, it was an innovative neighborhood, juxtaposing schools and shops, homes and undeveloped tracts. Mike Hogg, along with his sister, Ima, and their

father, were prominent leaders of Houston society, funding universities, scholarships, mental health programs, and symphony orches-
tras.[15]

Mike Hogg built a spectacular home along Bayou River in River
Oaks for his sister, naming it Bayou Bend. He later moved next door,
to the home he named Dogwoods. In the 1950s, Ima Hogg donated
her twenty-eight-room home and its collection of American paintings and crafts to the Museum of Fine Arts. Following Mike Hogg's
death, Dogwoods passed from one oil industry executive to another
until in August 2004 it was sold to John Arnold.

The following spring, the gas in the house was shut off. A crew
from an architectural antiques firm pried off the trim and hauled out
the arched windows, the claw-foot tubs, and a marble fireplace.[16]
When preservationists heard about the activity they knew there was
little time left to save the building.

One prominent River Oaks resident, Jane Dale Owen, mounted
a last-ditch effort to save the house. Owen's grandfather had been a
co-founder of Humble Oil, predecessor of Exxon—which, ironically, was one of the few oil companies that didn't embrace speculative derivative trading to hedge its oil production. Earlier Owen had
written to Arnold welcoming him to the neighborhood and inviting
him to a meeting of the River Oaks Committee, a group that discussed historic preservation, among other issues.[17] But he'd never
come.

When she realized how little time remained before Dogwoods
was to be torn down, she called on prominent people in the area to
help her. In mid-May a dozen or more residents of River Oaks, people not used to participating in protests, gathered by the huge gate
in front of Dogwoods. They carried little lanterns with candles that
gave off a warm glow. The weather was still quite warm, although it
was close to eight in the evening.[18] Several of those gathered gave
moving speeches, including Peter Brown, a noted architect and
urban planner, who would soon be elected to the city council. Brown
talked about how important it was for people to understand and
learn from their history.

But the candle-equipped protesters and Houston's anemic

historic-building recognition process offered little protection to Dogwoods. The house was torn down.

Soon after Hunter renegotiated his new Amaranth deal in the spring of 2005, he became curious about another natural gas trader, Robert "Bo" Collins, who was throwing his weight around in the market.

Knowing your competitors in the energy trading community is important. It is a fairly small group, one with less than two dozen traders dominating the marketplace.[19] Many have known each other since the days of Enron. When a new player enters the fray or a little-known trader becomes prominent, the others want to meet him.

One energy trader likens it to getting to know your opponents in poker. "Imagine sitting down at a Texas Hold'em game and you know everybody at the table except one other guy. You have a natural curiosity about what makes that guy tick, his strategies. In poker, they call it a 'tell.' These are tips, such as if he scratches his eye, you know he's nervous."[20]

And traders like to gauge how smart their opponents are. "If they were on the opposite side of a trade with me, it would make me stop and think hard about what they were seeing that I wasn't," says the trader. "Sometimes it can change or inform your strategy. Other times, it doesn't matter."

The previous Christmas, Collins had started his own natural gas hedge fund, MotherRock, and it grew quickly so that by spring 2005 it was trading hundreds of millions of dollars. It soon became one of the largest funds of its type, with $500 million in assets.

Hunter did not know Collins and wanted to meet him. So he asked a broker he did business with to include Collins in a dinner.

They dined at Del Frisco's Double Eagle Steakhouse, near Rockefeller Center in midtown Manhattan, a high-priced watering hole, which, with its rich dark wood bar and its virtually all-male clientele, had the feel of a men's club. It was the restaurant of choice for many energy traders, portfolio managers, hedge fund partners, analysts, and salespeople. In the skyscraper above the restaurant were offices of major financial firms and banks. Many more were in the buildings nearby.

Although his firm was relatively new, Bo Collins—a handsome man who carried himself with an easygoing self-confidence—was actually a veteran energy trader. Eight years older than Hunter and Arnold, he had started out as a banker at the Federal Reserve in Dallas, Texas. But Collins hated the politics involved with working for a bank and wanted to be a trader, where success was easily measured by how much money you made. So at age twenty-seven he headed to NYMEX to learn energy trading.

A few years later he returned to Texas to create the energy trading operation at El Paso Corporation, a major transporter of gas. Like other energy companies, El Paso was emulating Enron's enormously profitable business as a financial speculator in gas contracts. Collins, like John Arnold, engaged in hefty trades.

Collins quickly earned his firm and himself a fortune before moving on to become president of NYMEX—at the age of thirty-five, the youngest ever—just a few weeks before the September 11 attacks. As he was settling into his executive post, Enron and other giant energy-trading firms were collapsing and gas trading was slowing dramatically. Collins' innovations at NYMEX helped reinvigorate the gas trading business.

Collins was a man to know. But so was Hunter, who was now throwing some weight around in the energy trading markets. Collins, who was restarting his trading career, was interested in meeting the newcomer.

There was another reason as well. Brokers were talking up a trading war going on between Hunter and John Arnold, who were often on opposite sides of large trades. And Collins and John Arnold were friends. When Collins lived in Houston and worked for El Paso, the two had dominated natural gas trading. Often they'd engaged in friendly competition, trading against each other when they held different perspectives on how prices would fluctuate. Later, when Arnold set up his own hedge fund, he'd wanted Collins to join him, but Collins decided that he was still needed at NYMEX.

The night Collins and Hunter dined together at Del Frisco's,

Hunter waxed eloquent about his trading strategies. That was highly unusual for a gas trader. Generally, traders are supposed to lie low, especially those who trade huge positions, as Hunter was starting to do. They generally hid their actions, as Arora had learned to do trading currencies at Enron. If not, when they ended on the wrong side of the market the sharks would attack. For example, if prices tanked after a trader broadcast that he'd purchased massive amounts of gas for a certain month on a bet that prices would rise, other traders would immediately know he was in a bind and would hold back from buying from him, forcing prices even lower. Financial ruin could come quickly.

"There are some nice guys out there that won't trade against an injured party," says former Enron trader Gary Hickerson. "But come on. Once you know someone is bleeding and has to get out of a position, they're done."[21]

Hunter, however, liked to turn this threat on its head, publicizing his dominating positions, as he did that night. If other traders mimicked his actions, that would help push in his direction.

"Hunter was an attention hog, telling the rest of the market what he was up to because he thought that he would get other people to follow," says an energy analyst. "He expected them to say, 'Oh, Brian Hunter's so smart, if he's buying this spread we should too.'"

What Hunter discussed that night at Del Frisco's was a trade that only the most daring financial speculators engaged in. It could reap significant profits—or bring financial disaster. It was dubbed the "widow maker" because of the danger it posed to unlucky traders.

And it was a favorite of Brian Hunter, John Arnold, and Bo Collins.

The trade involved gas futures contracts for the months of March and April. Typically, gas prices between two consecutive months are not very different because the weather and supply situation in both tend to be similar. Prices are a little higher in the later month, however, to cover the additional cost of storing gas another thirty or so days, which runs a few cents per contract.

But this scenario does not play out for March and April. March is the end of the winter heating season. Supplies are already low and get lower through the month. April is considered the beginning of summer season, a time to refill the storage facilities. A glut of gas in March would be extremely rare. Supply might be a little higher than average if the winter was extremely mild, pushing down prices. But even then it's highly unusual for March gas to trade more than a dime below April. The opposite case is more likely. If the winter months are extremely cold, then by March there could be a gas shortage. If that happens, March gas prices skyrocket.

So traders who think it will be a cold winter buy March contracts, expecting the price to go up that month, and they sell April contracts, expecting price declines. But rather than lock in an absolute price level for these particular months, traders often use a strategy that involves relative prices between two months. They do this by linking their investments in both months, which is called a spread. Spreads are considered a safer investment, since the bet is on the difference between two months, not just on how one individual month will trade. They are also considered easier to analyze through mathematical models, since they are based on historical relationships between two months. When prices seem out of whack with where they usually have been, traders anticipate they will eventually return to their historical patterns. Betting on that, traders hope, will net them profits.

And trading spreads rather than individual months is also cheaper. To buy an individual contract a trader has to post collateral of around 10 percent of the value of the contract. At the time when Hunter was meeting Collins, the collateral cost, known as the margin payment, on spreads such as March-April was about half what it was for both months' contracts combined.

Say, for example, the March contract at the time cost $7.50 and the April contract was $7.25, the difference between them, the price spread, would have been 25 cents. The trader buying the spread makes money if the difference between the two prices widens. That can happen if either March prices increase or April prices decline. On the other hand, the trader selling the spread makes money if the spread between the prices declines.

That night at Del Frisco's, Hunter exuberantly told Collins and the others his theory that a trader could make a pile of money by betting on March prices being much higher than April's. It was almost a sure thing, since there was always a good possibility that winter prices would rise more than expected. Hunter's philosophy was that a trader should always play in this trade. It was an extended lecture, recalled those who were there that night—a sermon from a true believer. Hunter asserted that March prices could skyrocket—to "infinity" if the weather was cold enough or if gas supplies were disrupted.

Hunter seemed almost like a kid who made a great discovery and was eager to show off his intellect to his elders. Ironically, Collins had been one of the first major traders to invest heavily in this trade when he was at El Paso, earning hundreds of millions for his firm. And John Arnold had raked in Centaurus' first significant profits in early 2003 by betting on the "widow maker."

As they chatted at dinner that night, Collins cautioned Hunter that there were pitfalls in this strategy. For one, price differences of several dollars between the two months were extremely rare. And it mattered a lot whether the price differential was already huge when the trader placed his bets. Prices were more likely to return to the normal range than explode, Collins warned, and that could be disastrous.

But Hunter believed he could protect himself against significant losses if his huge investments in the March-April spread soured. It involved investing in other contracts further into the future, which he saw as a counterweight to the "widow maker" trade. Some traders saw holes in his argument—what he considered his counterweight trades didn't affect the risk inherent in the March-April trade. But the other traders and brokers present at that dinner listened avidly. One thing was clear: Brian Hunter would be betting big on the "widow maker" spread.

That spring, as Hunter came out from under Arora's wing, Maounis started to turn over more and more assets to him. Investing results for other traders at the firm were terrible during April and May, with losses of close to $300 million.[22]

The problem was convertible bonds, in which Amaranth was still heavily invested. They had their worst showing in decades that year. Many hedge funds, attracted by what they believed was easy money—provided they could do the calculations right—jumped into the investment strategy. But some firms made mistakes, and others were jolted by unexpected events and extreme changes in bond prices. A number of convertible bond hedge funds went out of business, and those still functioning barely squeaked by.[23] Amaranth's investments in General Motors bonds were particularly hard hit. The bonds were downgraded by bond-rating firms as speculation rose that the troubled automaker would file for Chapter 11 bankruptcy protection.[24]

Much of the mushrooming hedge fund industry was struggling as well. The CSFB-Tremont Hedge Fund Index was down 0.1 percent for the first four months of 2005—better than the S&P 500's 4 percent loss in that period, but not good enough for the wealthy and institutional investors who expected better for their "two and 20." Too much hedge fund cash was chasing too few good opportunities, it appeared, and there were predictions of a coming shakeout in hedge funds.

Maounis was worried and looked to Hunter for help to stem his firm's slide. "We need you," Maounis pleaded. "We need you to come through."[25]

Maounis began shifting more and more money into the profitable energy investment portfolio. In early 2005, 20 percent of the firm's assets were devoted to energy; by the summer it was up to 30 percent.[26] The multistrategy hedge fund was starting to look a little lopsided. What was billed as a diversified investment fund was starting to look like a heavily focused energy trading firm.

PITCHING TO GRANDMA

Nick Maounis was making his pitch.

In dark suit, crisp white shirt, and bright blue-and-white silk tie, Maounis was addressing the board of the San Diego County Employees Retirement Association (SDCERA). He came to San Diego that day—July 25, 2005—to tell board members why they should invest $175 million with Amaranth. The meeting had already been going on for some time, and people munched quietly on sandwiches as they listened to Maounis.

He was a bulky man now in his forties—baby-faced and balding, with a thin comb-over and hair that slightly overhung his shirt collar. He projected an air of calm and confidence and painted a picture of a firm at the top of its game.

"Amaranth is an organization which has $6.5 billion," he said. "But it also has 300 people. It has 140 investment professionals. It's able to commit capital across the globe—trade anytime, anything, anywhere in the world," he stressed, noting that he had just been in Hong Kong and Singapore.[1]

Amaranth was "multistrategy," he told the board. "We have expertise, for example, in technologies, utilities, financial services, insurance, health care, consumer products, cyclical and REITs." He highlighted the firm's convertible bond and merger arbitrage teams.

At no time did Maounis mention Brian Hunter and his burgeoning energy-trading arm. Indeed, Maounis didn't mention energy at all, despite the fact that close to one-third of Amaranth's assets were now devoted to the volatile energy-trading business.

Maounis sought to reassure the board about the care he took to safeguard Amaranth's investments.

"The most important thing for us, really, is to minimize the downside," he told the hushed meeting room. "We will typically give away upside. We don't want to hit home runs. We want to hit singles and doubles."

Usually the meetings of the pension association, which represented thirty-seven thousand county retirees—sheriffs, librarians, park rangers, social workers, among others—were businesslike and formal. But before Maounis took the podium, the July board meeting was highly emotional. The room was packed with retirees. There was an overflow room where a sound system had been hurriedly hooked up. Union leaders and twenty-six retirees came to the microphone, often in wheelchairs or hobbling on crutches.

Like many other counties throughout the country, San Diego County was in a fiscal crisis. Pensioners, especially those with health problems, worried that the board might eliminate a discretionary benefit that helped cover health insurance premiums. They besieged board members with emails, letters, and telephone calls before the meeting.

Brian White, the pension association's CEO, began the meeting that day by telling retirees they were misinformed. He gave a PowerPoint presentation aimed at convincing them the proposals under review by the board would not eliminate the medical benefits or a special cost-of-living adjustment.

Nobody seemed too reassured by his comments.

Neither program was guaranteed by the county. Instead, they were funded only if the county achieved "excess earnings" from its investments. Proposals before the board would give the county leeway to use this additional money instead to provide an extra cushion of protection for vested retiree pension benefits.

The county was assuming an 8.25 percent return on investments to meet all its commitments. Anything above that was considered "excess" and could be used for these benefits. But if returns were lower, the county or its employees would have to increase contributions or benefits might be cut.

Underlying the discussion about the discretionary benefits was a fear that the basic pension benefit itself was in danger. It was going to be difficult to meet investment objectives, board members cautioned, and that was the only way the pension had been fully funded in the past. Just that week, noted another member, Hewlett-Packard had announced it would phase out its defined-benefit pension plan, joining IBM, Sears, and Motorola, which had done so earlier in the year.

The 1990s bull market had been good to the pension fund: its ratio of assets to liabilities was very high. Investment income had risen almost 16 percent in fiscal 2000. Back then it could easily cover the benefits it promised. In fact, it was more than fully funded, with assets almost 110 percent of liabilities.

But, over the next five years, the retirement programs' investments returned only about 5 percent on average, well below its target rate.[2] True, there were a few terrific years, such as 2004, when returns blazed ahead at more than 21 percent. Even for fiscal 2005, which had just ended, investments were up by double digits. But overall, poor performance of the stock market had significantly hurt the pension fund.[3]

Now, retirees, worried that their benefits were in jeopardy, had come to the July meeting to make impassioned and tearful pleas to the board to maintain the health insurance and cost-of-living adjustment programs.

One of the more emotional was Keith Bailes, who worked his way to the microphone with his arms looped inside the tops of metal crutches to decry the "coldness and heartlessness" of the policies the board was considering. Deriding as "gobbledygook" the board's discussion of vested versus discretionary benefits, Bales said passionately, "When you've promised someone if they've worked twenty years they'll get their health benefits, I don't care what you call it. You're responsible for providing it to them."

Union leaders admonished the board for pitting employees against retirees. They criticized the board for putting these discretionary benefits in jeopardy. For nearly four hours the board heard explanations, criticism, debate, and denunciations.

Four of the board members were appointed by the county Board of Supervisors; four were current or retired county employees. The county's elected treasurer, a former stockbroker, also sat on the board. Only two or three members had investment experience. Others worked at or had retired from jobs with the sheriff's office, probation department, real estate division, tax assessor's office, and the district attorney's office. Although not explicitly stated, important philosophical differences divided the board members. In San Diego County, as in cities, counties, and states around the country, pension and health benefits for public employees were under siege. Conservatives made taxes a curse word and demanded drastic cuts in government spending. Public employees and their political supporters didn't counter with strong support for an expanded role for government in society. They didn't argue that government employees' benefits should be a model for the private sector. Instead, they were defensive, merely trying to hold on to their existing benefits.

At SDCERA meetings, conservative members such as Diane Jacobs, a member of San Diego's Board of Supervisors, angrily decried the idea of tax increases to shore up the pension fund or provide other benefits. Other board members fretted about which benefits were most endangered.

After the long, stressful discussions that morning about the state of the program's finances and the specter of benefit cuts, the board voted on the underlying issue: how should it use any "excess" money? Should it be used for supplemental benefits? Or, as the proposals directed, to shore up the guaranteed pension benefits? It was a tie. The members took another vote, and yet another. Every vote resulted in a 4-to-4 tie. In the end, the board delayed action until a meeting in September, when a ninth member was expected to be present to break the tie.

It had been a tiring meeting, but there was more to come. Next, the board was to take up the issue of how to keep up investment returns. On the agenda was whether to allocate investment money to two hedge funds, D. E. Shaw and Amaranth. Many people in the audience took a break to get lunch.

The hedge funds were being considered for what the retirement board called its Alpha Engine, the pot of money devoted to riskier investments with the goal of achieving results higher than average stock market returns. In 1999, the Alpha Engine was allocated $400 million—almost 11 percent of the pension fund's assets.[4] The amount in the fund expanded after the board hired an outspoken advocate of more aggressive "alternative" investment strategies, David Deutsch, as chief investment officer in 2004. By September 2005, the county had invested about $1.3 billion in hedge funds—nearly one-fifth its $6.8 billion in assets.[5]

Like many pension funds at the time, SDCERA was strapped for money and looking for better returns than it could get from just plain stocks or bonds. The fund's financial problems had also increased in 2002, when the Board of Supervisors significantly raised benefits, lowered the retirement age, and hiked payouts for various employees.

To help pay for the changes, the county issued bonds over the following two years, adding $1.2 billion to the retirement fund's reserves. But the pension fund was still in a precarious state. When the board met that July, the pension program was 80.3 percent funded.[6] Eighty percent was considered a critical funding level. Anything less raised significant concern about the ability of the program to pay future benefits.[7]

The board was under pressure to produce high returns. "You only get returns on stocks of 3, 4, 5 percent," explains one board member.[8] "We needed 8.25 percent to break even. In order to make even more money, you need to invest in riskier things, which is fine as long as you have the staff to keep watch on them day after day."

Not everyone on the board was that sanguine. Dan McAllister, treasurer of San Diego County and a former stockbroker, was more concerned. "The investment staff is forced to look under rocks that have never been turned over before for opportunities to invest our dollars," he worried. He believed that if an investment was too complex for board members to understand or explain, they probably shouldn't be putting money into it. "Even pretty well-educated people would have a difficult time explaining the alpha engine to a judge and jury," he warned.[9]

San Diego wasn't alone in turning to hedge funds. After the 2001–2 stock market collapse, a lot of underfunded pension plans—along with endowments for schools, hospitals, and charities—put some money in hedge funds. It was a marked change from how pension investments had been structured in the past. Until the late 1940s, the vast majority of pension money was in bonds, and only about 5 percent in corporate stocks.[10] This started to change in the 1950s, with publication of a thesis and book by Harry Markowitz describing what has become known as modern portfolio theory. Markowitz later won the Nobel Prize in economics for his concepts.

Conducting detailed analyses of investment returns, he concluded that more-volatile investments achieved greater profits over time. The more risk, the greater the potential profits. Combining investment types reduced the risk and still generated good returns. Pensions and endowments were encouraged to spread their investments among stocks, bonds, cash, real estate, and other types of investments in order to increase returns but limit risk.

The roaring stock market of the 1990s encouraged pensions to invest heavily in stocks. But when the market tanked, states and local governments suffered budget crises. For many, it was difficult to meet pension obligations, particularly since there was opposition to raising taxes, cutting benefits, or increasing employee contributions. Many pensions quickly embraced hedge funds, hoping to eke out profits through complex alternative investments, including arbitrage schemes, financial derivatives, and commodities. Hedge funds also avidly sought out pension money.

As of 2005, the Pennsylvania state employees' pension fund had invested almost one-quarter of its assets in hedge funds. The California Public Employees' Retirement System, the largest public pension fund in the country, started with an initial $50 million investment in hedge funds in 2002 and by 2005 had invested $1 billion.[11] Surveys show that by 2006, between 21 percent and 27 percent of pension funds had investments in hedge funds.[12] By 2004, pension money held in hedge funds reached $100 billion.[13]

Generally pensions were cautious about how much money they actually invested in hedge funds. Most only put in about 5 percent of assets. But for a few, such as SDCERA, it was more. Some invested as much as 30 percent.[14] (Endowments embraced hedge funds too. Schools with endowments over $1 billion had on average about 22 percent of their money invested with hedge funds by 2005. For endowments with less than $500 million, hedge fund allocations averaged about 12 percent.)[15]

But investing public pension money in hedge funds was controversial with many pension fund managers and public officials throughout the country. Like SDCERA, Massachusetts public pension managers turned to hedge funds. In 2004, its managers argued for taking some risks in pursuit of higher returns. The pension fund system invested $22 million with Amaranth in 2005. But hedge fund investments made Secretary of the Commonwealth of Massachusetts William Galvin uneasy. He warned that "there's an inconsistency between the concept behind hedge funds, which are high-risk, high-return, and the concept behind pension funds, which is little risk, guaranteed return."[16] They were, Galvin contended, "gambling."[17]

SDCERA, like some pension funds, employed an in-house investment professional, David Deutsch, to create and monitor its overall investment strategy, but it relied on a consultant, in this case Rocaton Investment Advisors Inc., based in Norwalk, Connecticut, to pick specific hedge funds.

Money invested with the help of a consultant is known on Wall Street as "sticky money." Consultants, who only advise clients on when to invest or withdraw money, are reluctant to admit mistakes and thus are slow to suggest pulling out an investment. Sticky money is good for hedge funds but not necessarily for the institutions that stay with losing investments.

Other pension funds invest through funds of funds. Funds of funds burgeoned in the late 1990s when investment consultants decided to manage money directly. Initially they focused on investing in Internet stocks, but as hedge funds took off, they increasingly started putting clients' money into portfolios of hedge funds to diversify the risks. These funds of funds grew quickly, from about 122 in 2000[18] to about 675 two years later.[19] By 2006 there were an estimated 2,500 funds of funds, controlling about 40 percent of hedge fund assets.[20]

"Funds of funds have a reputation for being 'fast money,'" explains hedge fund manager Selena Chaisson. "They actually manage the money and make the allocations to hedge funds. They are demanding; they are trigger pullers."[21] Often they pull out of a fund at the first sign of trouble, even if they have to pay a redemption fee, because they need to justify the hefty fees they charge clients—between 1.5 percent and 2 percent of assets invested. And that's on top of fees the hedge funds charge. This constant shifting of money by funds of funds puts more pressure on hedge funds to focus on short-term gains.

Funds of funds money was crucial to Amaranth, totaling about 60 percent of its assets, and much of this cash came from pensions and endowments. The New Jersey public pension system, for example, invested $25 million in Amaranth, through several funds of funds. Pensions that invested directly in hedge funds, such as SDCERA, were about 6 percent of Amaranth's funds. Direct endowment investments were 2 percent.

Generally the consultants and funds of hedge funds concentrated their clients in a limited number of investments, favoring larger firms. "There's real safety in numbers," noted hedge fund manager Richard Medley. "Once you get above $1 billion [in assets], that's the marker and people will allocate to you. If something goes wrong, they say, 'Well, look, everyone else was in it.'"[22]

On behalf of SDCERA, Rocaton executives met with Amaranth management and were impressed by what they saw. They liked the mechanisms it appeared to have in place to control investment risks, including its large risk-management team. And they were impressed with the firm's multistrategy investment policy. It held weekly investment committee meetings, Amaranth's executives explained, and continuously redeployed its capital into areas that appeared to have the best moneymaking opportunities.

SDCERA sorely needed good returns. The Alpha Engine had, in its first ten years, returned a measly 3.2 percent on average.[23] So Rocaton rated Amaranth a "buy" and introduced it to SDCERA's investment staff. In March 2005, Deutsch and SDCERA's assistant chief investment officer, Lisa Needle, flew out to meet Amaranth officials in Connecticut and tour its offices. They were shown around the trading floor, were introduced to portfolio managers, and spent time with the risk evaluation team. Three people, they were told, focused on monitoring the risk of the energy team's holdings—one of five major areas of investment at the time. Amaranth executives emphasized that this team not only tracked investments but also worked with portfolio managers as they were planning strategy to minimize risk.[24]

Amaranth, like most hedge funds eager to reassure the growing number of institutional investors that their money was safe, devoted pages of its offering documents to extolling its risk monitoring. And while some firms hired only a few risk managers, Amaranth employed more than a dozen highly trained people. SDCERA staff was as impressed as Rocaton. Deutsch and Rocaton decided to bring two hedge funds, Amaranth and D. E. Shaw, before the retirement board at its July 25, 2005, meeting. Deutsch wanted them accepted as part of the Alpha Engine. His intent was to invest $175 million in Amaranth.

It had been an emotional four hours that July day by the time Robin Pellish, the Rocaton consultant who vetted hedge funds, stepped to the podium before Maounis. She was well aware of board members' concerns regarding the riskiness of hedge funds. But the morning discussion had already focused on the necessity of keeping up investment profits to prevent benefit cuts or tax hikes. Pellish carefully constructed her remarks about the funds to address these issues. "We are going to monitor them carefully," she stressed. Rocaton would increase the frequency of calls to fund managers—traditionally done quarterly—to monthly, she told the board. They would review hedge fund performance, looking at their investment strategies, their diversification, and whether "risk of the manager is consistent with what we expect," said Pellish. Rocaton, along with SDCERA staff, would also conduct on-site visits with the hedge funds. They would evaluate any personnel changes or big monetary gains, not just losses, to understand what was happening at the firm.

"Due diligence is only going to be expanded and made more thorough," Pellish promised.

One board member raised a concern that many hedge funds were investing in the same strategies, creating less opportunity for each to make money. Could Rocaton monitor where its hedge funds invested, to make sure those allocations were still moneymakers? She assured him that Rocaton would monitor the flow of funds. And, Deutsch added, they looked for money managers willing to quickly move funds around if their strategies weren't working well.

Nonetheless, SDCERA's access to information about Amaranth would be restricted. The pension fund would have to sign agreements that allowed the hedge fund to share certain key information only with Rocaton—not with the pension fund itself. The reason was that the hedge fund, which jealously guarded information about its operations, feared its strategies would become too visible under California's freedom-of-information laws, which provide public access to documents of public agencies. SDCERA, they worried, could be a disclosure risk for proprietary information they didn't want shared with competitors. So Amaranth would limit the pension plan's direct access to information. What it meant, however, was that SDCERA would lose any ability to directly monitor the fund's activities, making it more dependent on its consultant.[25]

After Maounis' short presentation, his audience was wary. Board member and investment professional Laura DeMarco pounced. Her target: investment fees. At the time, Amaranth was charging a 1.5 percent management fee and a 20 percent incentive fee, and on top of that was collecting up to an additional 2 percent fee on investments. Why did Amaranth charge its investors such a hefty fee, more than the already outrageous fees of most hedge funds, she demanded? For SDCERA, a 3.5 percent fee meant spending more than $6 million on its $175 million investment, even if Amaranth didn't make it any money.

Maounis defended the extra fee as justified by Amaranth's multi-strategy approach to investing. It paid for the personnel and technology necessary to Amaranth's approach. Having some of its expenses covered, he argued, prevented Amaranth's money managers from taking larger risks in order to generate larger returns.

But DeMarco was not fully satisfied. "I'm used to one and one-half to two plus 20," she persisted. "Three and one-half [plus 20] is really rich."

"Greedy," interjected someone else.

Maounis forced a laugh and shrugged. "I think you really have to look at the net returns that are generated by the funds you are looking at. That's really what it comes down to."

DeMarco was still not convinced. "I invest in hedge funds, and this is the greatest fee I've ever heard of," she complained.

Deutsch backed up Maounis. He acknowledged that Amaranth's fees "were startling, to say the least." But he assured the board that the due diligence he and his staff had conducted took into account "all the fees" and investment results. Amaranth achieved the returns that the pension board wanted, he said. He stressed that its investment diversification would reduce its risks.

Pellish stated that high fees were common on the East Coast. "We visited these shops in New York and Connecticut, and they have huge staffs, IT, huge resources, and it's clear it's not a shop that is going to run on low fees," she argued. If the California pension fund wanted real Wall Street advice, they would have to pay Wall Street fees.

Maounis noted that his bonus, and those of the portfolio managers and traders, did not come out of the fees. Rather, Amaranth's bonuses were paid only when Amaranth made money for its clients, because it came out of the 20 percent of profits that Amaranth kept. If the firm loses money, "we don't get paid," he stressed.

Deutsch was reassuring. "A lot of the risk that we take on with an Amaranth—with any of the multistrategies—is diversified away in the portfolio," he said. "That is why we are doing this—to get diversified gains from going out in terms of risk and return." He didn't mention Amaranth's huge concentration in high-risk energy contracts.

So Deutsch and Pellish recommended that the board support investing in Amaranth.

"I make a motion that we move forward with this manager," said a board member.

The vote was all ayes and no nays—unanimous. Despite board members' concerns, SDCERA would invest $175 million in Amaranth.

But even before the vote was taken, Maounis' smile had disappeared and he had scooped up his papers from the podium. "Thank you," he said. He wheeled around and was gone in an instant.

Not all investors evaluating Amaranth at the time were as willing to invest in the hedge fund. Executives of Fauchier Partners, a British-based fund of hedge funds that managed about $4.3 billion on behalf of pensions, endowments, insurance companies, and wealthy individuals, decided they didn't like what they saw when they went to Connecticut to take a look at the hedge fund. The firm had just inherited a $30 million investment position in Amaranth that summer, after it took over a competitor.

Soon after SDCERA signed on as an investor, Fauchier Partners went ahead with plans to give Amaranth the required three months' notice in order to pull out its money that December. In fact, following meetings in Connecticut with Maounis and other Amaranth executives, Fauchier's "concerns were sufficient," it later told its investors, to justify paying a 1.5 percent penalty for early exit.

A year later, Fauchier co-founder Christopher Fawcett explained to his investors why he had pulled out from Amaranth. Fawcett's assessment is particularly important because he also chaired the Alternative Investment Management Association, the representative body for hedge funds worldwide.

Amaranth's problems, he wrote, were "anything but unforeseeable. Amaranth had just about every characteristic we do not look for in a hedge fund." He criticized Amaranth for insufficient risk controls. He scorned its highly leveraged investing, the lack of an independent entity to verify its profits and losses, and the difficulty of finding out exactly how it was investing. He said he was unnerved by a "hubristic" management team and concentration on energy. In summary, he wrote, Amaranth was "a fund with bad risk management and unattractive terms for investors."[26]

THE $100 MILLION MAN

I n the summer of 2005, Brian Hunter spied a bargain.

Natural gas supplies nationally were plentiful, gas production was unusually high, and by midsummer storage facilities were brimming with the stuff. Prices were low, hovering between $6 and $8 per MMBtu. Since investors didn't expect any reason for prices to shoot up, nobody was very interested in options that gave them the right to buy natural gas well above that. The options were going for bargain-basement prices. So Hunter swooped in, scooping up millions of dollars of options on the cheap.[1]

Energy was a growing colossus in Amaranth, and by August 2005 energy investments were tying up 36 percent of Amaranth's money.[2] Hunter was taking a huge gamble when he bought up his millions of dollars of options. He would profit only if natural gas prices rose dramatically. And that didn't seemed likely to happen.

Then Mother Nature came roaring in to Hunter's rescue.

On the evening of August 25, 2005, Hurricane Katrina struck. It hit the Florida coast between Miami and Fort Lauderdale first. Torrential rain, twelve inches or more, pelted the coast, and winds roared to 80 miles an hour. About a dozen people died, more than a million people lost power, and flooding was extensive.

Then, after crossing Florida, the storm surged into the Gulf of Mexico and strengthened. In the Gulf, it was classified a Category 5 storm, the most powerful. The damage to oil and gas operations in the Gulf was extensive. Four days later, the storm slammed into

Louisiana, with sustained winds of 125 mph. New Orleans was devastated.

Hurricane Rita came next. One month later, it too tore through the Gulf and ripped through Louisiana and Texas. The major delivery point for natural gas, the Henry Hub, was under water. Repair crews couldn't get to it because roads were flooded and covered by downed trees and power lines.

For Brian Hunter and Amaranth, the storms were welcome news. Katrina and Rita caused major damage to oil pipelines and rigs in the Gulf, which would affect natural gas prices. More than 450 pipelines were damaged. Drilling platforms—113 of them—were destroyed. There were close to 150 oil spills, six involving more than a thousand barrels of oil. Gas production dropped from slightly over 1.6 trillion cubic feet per month before the hurricanes to 1.4 trillion cubic feet immediately after.

Natural gas prices rocketed up. In June, the futures contract for the next month was selling for about $6. On October 25, a month after Rita struck, the price reached $14.33. Prices then went on a roller-coaster ride, falling, then peaking in mid-December at $15.38, then falling again to a little more than $6.

The undulating prices made a fortune for Hunter. His options to buy gas paid off handsomely when prices rose. But even his minor holdings—short positions he took as a hedge if prices fell—made money. "There were some fairly random occurrences after Katrina and Rita that also made money for Brian," says a former Amaranth employee. "Both his long positions, and where he was short as hedges. Where he was short, by chance he was locked into gas in areas where prices collapsed."[3] Whether it was because of luck or cunning, Brian Hunter could do no wrong.

The effect of Hunter's trading on Amaranth was dramatic. While the firm lost money for the first six months of 2005—down almost 1 percent—it gained more than 5 percent in August. In September, it was up an additional 7.5 percent.[4]

After months of shaky results, the firm turned itself around. It closed the year up almost 15 percent after fees. And it was all because of Hunter's investments. The energy book was responsible for 98 percent of Amaranth's earnings.[5]

Employees—down to the secretaries and limo driver—started calculating their bonuses. Because of Hunter's profits, the firm had earned money to divvy up at the end of the year. The largest bonus by far went to Hunter, with the farm-country boy from Calgary netting a bonus of $113 million.[6]

Everyone at Amaranth was making money because of Hunter. Wall Street was abuzz. Some traders were envious; others not yet invested in energy wondered if they should get in on it. A few were dubious about Hunter's trading. They warned that players betting a huge pile of chips could reap a windfall but could also be wiped out. More than anything else, however, there was disbelief that a guy as young and inexperienced as Hunter could make such a killing.

In its monthly newsletter to investors, Amaranth celebrated the destruction wrought by Katrina and noted that even though "sister Hurricane Rita did not have the same catastrophic impact," it did enough damage to keep gas prices up.[7]

John Arnold had been contemplating the upcoming hurricane season too, assessing where prices were headed. He thought there was a good chance they would rise, and he placed his bets. One large set of trades he negotiated was with oil producer British Petroleum, whose traders were worried prices might decline.[8] When the hurricanes hit, Arnold made money, lots of it.

Arnold also expected prices to quickly drop from their hurricane-sparked highs, say other traders. So he started to short gas prices. But he was too early. Prices remained high, and Arnold ran into trouble. As he lost money, brokers demanded he pay more collateral on his trades. Arnold struggled to meet their demands.[9]

But Arnold was willing to take the pain because he believed in his analysis. "When he feels he really understands the supply and demand, although his timing may be off, he's willing to ride through his analysis," says a fellow gas trader. "And if he's timed it wrong, even on large size, and he has a 30 percent drawdown in a two-week period, he's willing to live through it, whatever the short-term event is. And he's had investors that are willing to ride through that short-term pain with him."

Finally, in the second half of December, prices dropped, and Arnold ended up with blockbuster returns. His fund was up 160 percent for the year.[10] By the end of the year it was managing $1.5 billion.[11]

Bo Collins at MotherRock also was having a good year. His firm was up 23 percent.[12]

A few weeks after the hurricanes passed through and Hunter scored big, Amaranth's Calgary office was finally ready to open. Calgary, a major oil and gas center, wasn't an inappropriate place for Hunter to be, and Amaranth had several other offices abroad. But it took months to arrange, as business was booming in Calgary and office space and staff were hard to find. By October 2005 everything was finally ready, and Hunter and his family, after living for four years in the New York/Connecticut area, moved back to Calgary, near his parents and other family. He already owned two and a half acres in a suburb west of Calgary, bought when Maounis had hired him, although it would take some time yet to build a house.[13]

Initially he was the firm's only employee in the office. Later on, he hired several traders to work with him. There was an electricity trader who invested in California and Rocky Mountain power, and a trader of propane, ethane, and butane—natural gas liquids. Several others worked with Hunter on natural gas. There was administrative staff. But there were never any risk management people sitting in the office, talking with the traders and evaluating the trades. That was still done from Greenwich by David Chasman, who was the primary risk manager for the natural gas portfolio. When Hunter had been working in Greenwich he sat three or four seats down from Chasman.

Chasman—short, portly, and opinionated—had earned his PhD from MIT in physical chemistry. He had previously worked as a risk manager at San Diego–based Sempra Energy Trading, which specialized in trading and marketing natural gas and other energy commodities. Chasman's job there was similar to what he did at

Amaranth—working with natural gas traders to determine the value of their portfolios and monitor the risk of their positions. Another guy brought in by Chasman, Karl Koster, devised the computer system that tracked their holdings.

Chasman reported to Rob Jones, the head of risk management. The tall, soft-spoken Jones had an air of the academic about him. He had joined Paloma in 1989 to manage an international arbitrage portfolio and worked with Maounis during his last four years at Paloma. Prior to that, he had worked at Goldman Sachs with Fischer Black, developing arbitrage strategies and techniques to limit portfolio risks. He was well known in his field. Indeed, he helped conduct a study for the New York Stock Exchange evaluating market risks brought to light during the 1987 stock market crash. However, he had no experience in energy trading, with its acute volatility and high risks.

Chasman believed in Hunter. He told Maounis Hunter was the best commodity trader he had ever seen. "He has a very strong understanding of the underlying trading instruments and a good grasp of market supply-and-demand fundamentals," he later testified.[14] Chasman was responsible for monitoring Hunter's trades, evaluating his portfolio, and assessing what would happen if prices didn't go his way. He calculated the value-at-risk of Hunter's holdings. Chasman was hired to be a tough watchdog over Hunter and his team, but other traders say they seemed more like friends.

When Hunter was in Greenwich, Chasman could follow his exchange trading in real time, questioning his strategies, making suggestions, warning about pitfalls. Chasman could easily hear about over-the-counter trades. When Hunter moved to Calgary, there was no computer system at the firm's Greenwich headquarters capable of viewing Hunter's trades in real time.[15]

Hunter provided Chasman information on his trades, although sometimes there was a wait on details. Their interaction—give-and-take about the markets, discussions about strategy—was now more difficult. Chasman later told government officials he recognized a need for risk personnel "on the ground" in Calgary.[16] But no one was sent, or hired, to work out of the Calgary office. Instead, the firm relied on email, instant messaging, and phone calls to keep abreast of what was happening there. Hunter and his traders spoke to Chasman and his guys daily, frequently more often. But the Federal Energy Regulatory Commission later charged that the lack of on-the-scene risk managers significantly hurt the firm's ability to constantly monitor exactly how risky its investments were.[17]

As 2005 wound down, Arora's misgivings about his role at Amaranth and about Hunter grew. He acknowledged that Hunter had turned around Amaranth's losing year, resulting in double-digit profits. And he thought Hunter had some good investment strategies going into the hurricane season. But the size of Hunter's positions was growing. They weren't yet a danger to the firm, but they were larger than anything Arora would have put on. And while Hunter's main bet on prices rising had paid off after the hurricanes, a colleague remembers Arora pointing out that the trades easily could have gone the other way if the weather had been different.

Other things were bothering Arora too. Nothing had come of his talk with Maounis about setting up a separate commodity fund. Now, with the firm's attention focused on Hunter's trading, Arora was certain it was not going to happen.

Although he didn't have any say about Hunter's trades, Arora generally was called in by management to speak with investors about the complete energy portfolio. He was the face of the energy desk. Even if both Hunter and Arora were in the room with investors, Arora usually did most of the talking. He was the more seasoned portfolio manager, more at ease expounding on micro and macro issues. But discussing the entire energy desk bothered Arora. While he understood his book of business, knew his strategies and the size of his positions, he had no control over what Hunter was doing.

He had been thinking for some time about starting his own firm. Now his interest in it grew more serious.

The Amaranth Christmas party at a nearby hotel was festive that year, an elaborate celebration that featured Russian caviar, quail foie gras, and sixteen musicians. Along with its annual Christmas card, the firm sent out little gasoline pumps.

But beneath the smiles and gaiety at the party, tension was starting to build. Capital allocations were cut for some portfolio managers and traders in order to funnel more money to Hunter. The other traders had not necessarily lost money; some just had longer-term investment strategies, which would take a while to pay off. Some employees with profits as high as 15 percent for the year found their capital reduced by as much as 25 percent. There was significant dissatisfaction. After bonuses were paid out, a number of people left the firm.[18]

Twelve hundred miles away in New Orleans, Christmas 2005 was grim. The hurricanes that had given Hunter his financial bonanza and Amaranth the means to celebrate so extravagantly had left more than eighteen hundred people dead and thousands without jobs and homes. For the residents of New Orleans, still putting up shingles and siding instead of Christmas lights, the storm that destroyed oil rigs and gas pipelines only meant loss of jobs, collapsed houses, and financial ruin.

At the start of 2006 money was rolling into the firm, both from Hunter's dramatic investment profits and from investors eager to ride the gravy train. By the end of January, the firm was managing close to $8 billion.[19]

Hunter personally was managing between $2 billion and $3 billion.[20] And because he needed to put up only a small amount of cash to place a trade, he was directing many billions more. It was a huge amount of money for anyone to oversee, let alone a thirty-one-year-old trader who had been at his firm less than two years. Profits seemed to spew from his trading screen like it was an ATM run wild. He was raking in more than half of all the firm's earnings.

Maounis was earning so much money from Hunter's profits and the 1.5 percent management fee that "he didn't want to be bothered with other things at the firm. Now he just wanted to sit on the desk," says a trader. He would lean back in his chair on the trading floor, put his feet up on the desk in front of him, and joke that he was going to get rich enough to own the Yankees.

Maounis "had the real-time profit-and-loss [report of Amaranth] screen up on his computer, and he knew constantly how much he was earning," recalls another employee. "We joked about how many thousands of dollars he was making as he read every letter of the *Wall Street Journal*."

When he came back to the Greenwich office periodically, Hunter's manner was the same as before. He was polite and respectful to the senior managers. He still walked with the usual slouch that made him look shorter than his six feet four inches, and he dressed as always, in jeans, sneakers, and hockey jersey. But he started talking about earning a bonus of $500 million. Then $1 billion.

In Calgary, Hunter put together what would be called "Team Hunter." Eventually as many as seven people were working with him there. Hunter surrounded himself with guys his age, several of whom he knew from school or previous jobs. They included Shane Lee, from his days at TransCanada Pipelines, and his university buddy and fellow Canadian Matthew Donohoe.

Hunter was the nucleus of the group and planned the natural gas investment strategies. He preferred the cerebral aspects of the game. "I never enjoyed the trading, I liked the design," he said later. "Most of my models would be option-based models and scenario models." He didn't like implementing his stratagems—the technical aspects of trading—saying later it wasn't his strength.[21]

Donohoe executed most of the trades that Hunter devised. Hunter considered him good at the nitty-gritty aspects of trading, which required good people skills—getting to know the strengths of various brokers and being able to negotiate complex deals with other traders—along with the agility to process electronic trades.

The Calgary group operated out of what Hunter called an "office in a box."[22] Amaranth leased a couple of small rooms on the tenth floor of Bankers Hall that were part of a ready-made office suite run by a private company. The offices shared receptionists, telephone answering services, mail delivery, conference rooms, and a kitchen area with other businesses. Dozens of other company offshoots or small firms also worked on the floor, many involved with the oil and gas industry.[23]

Amaranth leased a corner office—a larger room about fifteen

feet square and a smaller side office about ten feet by six. Traders were wedged in tightly in the larger room. Hunter faced a wall, and at his back sat Donohoe.[24]

Arrayed in front of Hunter were five computer screens. One displayed real-time trading on global markets for a variety of investments, including currencies, stocks, and bonds. On another screen, Hunter tracked U.S., Canadian, and European government weather forecasts, which drew on vast quantities of data churned through by giant supercomputers. A third screen was open to the IntercontinentalExchange, showing trading volume and prices on a multitude of contracts. Hunter also watched a fourth open to the Bloomberg service providing real-time price information on futures and options traded on the floor of NYMEX. Finally, Hunter also had open an instant-messaging screen, where he kept in contact with as many as fifty different people. They included his Amaranth colleagues, brokers, and traders. He was always messaging someone—a broker who wanted to get his bid or offer on a trade, Donohoe or another Amaranth trader who wanted his advice or direction, outside traders who were speculating on how prices would move or were wondering what Hunter was trading.

Hunter's communications with traders outside the firm were somewhat unusual. He speculated about what other competitors were up to and who was responsible for prices moving in a certain way. He even talked about his own trading. Bo Collins and John Arnold didn't do that. They used instant messaging and emails mainly for perfunctory communication with brokers, getting prices and giving directions, and generally were circumspect about their trading.

Hunter and his team were feeling pretty good about themselves. They had made their firm, their investors, and themselves a fortune the previous year. Hunter was back in his hometown, among friends and relatives. He was building his planned $2 million house with its stunning view of the Rockies. He tooled around town in his Bentley and his Ferrari. He enjoyed fine cigars after meals at high-end restaurants.

Hunter's team gloated over how well things were going, how

they were exerting their muscle on the market. They referenced favorite jokes often, in instant messages and conversations. One stemmed from Hunter's baby son acting like a "muscle man." When Hunter's son was an infant just starting on solid food, Hunter asked Donohoe to babysit. Donohoe tried to feed the baby spinach, but he refused to eat it. "Don't you want to grow up big and strong like your dad?" he asked the baby as he kept offering him the spoon. But instead of eating or crying, Hunter's son flexed his arms and legs and grunted, sounding more like a tough guy than a baby. So, anytime they could, Hunter and Donohoe threw references to that into their conversations and instant messages. They joked about "flexing" and wrote "rrrrrrrrrrrrrrrrrrrrrrrrrrrrrrr" to each other when they were happy with how their trading was going.[25]

Flush from his stunning success following the hurricanes in the fall and newly ensconced in his Calgary trading room, Brian Hunter began to plan for the year ahead. January 2006 was turning out to be the warmest January on record for the United States, with an average temperature of 39.5 degrees—8.5 degrees higher than the mean temperature for the previous 110 years. Even the coldest regions of the country, including the northern plains and the Midwest, experienced record-high temperatures. Outdoor ice rinks in Wisconsin closed, and Super Bowl event planners worried that the mild weather in Detroit would melt the two-hundred-foot snow slide they were constructing as part of the pregame Motown Winter Blast.

Although Hurricanes Katrina and Rita had destroyed or closed down significant infrastructure and natural-gas supply that past summer, the warm winter weather kept gas in storage, mitigating the storms' impact. Hunter, along with his team of traders, believed gas supplies would remain plentiful and demand low all that current winter and into the summer of 2006. "We thought that a price upside potential for the next several months was muted by all this extra storage," was how Hunter put it later. "The summer prices couldn't go up in crazy amounts."[26]

But Amaranth's traders anticipated a changed scenario the following winter, in 2007. They predicted that the natural gas supply would be tight and demand strong. If the winter of 2007 turned out to be very cold, then gas supplies could get very low, even run out. Their view seemed to be supported by the activity of other traders, such as a major Texas utility that was hedging massively. If there's only enough gas to heat 80 percent of homes, Hunter liked to say, "what will the other 20 percent pay to keep their families warm?" In such a scenario prices would "skyrocket."[27]

With this overall view of supply and demand, Hunter started placing his bets in early 2006. Initially he focused on trades that would make money if that winter continued to be warm all the way into the spring, causing a glut of gas. He shorted gas for March, and by the end of January had shorted 40,000 contracts. As the weeks wore on and the mild weather continued, he switched from shorting March to shorting April contracts. Hunter expected the resulting gas excess to carry all the way into the upcoming fall, 2006. That would cause autumn prices to be lower than other traders probably expected. So he began to work on November gas contracts too, shorting more than 25,000.

While lower than expected prices might carry into November, Hunter believed that by January 2007 cold weather would return and supply would be tight, forcing gas prices up. So he started buying January contracts, more than 25,000 of them. By buying and selling the same number of contracts in this way, he created a spread position between November and January, betting that January 2007 prices would be much higher than November 2006 prices.

These positions were huge. By the end of February, Hunter alone was responsible for 70 percent of all the November contracts shorted on NYMEX. He had bought 60 percent of all January 2007 NYMEX contracts.[28] His holdings would grow even larger in the months to come.

Also in February, he bought thousands of contracts for other winter 2007 months, particularly February and March, and he shorted other fall months. On top of that, he started to trade the "widow maker" spread for 2008, buying thousands of March 2008 contracts and shorting April. That trade was a gamble that winter

2008 would see high gas prices extending into March, then falling in April.

He also expected that the high winter prices of 2007 would cause average prices that year to be higher than for calendar 2010. He bought contracts that would pay off if that happened.

Hunter was dealing with tens of thousands of contracts. (By comparison, a small steel hardening company, one that relied heavily on natural gas for its operations, used less than one contract worth of gas a month.) The value of these holdings and the potential profit as prices moved was huge. One contract represented 10,000 MMBtus, so if the price of gas was $8 per MMBtu, then one contract was worth $80,000, and ten thousand contracts would be worth $800 million. A change of just 1 cent would mean $1 million more in profit or loss. With contracts for the upcoming winter in the $9 to $10 range per MMBtu that February, Hunter was trading billions of dollars' worth of gas.

Hunter faced few limits from regulators on his trading. ICE was exempt from any government regulation and didn't impose any limits on trading. NYMEX was regulated by the CFTC, but that agency, which set firm limits on what traders of wheat, corn, and other farm products could hold, did not do so for most energy trading on NYMEX. Instead, it allowed NYMEX to set loose guidelines, called "accountability levels," for what a trader could hold of one month's contract or for all months combined. The only firm limit set by NYMEX, under CFTC guidance, was on how many expiring contracts a trader could hold during its last three trading days: one thousand. But traders did not have much trouble getting permission to exceed these limits. Indeed, in September 2005, Amaranth's limit for such trading was raised to twenty-five hundred.[29] If traders exceeded these limits, they received a warning letter after each of the first two violations. If it continued, they could be fined or lose trading privileges.

Other than that, Hunter was subject only to the less strict NYMEX accountability levels. Traders weren't forbidden to exceed them. Some did so occasionally; others exceeded them daily. When

traders did that, NYMEX reviewed the situation, assessing the overall size of the market, whether a contract was near expiration, and a
trader's other holdings. Frequently, rather than require a trader to
cut back positions, they agreed the trader could exceed the accountability levels. At the time, NYMEX allowed a net position of twelve
thousand (adding up all the long futures contracts and subtracting
all the short contracts) in one month's contract, and a net position of
twelve thousand for all months combined.

As Hunter bought and sold over the following months, he rarely
changed his strategy; he just kept adding to his positions. It was a
very different trading style from that used by most other gas traders.
Usually a trader just picks and chooses some positions he believes
are really good, then waits to see if he is correct. John Arnold "puts
on two or three big positions a year," Bo Collins later told a reporter.
"He has discipline that other traders don't have and is aware when
there are just no good trades around. He won't overtrade."[30] But
Hunter seemed to believe every trade he did was a good one. Furthermore, he had no plan for when to exit them, cashing out and
taking his profits. Until he did so, any profits were only on paper.

"You have to know why you think the price will change and
when, and then get out when it does," says a longtime successful
commodity trader.[31] "But he had a Master of the Universe, 'I'm always right' mentality. Other traders will take off all their risk for a
time, get out of their positions, in order to reflect or take profit. You
must say to yourself, 'If the portfolio is X, what would I get out at?
Would it be a $1 billion profit?'"

Maounis seems never to have pressed Hunter on that. "They had
no idea how much it would give them in profits," says the same
trader. "They just knew, or thought they knew, it would keep going
up. The idea that you can speculate and always be right is a crazy
idea."

As the size of Hunter's positions soared in February, Arora
grew even more worried. He saw the daily profit-and-loss reports.
Hunter's profits and losses could change by tens of millions of
dollars from day to day. On February 24, for example, he was up
$45 million; for that whole week he earned $163 million.[32] Arora

knew Hunter's holdings must be huge. So he decided to open up Hunter's spreadsheets and take a look at his book.

Arora was very troubled by what he saw there. Hunter's holdings were very large, and they were concentrated in only a few ideas. Diversification didn't guarantee he wouldn't lose money, but it was generally considered safer than going all in on one strategy. But Hunter loved winter/summer spreads and March against April. Hunter's strategy wasn't necessarily wrong, thought Arora. But his size and concentration were.

Arora went to Jones to express his concerns over the size of Hunter's positions. A little while later he also brought it up with Maounis. "They reacted positively and told me that they appreciated my input," Arora later said.[33]

"Harry has a good nose for smelling danger," says an analyst who knows him. "Harry saw that what Hunter was doing was so risky that it was dangerous."[34]

But Hunter was minting money. "Most people were just amazed at how much money he was making," remembers a former Amaranth trader. "You don't want to kill the goose that lays the golden eggs. It was good for everyone when he was making money."

Other traders, back-office staff, and executives could see Hunter's profit-and-loss statements and could guess at the amounts of money he traded. Some could see his spreadsheets. Other portfolio managers raised an eyebrow as they watched the volatility in his book. But there was little incentive to say anything. Everybody could see their bonuses growing. If Hunter was trading outsize positions, he was also earning outsize profits—he earned the firm $320 million in February.[35] He must know what he's doing, people told themselves.

"Human nature is such that when someone is making a lot of money, you don't question them," says another Amaranth trader.

Nothing was done about Arora's concerns.

KING OF GAS

rian Hunter knew John Arnold traded in dangerous shoals—the last thirty minutes of trading for an expiring futures contract. It is a high-risk game that few financial traders like to play. If it's not handled well, traders who usually deal only in paper run the risk of actually having to take possession of or supply physical gas.

March futures, for example, expire at the end of February. Trading on them stops three business days before the end of the month. That last trading day is known as "the settlement day," and the last thirty minutes are known as "the close."

Traders conducting business then are not creating new positions in the contract but rather are closing out whatever positions they have left. If a trader still holds contracts of gas at the close of trading, he could find himself scrambling to locate a place to store huge amounts of physical gas. Or if he has not closed out contracts he sold, then he has to desperately find physical gas to deliver. It is harder to exit positions in the last half hour of trading on the settlement day. There are fewer traders and less activity, because most traders have already exited their positions. But because of this, and because trades conducted in that thirty-minute period are averaged to determine the final price of the expiring month's contract, a trader buying or selling significant positions at this time is an important part of the marketplace and might find ways to make money.

Arnold had traded in the close since his Enron days as a market maker. In the months following Hurricane Katrina, Arnold traded often and heavily in the close, and frequently was the largest trader.

In seven out of the ten months from August 2005 to May 2006, for example, Arnold was the largest-volume trader in the settlement period. In two of those months he was responsible for about one-third of transactions at the close.[1] Hunter considered Arnold skilled at this trading, later dubbing him "the master of moving the close."[2]

Hunter himself never traded more than a few expiring futures contracts in the half hour settlement period. In fact, no one at Amaranth had sold more than fifty contracts or bought more than five hundred contracts during settlement for as long as Hunter had been there. The firm had a near catastrophe in July 2005 when its arbitrage traders decided to stick their toes into energy trading and got stuck with between one and two hundred contracts at the end of a settlement day. Unable to store or transport the gas they suddenly owned, they frantically scrambled after the market closed to find a buyer to take the gas off their hands, at a significant cost to the firm.[3, 4]

Arora did not trade at all in the close; the tactic bothered him. In fact, he was so concerned about the risks it involved that generally he liked to have all his expiring futures contracts settled two to four days before the final trading day. There was no need to trade during that time period, he believed, because Amaranth's investment strategy was based on a longer-term view of the market.[5]

February 24, 2006, was the settlement day for the March contract. As usual, at ten o'clock that morning the opening bell sounded on the NYMEX trading floor, four stories above the Hudson River at the lower tip of Manhattan. A frenetic dance began. Standing on the steps around the circular trading pits, 816 men and one or two women began pushing, shoving, and waving their hands as they screamed out orders. The traders were always stressed and tense. Sometimes fistfights broke out if someone was pushed off a step or thought his hand signals had been blocked by someone's arm. That February day was particularly hectic with more activity than usual among the 150 or so gas traders. There were wild swings in prices during the day, and trading was volatile.

Hunter thought he and Arnold would be on the same side of the trading, in synch on strategy, but it didn't turn out that way. In fact, they ended up locked in a battle that would be important in determining closing prices. The contest between Hunter and Arnold that day caught the attention of traders around the pit, and they would discuss it later.

Brian Hunter was eager to try his hand in the fray. Early on in the day he bought nearly 4,900 expiring contracts to sell toward the close of trading. He and Donohoe discussed whether Arnold would try to drive prices up or down. Hunter speculated he would try to punch them down.

Hunter told another trader he planned to do just that himself.

"We have 4000 to sell MoC [market-on-close]. Shhhh," wrote Hunter. The trader asked why he was planning to sell. Hunter told him, "Bit of an experiment mainly. I think John and Sempra [Energy Trading Corp] are sellers too."[6]

But Hunter was wrong about Arnold. The action started earlier but heated up in the settlement period. Traders in the pit watched as Arnold bought and Hunter sold dramatically. Many eyes in particular were on a broker who they knew did business for Amaranth. He was frantically selling, at virtually any price.

Traders around the gas pit witnessed "an apparent battle going back and forth between Amaranth and T. Boone Pickens and John Arnold," remembered one of the largest pit traders, Eric Bolling, who watched the action.

In the last thirty minutes, prices swung wildly as each trader sought the price position for himself.

"Prices would go up; prices would go down," said Bolling. "If one side was going to throw the towel in, the other side would prevail, and the price would probably go in that direction."[7]

In the close, Hunter sold about 3,000 of the contracts he had just bought.[8] He was the largest seller, accounting for one-fifth of the market volume. He sold three times more futures contracts in the close than any other trader had done before.[9]

The largest buyer was John Arnold. He purchased 2,310 contracts.[10]

Prices went Hunter's way: profits for Hunter and his team that day were $45 million.

Hunter later argued that his decision to trade in the close was based on the way prices had changed the previous day. But a judge later ruled that Hunter's "bit of an experiment" was actually a calculated attempt to manipulate prices down.

High-volume trading in the close is not illegal. But using trading to artificially move a price to benefit some other position can be. By selling in the close Hunter sought to affect prices and benefit on contracts he held on the unregulated ICE exchange, the judge said later. On February 24, Hunter held massive short positions, 14,000 contracts, on ICE. These ICE holdings settled based on the NYMEX final price. The lower the final closing price of the March contract on the NYMEX, the more he would make on ICE. If he could sell heavily on NYMEX during the close, saturate the market, and sell below other traders, he would drive down the price of the expiring contract to the benefit of his ICE holdings, concluded the judge.[11]

Indeed, for Hunter it was a hugely profitable day and a fantastic month. Hunter, who was in Calgary, and Donohoe, who was in Greenwich, did some high-fiving via instant messaging.

> HUNTER: "Today came together quite nicely."
> DONOHOE: "Nice."
> HUNTER: "I am flexing here."
> DONOHOE: "Looking pretty bang on . . . lol . . . rrrrrrrrrrrrrrrrrrrrrrrrrrr."
> HUNTER: "hahahahaha."
> DONOHOE: "2nd best . . . Sept/Oct last year still the best" [a reference to their billion-dollar windfall after the 2005 hurricanes].[12]

Hunter had profited mightily in his first go-round with Arnold in the thirty-minute settlement period.

The next settlement day was March 29. The day before, Arora was overseeing Donohoe in carrying out his task of ensuring that all natural gas contracts in the firm were closed out before settlement. Hunter was overseas on vacation.

They were sitting next to each other on the trading desk in

Greenwich at the time.[13] Hunter's portfolio still held more than 1,600 contracts that he needed to exit before the end of the next day. Arora wanted them sold. Donohoe refused, keeping them for the settlement day. Arora was livid, but there was little he could do. Hunter was a force unto himself in the company by now, the high-flying golden boy.

Later that day Arora met with Maounis and told him he was leaving to start his own hedge fund. Bonuses had been paid and Arora was up for the year, something he could tout to investors. It was an opportune time to leave. Maounis wished Arora well, asked to be kept updated on his progress, and indicated he might want to invest in the new firm.

Then Arora walked around the Greenwich office saying good-bye. One colleague remembers him warning that Amaranth was a house of cards.

"Brian's positions are too big," Arora presaged. "He could blow up the entire firm."

But the hedge fund was raking in money. The colleague discounted the comment, attributing it to jealousy.

The next day, March 29, during the final half hour of trading, Donohoe sold 1,300 contracts. And while Amaranth was selling, John Arnold was a major buyer, second only to Sempra.

That day clients also received an unexpected email announcing that Arora had left and that Hunter was going to lead energy trading.

"We wanted to let you know that Harry Arora decided to leave Amaranth last night," the email said. "Although we are all sad to see Harry go, we wish him the best of luck in whatever he chooses to do next . . . we expect the team's great success to continue under Brian's leadership."[14]

The San Diego County Employees Retirement Association was troubled by that news. Executives at the association knew nothing about Hunter. In fact, they had not heard his name when they visited Greenwich back in March 2005 to check out the hedge fund. They had met with Maounis, other executives, and certain portfolio managers. They were also given bios on all the portfolio managers. But since Hunter did not yet have that title, SDCERA learned nothing about him until the email announcing he would replace Arora.[15]

When Arora suddenly left, Hunter was halfway around the world in the Maldives, an archipelago in the Indian Ocean. Donohoe emailed him on March 29: "Call me ASAP. Book fine. Attention needed elsewhere unfortunately." Hunter had no email service in the isolated island chain, but soon after arriving at the remote Kanuhura Resort by private seaplane, he called his office and found out that Arora had left. He walked the beach long into that night, his ear to his cell phone, discussing with Amaranth executives how to handle Arora's investments.[16]

Within the next few days, Hunter called in again from his Maldives vacation and doubled the bonus for some of the energy traders Arora had supervised. They would be paid 15 percent of their profits—the same percentage that Hunter had negotiated for himself the previous year.

Arora had screwed them, he told the traders now working for him. They deserved more money. Still resentful that Arora had shared his profits a year earlier, Hunter assured his new trading team, "I'm not going to make money off you."[17]

When Hunter returned from vacation, the large bets he had made seemed to be paying off. The prices of the spreads that Amaranth was expecting to surge, such as the November-January spread, were at record-high levels. The price differential between the two months had more than doubled since Hunter started trading the spread. By April, it had soared to as much as $2.22, way beyond what it had been during the previous four years, when it mostly hovered around 25 to 50 cents.[18]

In fact, it was Hunter's trading that was a significant factor in the volatility and the hike in prices. Exactly how much he was responsible for that is hard to calculate. But prices are determined by the interaction of buyers and sellers. When there is heavy buying, prices move up, just as huge selling causes them to drop. Amaranth was the predominant buyer of winter contracts and by far the largest seller of summer positions. When Hunter traded big, prices moved in his direction. Because he kept his positions in place, not moving in and out of them for months, prices stayed in his favor.[19]

Signaling his strategies seemed to be part of Hunter's plan. Was it ego? Was it an effort to bolster his position by convincing others to trade with him? "He wanted people to know where he was at," says an energy analyst at another investment firm, "hoping that everyone thought he was so smart, since he had made a billion dollars last year, they were going to follow him. Kind of like the Warren Buffett effect. Stocks go up that he owns after people know he bought them. Then other people want to pile in."

"Brian's chatter in the market encouraged others to speculate as well," says an energy trader who was investing at the time. "There was a whole cottage industry based on 'let's just get in the wake of Brian and do whatever he's doing.'"

Hunter messaged one trader, for example, "7/10 coming in and I am making $$$," referring to the 2007–10 spread that he traded. "Beauty."[20]

Buying more and more of the same positions month after month is not what traders usually do. They establish their holdings and wait to see if they are right. "These are commodities that go up and down," explains a trader. "It's unusual for people to add to it and grow it throughout the whole year. It's like buying crude oil at $50 and continuing to buy it at $150. I guess if you thought it was going to $500 that would look rational. It didn't seem rational to me."

Smaller players were in a quandary about how to react to Hunter's massive trading. Some who went against him were badly hurt, because Hunter maintained his positions for so long and kept prices in his favor. "They wouldn't just go up for two days and then flame out," says another energy trader. "Nobody could stay in a position losing that long. People would knock themselves out. I think some people tried that. And they got knocked enough that they said, 'Screw it, it's obvious what he has on. I'm going to be positioned in a similar fashion.'"[21]

Some investors measured firms by whether or not they were following Hunter's lead. One hedge fund manager, just setting up his company at the time, recalls a fund-of-funds investor who decided against investing in the new firm when he found out the manager disagreed with Hunter. He "came into our office and asked, 'What do you guys think about the March/April spread?' We said, 'We hate that trade.' The investor said, 'Well, Brian Hunter likes that trade.' At which point the meeting was over."[22]

"He certainly didn't disguise putting his positions on, there's no doubt about that," according to another energy trader. "So you had two choices. You either chose to trade with the guy or you chose not to trade at all."

That was the decision of prominent hedge fund manager Paul Touradji, who had been a well-known trader at Tiger Management and was just starting his own hedge fund as Hunter began dominating gas trading. Touradji said that he exited natural gas trading for a year because of Amaranth's huge positions. He compared Amaranth to a well-financed poker player sitting down with poorer players and making big bets. "I can't think of a right counterstrategy other than to say, 'I'm going to be at the bar until you're done.'"[23]

John Arnold in Houston and Bo Collins in New York were also wondering how to trade. They watched with dismay as the prices for winter gas climbed. Something was wrong. Winter gas was way overpriced. The fundamentals of supply and demand just didn't warrant it, they thought.

In mid-April the price of gas futures for the upcoming winter of 2007 was over $12. That was close to the high price set the previous autumn, when Hurricanes Katrina and Rita devastated Gulf Coast facilities. Back then, when production disruption was at its worst, prices for winter gas had been between $13 and $14. That was high, but the hurricanes had been devastating and even the Henry Hub area, through which about one-third of natural gas used in the country flowed, was under water. At the time, traders didn't know when production and delivery would get back to normal.

But now it was April, and natural gas production was back to pre-hurricane levels. There was no hint of a gas shortage on the horizon. The winter just ending had been warm, with January temperatures setting record highs. So there was lots of natural gas still in the ground. Inventories were nearly 40 percent above the average for the past five years.[24] Yet the price was still way up.

Arnold and Collins didn't share Hunter's view that weather-related disruptions, maybe another hurricane or two, along with supply shortages and delivery bottlenecks, would boost upcoming winter prices.[25]

"The market is, in a sense, trading in conflict with the fundamentals," John D'Agostino, one of the principals of Bo Collins' firm, MotherRock, told a reporter early that April. "We obviously have a ton of gas in the ground, which everyone is well aware of."[26] It would be surprising to have a repeat of the severe hurricanes that had hit during the previous year, he said, but even if it occurred, producers would be better prepared to avoid damage and disruptions.

Long-term supply was not likely to be a problem either, Collins thought. He joked to colleagues that everyone and their mother, even his, seemed to be discovering gas in their backyards. He had recently gotten a call from her about an old piece of forgotten property inherited from his grandmother. Mobil had just started drilling for oil and gas a half mile down the road, she told her son. Should she hire a driller or someone to sell off the mineral rights?

Arnold and his traders at Centaurus also saw this same frenzy to get in on the oil and gas bonanza. Bill Perkins, a Centaurus trader, later joked that "when you have cab drivers quitting their jobs to search for oil and people drilling through their bathtubs in Piscataway, New Jersey you know that prices are way too high."[27]

But while Arnold and Collins believed fundamentals dictated lower prices, the market seemed to have a life of its own. People bought into the hype of higher winter prices. And Arnold and Collins were fairly certain Hunter's large-size trading was leading this. Although trading was supposed to be anonymous, for the handful of really large traders who dominated the marketplace, it didn't work that way in practice. About 80 percent of market activity was driven at that time by fewer than two dozen traders, according to a NYMEX official.[28]

While Arnold and Collins couldn't know for sure what other traders were doing, since some trading was done through the electronic exchange, or directly between two traders, a large part of trading was conducted through brokers, and Arnold and Collins, as well as other traders, usually knew what was going on in that world.

Traders used two types of brokers. One was a floor broker, positioned on the edge of the trading pit at the NYMEX, who handled trades of futures contracts or options. The other was a voice broker, someone they called to arrange over-the-counter deals with other traders. Any given trader generally relied on just a few brokers. And the brokers gossiped like teenage girls at a sleepover. They bragged about their best customers and tried to impress traders with how much insight they had on who was trading what positions. It was a way not just to drum up business but also to make their day more fun.

When a client asked a broker to find someone for a specific trade he wanted to conduct, the broker shopped it around, and often told prospective purchasers which trader wanted to do the deal. (That information would become public anyway, if it was cleared through the NYMEX, when confirmations were sent.) Colleagues sitting nearby would overhear, and in turn they called customers with chitchat about the trade.

On the NYMEX floor, brokers stood near banks of red, green, and yellow phones, reserved for specific clients. The space was small and voices were loud, so brokers who worked side by side for years and often hung out together after work developed a good idea of which clients called on which phone, and they could see the trades executed as a result of the call.

Large traders were informed about the market in other ways too. Arnold, a market maker, gleaned information on producer supply and user demand from the clients he traded with. And all traders knew the total number of open contracts, spreads, and options traded through NYMEX. Large traders knew what percentage they held of total trading in certain positions and watched what was bought or sold. Market chatter told them which brokers did different trades, and often how many lots. One experienced trader compares figuring out what positions major traders held to counting cards in poker. It's not an exact metaphor and counting cards is viewed as less than playing fair, but the comparison is apt. A trader had to keep track of a lot of data from many different avenues all at once, but if he did it well, he had a good idea how to play his hand.

"[Hunter] was public about it," says an energy trader. "Everybody knew what brokers he was using. Everybody knew he was one of the few people who could trade the size he was trading. The industry is small. So everybody says things like, 'Don't tell anybody, but . . .'"[29]

While Arnold and Collins were puzzling over prices and picking up clues on Hunter's trading, they, along with other traders, were also hearing from brokers that Hunter was out to crush John Arnold. "I was aware of Hunter's almost unnatural kind of intensity, almost of a personal nature, that he was going to bury Arnold on a trade," recalls an energy trader.

Arnold wondered whether he had done something to cause such seemingly personal animosity. Whether or not he had, one thing is clear: Brian Hunter aspired to be the preeminent natural gas trader, say former colleagues. And to do that, he needed to topple Arnold.

With just a few top traders, "If you want to succeed and make money, you want to destroy someone else," explains a trader. "That's just how it works. If I want to be successful in this industry, I'm going to want to destroy five guys."

"Everyone was gunning for John Arnold, because he's the wonder boy," says an energy trading consultant. "If you want to be the next Michael Jordan, you have to take down Michael Jordan. John Arnold is Michael Jordan. I have no doubt Brian saw him as a competitor. I don't think there's a single trader in the world who trades this market who at one point or another hasn't thought or verbalized that they were going to beat John Arnold on the Street, 'cause that's what everyone aspires to do."[30]

Arnold and Collins continued to gauge the market frenzy on the summer-winter spreads. They intended to stay out of the way of Hunter and his followers until they saw an opportunity to profit. Still, they nibbled on trades.

Collins put some money toward shorting the March-April spread. Early in his career he had made a lot of money on it, when the two months' contracts differed in price by about 60 cents. Now the difference was between $1.50 and $2.25. So he did some trading.

But Collins got burned on his trades. Hunter messaged another trader: "Bo's attempt to sell in H8/j8 [March 2008–April 2008] hasn't worked." "Not a bit" was the reply.[31]

Arnold concentrated on the other summer-winter spreads. For the past four years the October-January spread had traded under $1.00 throughout the first four months of the year. Now, in early April, it was hovering close to $3.00. John Arnold expected the price to go down, so he started selling the spread. But instead of dropping back toward more historical norms, the price shot up to over $3.50 by the end of the month.

Hunter gloated to another trader that Arnold had been "squeezed out" of his holdings. Arnold had shorted the spread and when the price suddenly rose, he had to get out of his holdings in a hurry. Another trader messaged Hunter about it: "What do you think buddy classic short squeeze?" "Yup," Hunter replied. The other trader urged Hunter to heavily trade the October-January spread to "teach Arnold a lesson on what's right and wrong."[32]

As Hunter's trades grew larger and larger over the first four months of the year, executives at the firm started to worry. Arora had warned them about the size of Hunter's holdings. Rob Jones, the head of risk management, and David Chasman, who was responsible for energy, were also troubled by the risk of Hunter's positions. They discussed it with him in early April, Chasman later testified, and they all agreed that the risk had to be reduced.[33]

Amaranth's treasurer, Artie DiRocco, responsible for ensuring Amaranth had the cash available for margin calls, was worried about meeting requirements if the market turned against Hunter. DiRocco, who had a forceful personality that matched his massive physique, was known in the firm for speaking his mind. And as the spring wore on, he too grew more vocal about the firm's leverage and the potential for devastating margin calls.

Margin requirements were adjusted daily. If the value of the holdings went up, an investor's margin account was credited. If the trades lost value, a trader could be asked to cough up more cash overnight. Given the size of Hunter's holdings, DiRocco feared that if prices turned against the firm, it might not be able to come up with sufficient cash.

So the executive committee, which included Maounis and some of his top traders along with DiRocco and others, decided that Hunter should cut back his positions. He was told to slash his holdings by around "$1 to $2 billion," Hunter later said. "They kind of wanted to [eliminate] 10,000 to 15,000 summers, 10,000 to 15,000 winters," he explained.[34]

Chasman pressed Hunter to cut his holdings 20 percent to 30 percent by the end of April. Hunter agreed to do so, Chasman later testified.[35]

On April 21, Matthew Donohoe received an instant message from Chasman asking, "Hey can you and Brian sit down and give me the trades that you are going to do to reduce your position by 25%?"[36]

Hunter felt the pressure. He emailed a Canadian executive committee member the same day, assuring him he would "take the book down from here on month end." But he added, "It's a little tricky this month since every commodity in the world is bouncing like crazy."[37]

He still believed, however, that his investment strategy was correct, and he was clearly unhappy with the firm's change of direction. "My thoughts were I would prefer not to reduce it. I thought there was definitely some room to run, and frankly, I saw no reason to reduce the portfolio in any significant way," he said later. "Basically, I thought there was—we could actually make quite a bit more money under the current position. We were planning to keep on going the way we were going if we hadn't been told to reduce."[38]

Chasman argued with Hunter about scenarios for his energy book. He was frustrated that Hunter was not seriously discussing strategy with him. The morning of April 25 Chasman sent Donohoe an instant message: "You guys need to set aside an hour a day to talk w/me. That's why we have these problems . . . everybody is busy, but a lot of the reason that I'm busy is cuz you and BH [Brian Hunter] do not take the time to talk—then we end up w/those silly conferences."[39]

In fact, that entire week the risk management team had trouble reaching Hunter and his traders and monitoring their holdings. They weren't getting timely reports of trades, hampering the firm's ability to run risk assessment programs. "And when it came to the energy book, I wanted to make sure that the Chasman-Koster risk reports have the correct positions in them and that we know that the positions that we're seeing are the correct positions," Jones explained later.[40]

Jones sent Hunter an angry email on April 24 telling him, "You need to have someone on the desk by 8:30 EST every day. Ideally someone who has a qualified opinion on your portfolio or who can quickly contact someone who has." To emphasize his annoyance, Jones resent the identical email to Hunter every day that week.[41]

In the midst of this pressure, on April 26, the closing day for May contracts, Hunter and Arnold again dueled it out. That morning, Hunter instructed Donohoe to short 10,000 May contracts and buy 10,000 June contracts. He later said it was part of a complex plan to reduce his winter and summer holdings, as Amaranth's risk management staff was instructing. A judge ruled later that it was actually part of another attempt to benefit his ICE holdings by manipulating the market in the settlement period.[42]

Donohoe contacted a broker and asked him to find people to engage in this type of swap. Because of the size of the deal, Hunter expected to complete it in pieces, with several different traders. But one trader was ready to conduct the entire transaction: John Arnold.

Trading 10,000 contracts with Arnold provided Hunter some insight into his holdings. Hunter now knew for sure that Arnold held a large position of May contracts that would benefit from May prices rising in the closing minutes of trading. And he knew Arnold would benefit on his 10,000 short June contracts if those prices were to decline.

Hunter started to worry. He knew that Arnold was a major trader during the settlement period. If he was a heavy buyer of May contracts during that time, Hunter, who had just shorted May, could be hurt.

A little after noon on April 26 Hunter sent instant messages to Chasman expressing concern that Arnold had positions opposite his own. "I am worrie[d] that Arnold has taken the other side of everything," he said.

But his real fear was that Arnold would trade heavily in the closing period, to benefit his holdings. He told Chasman, "[He] may try to help it by running the market up on the close. Arnold is the master of moving the close."[43] A little later Hunter told another trader, "I think john [Arnold] wants to bid it on close"[44]—in other words, buy.

Hunter's fears turned out to be correct. He sold 3,044 contracts during the settlement. And in those last trading minutes, Arnold bought 3,000 contracts.[45] Hunter believed Arnold's trading cost him $17 million additional profit. If Arnold had not been buying, Hunter believed, the price would have fallen more in his favor.

Hunter shot off an instant message to a trader friend at a Toronto bank complaining that Arnold had bought heavily and was able to "jack the settle," referring to hiking prices in the settlement period. "It worked," his friend agreed.[46]

Hunter was also irate that Amaranth executives had ordered him to start reducing his positions. He believed that following directions from management to cut holdings had lost him money. Just after trading ended, he angrily wrote Chasman that "we got smashed on the stuff we rolled off," referring to the May-June trade. Two days later, when Chasman commented on trades that had lost Hunter money, Hunter snapped back that what really had cost him money was following orders to cut back his positions. "For your information if we hadn't expired anything off we'd have made a mountain of money."

Hunter made close to $42 million on the April 26 settlement day. But he was smarting that he had been forced to trade away 10,000 June contracts. In the two days following that trade, prices moved in a way to benefit those contracts. Hunter believed that if he hadn't been forced to trade them away, he would have actually made $70 million to $80 million.[47]

That settlement day Brian Hunter and John Arnold were not the only ones closely watching their computer screens to monitor how prices were moving during the last half hour of trading. In a glass and cement office building a few blocks from the Capitol in Washington, D.C., a small group of staff in the enforcement division of the Federal Energy Regulatory Commission were sitting before a computer screen, watching trades being reported from the floor of NYMEX.[48]

FERC is responsible for preventing or stopping manipulation of physical gas prices. And since the settlement price of a futures contract is used in a number of ways to set actual physical natural gas prices, FERC staff watches for unusual trading in the closing minutes on settlement days.

That April they saw a sharp rise in prices, followed by a steep decline. Throughout those thirty minutes, the price was unusually volatile, bouncing up and down as much as 30 cents. It closed lower than it had been earlier in the day. FERC staff decided to analyze the trading data in more depth and compare it to settlements going back several years. They requested data from the CFTC identifying which major firms were trading then.

Within a few weeks, FERC had initiated a formal nonpublic investigation into suspicious trading by Amaranth. The CFTC soon followed FERC's lead with its own review and the two agencies coordinated efforts.

Unaware of this, Hunter was focused on the staggering profits his trading had generated that month. He'd earned Amaranth more than $1 billion.[49] It was the primary reason the entire fund was at that point up more than 30 percent for the year.[50] Of course, most of the earnings were on paper. Amaranth executives did not cash in the energy holdings to realize all this profit. But virtually everything Hunter held was moving his way. For example, his March-April 2008 holdings—the "widow maker" spread—made him a lot of money as the price of the spread widened by 51 cents.[51]

By the end of April 2006, about 38 percent of Amaranth's capital was directed by Brian Hunter. Money was rolling in to the firm. Investors were eager to jump on Hunter's gravy train. The firm was managing between $8.7 and $9.2 billion. "April was outrageous," Hunter gloated to another trader.[52]

As Hunter watched his profits jump, the spring issue of *Trader Monthly* landed on investors' desks all across Wall Street. This glossy, gossipy magazine glorifying the life of Wall Street's fast-living traders—the cars they drove, the wine they sipped, their messy divorces and busts for cocaine—was sent free to a hundred thousand traders. The much-touted spring issue was highly anticipated because it listed the previous year's one hundred highest-paid traders, and word of who made the list spread quickly. That year energy traders were abuzz with the news that Brian Hunter, trading from the energy capital of Canada, and John Arnold, in the energy capital of the United States, were two of the most successful traders in 2005, each earning between $75 million and $100 million.

"In 2005, Hunter was certainly among the top natural-gas traders in the world—or, at the very least, the most buzzed-about," panted *Trader Monthly*.

As for Arnold, it gushed: "As ex–Big E biggies Ken Lay and Jeff Skilling finally face the music, Arnold and his boys are making beautiful noise."

Among all traders, Arnold and Hunter were tied for twenty-ninth place. Given that Wall Street has thousands of traders, just getting a slot on the coveted list was impressive, let alone ending up in its top third.

But even more striking was the fact that Arnold and Hunter made the top tier coming from the world of energy trading, recently rediscovered by banks and hedge funds. *Trader Monthly*'s editors gloated in their introduction to the list that they had "uncovered a crop of red-hot traders" on the energy commodity exchange. Except for oil and gas mogul T. Boone Pickens, who headed the list overall, Arnold and Hunter were the top energy traders. For Hunter, hearing that he was taking home as much money as John Arnold was particularly sweet.

When word of Hunter's huge profits spread through the trader networks, another trader sent him an effusive instant message: "You are the talk of the town these days . . . between the article and other rumors. Latest jiberish is that you made 1Billion+ and pulled in 300MM for you and your wife." Hunter seemed to love the banter, replying, "Hahahahahahahah. 30% payout nice." And the other trader quipped, "Was hoping you could spare a few for a good friend?"[53]

The enormous profits, the adulation of other traders further encouraged Hunter. Like Icarus on his wings of wax and feathers, he headed higher.

PAYING THE (INFLATED) TAB

Speculative traders such as John Arnold and Bo Collins were not the only ones who believed there was a major disconnect between gas supplies and the prices of gas contracts for the upcoming winter. In a small town on the outskirts of Atlanta, Georgia, Jeff Billings was closely monitoring the prices of NYMEX contracts.

Billings was the head of risk management for the Municipal Gas Authority of Georgia, an organization formed by Georgia's small-town gas delivery systems to purchase gas on their behalf at decent prices. Back in the 1950s, local villages were forced to create their own pipeline systems because large investor-owned utilities weren't interested in extending their systems into rural areas. People living in rural areas and the small firms operating there still needed gas even if they weren't large consumers. So they demanded that their town governments build the pipelines. These localities operated their gas systems as a business and provided a critical service for residents. Profits were plowed back into the municipality. The Municipal Gas Authority, formed in 1987, explained on its website that "the benefit of a city-owned system is that the local consumer's dollars stay on Main Street—they don't flow to Wall Street."

By 2006, the gas authority was the largest nonprofit gas agency in the country, made up of seventy-six citizen-owned distribution systems in Georgia, Alabama, Florida, Pennsylvania, and Tennessee. These, in turn, supplied the gas needs of 243,000 customers.

Billings' job was to keep the lid on the authority's cost of natural gas and keep extreme price swings in check. He worried most about winter prices, since that was when his members had to have gas for heating. And it was when supplies could be tight and prices might jump. So traditionally he hedged at least some of each winter's gas costs by trading futures contracts.

In the spring of 2006, Billings knew prices for the upcoming winter were high, and way out of line with prices of physical gas on the spot market. Was that an indication of where physical gas prices would be in the upcoming winter? His members couldn't buy physical gas in the spring and store it for the winter. So he needed to buy financial contracts to protect his customers against the prospect of higher physical gas prices in the months ahead.

"There's a lot of risk if you wait until winter," says Arthur Corbin, president of the Municipal Gas Authority.[1] "We have a disciplined approach, where we hedge our members' prices systematically over time. Our time parameters push us into the market in spring and summer, in advance of the winter. Winter is when our members' consumption is the highest, so that's the period of time we try to take away the risk of price spikes."

Financial contract prices kept increasing, week after week. And so did the difference between those contract prices and what physical gas was selling for in the spot market. In the middle of February 2006, contracts for a year later, February 2007, were selling at $10.10, which was $2.80 above the price of physical gas for immediate delivery. By early March, the February 2007 contract was up to $10.43. By mid-May contracts for the following winter heating season had jumped to $10.98. That was $4.48 above what gas was selling for in the spot market.[2]

Billings watched the price hikes and volatility all through that spring. He didn't know what to do. Prices were severely inflated both from a historical perspective and from what supply fundamentals seemed to warrant, and Billings didn't want to end up in the winter faced with even higher gas prices. Usually he would buy contracts little by little, spreading them out over weeks. "But here we were in the market in 2006, and prices were insanely high, to the point where you start second-guessing your program." He ended up doing trades he really didn't want to do but felt were prudent at the time.

That spring Municipal Gas Authority of Georgia officials hedged winter 2007 gas needs by purchasing futures contracts, even though they believed those prices were unjustifiably high. In fact, the Gas Authority hedged half its winter gas prior to September 2006. It was a decision that ultimately cost the member municipal gas systems millions of dollars.

If Hunter had been trading stocks, most investors would have been happy to see prices soar. And if it had been another commodity, say cotton or cocoa, escalating prices wouldn't have mattered so much to individuals and companies. But natural gas played a critical role in the American economy, for millions of individuals as well as corporations. It generated almost one-quarter of all electricity. About half of all households used gas for heating. Three-quarters of restaurants and hotels used gas, as did half of all hospitals, offices, and retail stores. It was also a key ingredient in many important products, including pharmaceuticals, medical equipment, computers, auto parts, clothing, and sports equipment.

Bob Easterbrook Jr., general manager of the steel-hardening company his father founded in 1976, was also dumbfounded by how gas prices did not seem to reflect supply and demand. "We have a warm winter and a cool summer and record amounts of natural gas sitting in reserves," Easterbrook says, "and the price runs up. There's no sense to it, no rhythm or reason."

Easterbrook got the shock of his life in early 2001 when the monthly gas bill for his family business came. Back then, gas bills were just something the comptroller routinely paid, and normally the general manager didn't bother much with it. But that day Easterbrook glanced at the invoice. Then he looked again. "This can't be right," he said and he looked at his father, dumbfounded.

Their bills were always in the $10,000- to $20,000-a-month range. But this bill was for $45,000. Easterbrook ran to the phone and contacted his gas supplier. "What's going on?" he demanded. He learned that the gas company's costs had increased drastically and it needed to severely hike prices for its customers.[3]

It was devastating to the Easterbrooks' company, East-Lind Heat Treat Inc. of Madison Heights, Michigan. The company relied heavily on natural gas to run its furnaces, which in turn hardened steel parts for manufacturers throughout the Detroit metropolitan area. The firm's eight hundred customers ran the gamut, from small mom-and-pop shops to major auto companies, military contractors, and medical equipment firms. East-Lind hardened everything from simple springs to crash test dummies and sophisticated medical instruments. It took less than one contract—10,000 MMBtu—per month to keep those furnaces running. That was a tiny fraction of the thousands of contracts that traders like Brian Hunter or John Arnold traded per day.

For the Easterbrooks' company, the going rate for gas for years hovered around $2.50 per MMBtu. Sometimes it hit $2.60. Sometimes it dipped to $2.40. But suddenly to get a gas bill for $45,000 for one month—it was a "punch between the eyes with a sledgehammer," says Easterbrook.

What Easterbrook didn't know at the time was that the natural gas market was undergoing a major transformation, and speculators were becoming a major part of it. Enron and the other merchant energy companies were at the height of their activity, trading energy futures and derivatives. John Arnold alone was placing $1 billion in trades on some days. And a newly enacted law put much of energy trading out of the reach of regulators.

And it was the period when the large merchant energy trading companies were manipulating prices. Over the next few years, two dozen companies would settle more than thirty complaints by the Commodity Futures Trading Commission for earlier manipulation, or attempted manipulation, of the natural gas market. They were fined more than $4 billion.[4]

The biggest change in the gas market since NYMEX natural gas futures began trading in 1990 had hit the industry.

Commodity futures exchanges first came into existence in the United States just before the Civil War. Chicago was the center of the grain trade, which was a boom-and-bust industry. When harvest time arrived and the city was flooded with wheat and corn, prices were low, and often farmers burned the grain for fuel or dumped it rather than further depress prices by selling. When winter came, grain was scarce and prices high. A group of businessmen set up the futures exchange to bring some order to the market. The idea was farmers and grain buyers would negotiate prices for future deliveries. The exchange established standardized futures contracts in 1865, which detailed where, when, and what would be delivered.

The commodity futures exchange was important for two reasons. First, it set stable advance pricing, allowing both producers and users to protect themselves against unexpected and extreme price fluctuations. This, in turn, not only prevented financial catastrophes but also allowed buyers and sellers to plan their business activities. Second, it was a means to determine fair prices by allowing all sellers and buyers to negotiate on an open exchange.

The marketplace was created for the producers and consumers, but there was a third type of participant as well—the speculator. A certain degree of speculation was needed in the market to allow it to function efficiently. If a farmer went to sell futures contracts but there were no cereal companies or other users in the market at the time, the farmer might have a problem. But a speculator who thought he could make a profit by buying from the farmer and holding it until he could find someone to take the grain off his hands at a higher price provided liquidity to the marketplace. The speculators were expected to base their prices on what they thought was happening on the farms and with the users—in other words, based on the real dynamics of supply and demand.

That was how it was supposed to work. But some speculators got carried away with the prospect of making money by manipulating prices, and weak federal laws did not rein them in. There were scandals involving rogues hoarding futures to drive up prices or force a sell-off. During World War I it got so bad that emergency legislation was needed to halt wheat futures trading and stabilize prices. A few years later Congress required that commodity exchanges be licensed, and regulations were put in place to oversee grain trading. But they were not very effective.

During the Depression, speculators were blamed for exacerbating agricultural crises. President Roosevelt pressed Congress to control commodity exchanges and eliminate "unnecessary, unwise and destructive speculation."[5]

Along with a host of other New Deal legislation, Congress passed the Commodity Exchange Act in 1936 to oversee trading in grains and other farm products, including cotton, butter, and eggs. Over time, other agricultural commodities such as wool and livestock were added to the list. The law was enforced by the Commodity Exchange Authority (CEA), which was part of the Department of Agriculture.

The CEA required that these commodities be traded on regulated exchanges, and it prohibited options trading. The government was also empowered to set limits on how much speculators could trade. It warned that "excessive speculation" harmed interstate commerce. These limits initially focused on grain trading and regulated how much of the market an individual could control as well as how much traders could buy or sell in a day. Over time, trading limits were set for a few more products. For decades the Commodity Exchange Act worked fairly well.

But as the decades passed, futures trading ballooned and expanded to nonagricultural products including Treasury bills, precious metals such as gold and silver, currencies, and government-backed housing mortgages. In 1974, Congress decided to broaden federal oversight of commodity trading.[6] It created an independent agency, the Commodity Futures Trading Commission, giving it authority to regulate all commodity futures contracts and options, deciding what could be traded and where.

For several years the CFTC debated whether to expand limits to all types of holdings. In the early 1980s, in the wake of massive manipulation of the silver market, the CFTC ruled that the commodity exchanges had to curb the size of a trader's position. But over time the CFTC, under pressure from the exchanges, backtracked on this, first for financial instruments, then for energy and metals. Ultimately, the CFTC ruled there would be no fixed trading limits except on those contracts expiring in the following month. Otherwise, trading above certain levels would only trigger a review by the exchange involved, which would then determine whether to ask a trader to limit his holdings.

A watershed in the regulation of commodities occurred late in the Clinton administration. CFTC chairwoman Brooksley Born and Michael Greenberger, director of CFTC's Division of Trading and Markets, were threatening to regulate new financial derivatives, such as credit default swaps, that were starting to trade. Banks were lobbying hard to keep them out of CFTC purview. Simultaneously, Enron was pressing for legislation that would guarantee the deregulation of electronic commodity trading, to keep EnronOnline away from regulatory scrutiny.

Treasury secretary Robert Rubin and Federal Reserve chairman Alan Greenspan were opposed to regulating the financial derivatives, but according to Greenberger, no one in the administration was talking about deregulating aspects of physical commodity trading.[7] Despite Enron's efforts, the fight was only about financial derivatives. In fact, Greenberger says, when the concept of physical commodities came up in a group meeting that included Rubin's successor, Larry Summers, and Greenspan, "the group said, 'Absolutely not. There is a limited supply, and those markets can be manipulated. We strongly recommend against it. You cannot deregulate physical commodities.'"[8]

Even the banks opposed Enron's efforts, seeing it as a distraction from their campaign. Only one House committee had agreed to the idea. But late on December 15, 2000, the final day of a lame-duck congressional session, as the Senate was about to pass a massive, important appropriations bill, Texas senator Phil Gramm introduced an unrelated rider, the Commodity Futures Modernization Act (CFMA). With no time for anyone to study Gramm's bill, it passed as part of the budget bill. With adoption of the measure, much of energy trading was put outside the reach of regulators.

A provision in the bill, known as the Enron loophole, guaranteed EnronOnline would not be regulated. Although many observers held Gramm personally responsible for the provision, because his wife, Wendy, sat on Enron's board, he later denied it.[9] Another section of the law allowed Goldman Sachs, Morgan Stanley, and several U.S. and European energy companies to operate their electronic commodity exchange, the IntercontinentalExchange, without oversight. The law also strengthened the legality of over-the-counter energy deals pioneered by Enron, which had never been subject to oversight, and ensured they would continue to be unregulated.

Shortly after the CFMA passed, the price of gas, which had been between $2 and $3 per MMBtu for years, suddenly spiked to more than $9, and the speculative energy trading business took off. In particular, gas became the most volatile commodity traded. Exactly what caused this change has been widely debated. But many industrial users and two key congressional investigations have largely blamed speculators for short-term price spikes and for contributing to long-term price increases.

Basic supply and demand didn't change radically between 2000 and 2006, not in any substantial way that can explain "the sharply higher prices of recent years," noted a report by Robert Shapiro, an economist and former undersecretary of commerce for economic affairs, and George Washington University economics professor Nam Pham.[10]

And the difference between the price in the spot market and futures prices widened more than in the past. In the 1990s, when natural gas prices were usually stable, spot gas prices and futures prices were almost the same. But the gap between the average spot price and the average of all futures prices increased dramatically from 2.1 percent in the 1990s to almost 38 percent in the 2000–6 period.[11]

When gas prices started their climb, Bob Easterbrook Jr.'s life changed. He really wanted to just focus on his customers, take care of his employees, "and do what we do best," harden steel. But instead, he learned all he could about the natural gas futures market, talking with experts and attending trade association meetings that dealt with the issue.

The East-Lind Heat Treat firm wasn't big. It employed thirty-five people, with revenues in the $4 million to $5 million range. Easterbrook considered his employees like a "big family." He didn't lay people off when times were bad. He tried to treat employees fairly. But after big gas price increases, he was not able to provide the compensation packages that he wanted.

"You have to cut somewhere because one thing we must have is natural gas to run our processes," he says.

Price volatility, even more than increased prices, made it very difficult for him to operate. From May 2000 to September 2006 a standard measure of volatility showed that it increased 475 percent.[12] One can see how volatile the market became after 2000 by looking at what is called the "forward curve," a graph of prices for every month going out several years. For 1999, the three-year curve looks almost like a straight line, with a slight wave showing prices between $2 and $2.50 per MMBtu. But the graph for 2006 shows wide gyrations, from prices in the $6 range to more than $10, then back to $8 and up to $11.[13]

Easterbrook couldn't gauge what his expenses would be in the future. More troubling still was that he didn't know what his competitors were doing. Were they buying gas at lower prices?

"You don't really know if you are playing on an even field," he says. "Did you buy your gas a year ago or are you buying it now and the price is doubled? I may be paying $13 for gas and my competitor $8 or vice versa. And if I try to raise my prices to cover the costs, I am out of business. The heat treating business is fairly competitive."

Easterbrook learned from his industry trade group that he could buy gas in advance, using the futures market. He hired the Legacy Energy Group and became a hedger—someone who tries to protect himself against future price changes that could hurt his business.

Hedgers—unlike the similarly named hedge funds—are users or producers of natural gas. While speculators such as hedge funds are trying to make as much money as possible by betting on the price swings of natural gas, hedgers are actually trying to protect themselves from wide price swings. They use futures, swaps, and options as a form of insurance against price changes. They generally are not interested in making lots of money by speculating on the price of gas and are not rapidly and continuously trading. Generally, they buy or sell quantities that directly relate to their underlying physical needs. They just invest in gas contracts and monitor how market prices move, trying to make sure they don't experience sudden, unexpected cost increases. Sometimes they actually deliver or take delivery of the gas when the contract comes due, but often they just buy or sell futures, as well as options, spreads, and swaps, trying to earn a profit on the paper product to offset any losses they may incur on the physical product.

Easterbrook and other hedgers saw a drop in prices for about a year after the merchant energy companies exited trading, amidst charges they manipulated gas supplies and prices. Wellhead prices dropped about 25 percent, although they were still roughly 50 percent higher than they had been in the 1990s.[14]

Then in came Wall Street.

Attracted by the newly deregulated field, now cleared of competition by the collapse of the merchant energy companies such as Enron, banks and hedge funds rushed into energy trading. Some, like Goldman Sachs and Morgan Stanley, were already in the energy business but expanded their role. Morgan Stanley had been in the physical energy business since 1986. By 2005 its plants were the second-most-active generators of electric power, and it controlled a quarter of all U.S. home heating oil reserves. It delivered more than twenty million barrels of heating oil between 2002 and 2004.[15] Goldman Sachs got into commodities trading in 1981, after it acquired a firm with a seat on the futures exchange in order to trade financial futures. But in 2003 Goldman also delved into the physical energy market, picking up thirty power plants cheaply from troubled energy giants.[16] In 2004, Goldman Sachs and Morgan Stanley together earned about $2.6 billion from commodities trading—most of that from energy.[17]

While some hedge funds at first had trouble finding enough qualified traders, it didn't take long before they too were major players in energy markets. Analysts estimated that by 2006, the number of energy hedge funds—those that held more than 25 percent of their assets in energy—had risen to five hundred from one hundred three years previously.[18]

Energy trading soared. The number of oil and gas and other energy contracts on the exchanges quadrupled between 2002 and 2005.[19] Speculators were a driving force behind this. By mid-2004 noncommercial traders—hedge funds, money managers, and other speculators—made up 42 percent of all traders, according to the CFTC. Because the CFTC lumped swaps traders in with producers and other commercial users, the role of speculators was probably even higher.[20] As of April 2005, hedge funds held at least 31 percent of all NYMEX natural gas holdings; altogether, speculators held 47 percent of NYMEX gas futures contracts. Again, that is probably a low figure because of the way swaps dealers were counted.[21] ICE, which soon rivaled NYMEX in the value of contracts traded, reported that hedge funds and other speculators were more than 30 percentage of its traders, based on the percentage of total commissions they paid.[22]

Free market advocates argued that speculators lubricated the markets, guaranteeing hedgers the liquidity they needed to trade. But increasingly utilities, small companies, and local distributors came to regard speculators as a major problem for them. Paul Cicio, head of a trade group representing cement, food processing, chemical, steel, glass, pharmaceutical, and other industrial users of gas, said that the system had been working fine until about 2000. There was enough liquidity, provided by locals in the trading pits and others, so that hedging was not a problem. And because there was very little volatility, there wasn't a great need to hedge. But then the system changed. "Unfortunately, it appears that speculators are trading with other speculators, betting on the market as if it's a gambling casino with little regard to the fundamentals of supply and demand of the commodity," he said.[23]

"You need a certain amount of speculation for the market to work," agrees Michael Masters, a portfolio manager who has studied commodity trading extensively, "and in fact, ten years ago, the market worked fine. Nobody was complaining about lack of liquidity."

But then suddenly there was excessive speculation. And that in turn caused excessive volatility, which in turn required more hedging, he explains.[24]

"Many, many hedgers were driven out of business from the excessive volatility," he says. "Imagine you were trading based on supply and demand for ten years. And then, all of a sudden, large flows of money come in. You are going to lose . . . because you didn't realize the significance of the financial flows on the commodities you were trading," explains Masters.

"What I think Wall Street saw, right then and there, was, 'We can run these prices up,'" says Thomas Ihrig, vice president of the Legacy Energy Group, a Virginia-headquartered company that manages its customers' energy price risks by buying energy futures and options for them.[25] It represents commercial and industrial companies such as Bob Easterbrook Jr.'s firm, as well as schools.

"What Wall Street does now . . . is they put the worst-case-scenario risk in front of everybody," says Ihrig. Actual energy users usually don't buy into the scare stories about supply and demand, he says, but they have to consider buying overpriced gas because of fears it could spike further. "If we had a major hurricane . . . you're sitting there saying, 'Gee, gas could go to $18.' But yet the fundamentals are telling you we are in okay shape, so what do you do? The minute a hurricane comes in and knocks out production, you are going to $18. So the end user is saying, 'I've got to buy gas at $13.' And then two weeks later it's valued at $7 . . . it makes it very, very, very difficult for that end user to manage his energy costs."

Aubrey Hilliard has been helping clients in industry, commerce, and local governments meet energy needs for more than thirty years.[26] Much of that time, he has been at Texican Horizon Energy Marketing, the largest gas supplier in the Carolinas. When NYMEX started trading gas futures in 1990, recalled Hilliard, the market was dominated by producers and users. There was so little activity that the head of NYMEX invited Texican up to the trading floor to see what was going on because, small though it was, it was one of the largest traders there.

"And I mean to tell you, we traded in hundreds, not in thousands, of contracts," says Hilliard. It was that way until about 2000, he says, when "there seemed to be a shift in the marketplace, where the volatility was greater . . . because there were speculators in the market. And we couldn't tell who they were or where they were, because they were doing a lot of their trading OTC [over the counter]."

Echoing Easterbrook, Hilliard recalls that in the 1990s the market never saw big price spikes. Then suddenly it went up to $10 in 2000. "And from then on, you had ranges that went from $5.50 to $15 when you had Amaranth involved in the market." Hilliard wanted regulators to shine a spotlight on the unregulated over-the-counter market because he believed "there were outsized positions that were causing the prices to run up."

In his newsletter to the companies and local governments whose energy costs he was helping manage, Hilliard repeatedly inveighed against hedge funds and banks, which he suspected were driving up prices. But because so much trading was being done either directly between parties or on the unregulated ICE platform, he didn't know for sure.

In July 2005 he told his clients to "look for hedge fund buying to run oil and gas up the next few weeks . . . Were it not for fear, energy prices would surely be lower" because of huge inventories.

The spike in prices exasperated Hilliard. The next month he wrote customers, "Where is Eliot Spitzer when we need him? Hedge funds, pension funds and commodity funds are buying energy futures like never before . . . Gas and oil have become the NYMEX equivalent of beach property. You can pay anything you want today because someone will be willing to pay more tomorrow. Never before have I seen a greater disconnection between fundamentals and the futures market, and I've been trading oil since the '80s."

When representatives of commercial, industrial, and municipal gas users went to the CFTC and the White House during the presidency of George W. Bush, seeking better oversight of energy trading, they were stonewalled. "If we took it to the guys at the CFTC," says Hilliard, "Bush's people were all about, 'Hey, let the free markets go.' The guys that ran the CFTC . . . were all saying, 'No, you can't do this, this is the free market, no one's going to manipulate it.' And I kept saying, 'Hey guys, remember the Hunt brothers?' Everyone on our side of the market was of the same thought—that there's something crooked going on here."

"GONNA GET OUR FACES RIPPED OFF"

For Amaranth, April was a banner month. Its energy portfolio gained $1 billion, and Hunter was riding high.

But some of his investors were not so ecstatic. In fact, the money made by the firm that spring unsettled them. Investors and traders knew that earning a billion dollars doesn't come without huge risks. So when the hedge fund suddenly had a massive win, it raised a red flag—at least in some quarters.

The spring's earnings volatility, even before the end of April, added to the concerns of BlackRock, a huge New York–based investment management firm. It was already troubled by Amaranth's huge profits the previous fall when the hurricanes hit. In the first quarter of 2006, it paid a 3 percent penalty fee to withdraw its holdings earlier than the date set in its contract. Larry Fink, BlackRock's founder, later explained that "when you see aberrant success, you have to ask, did I take too much risk?"[1]

Soon after the April investment results went out to clients, telephones started ringing at Amaranth's Greenwich office. Funds of funds, including three that managed money for the New Jersey state pension plan, had questions for Maounis and other executives about April's results.

In mid-May, SDCERA received Amaranth's report about its April profits. The San Diego pension fund's original $175 million investment, which had grown to $218 million at the start of April, was now worth more than $244 million, even after the 20 percent profit fee and 1.5 percent management fee taken by the hedge fund.[2] The fund's investment officers were happy with the profits but harbored some concern about Amaranth's volatility. It would be a few weeks, though, before SDCERA officials spoke with people at the hedge fund.

Amaranth's April update to investors acknowledged the increased volatility of its returns and indicated that it was trying to cut the risk and bank some of the profits. "Our energy and commodities portfolios generated outsized returns due to unusual volatility across the crude oil, natural gas, and metals businesses," it said. "As volatility increased during the month, we took the opportunity to reduce exposure in our natural gas and metals portfolios and realized profits."[3]

Still, some investors must have raised an eyebrow when that same letter revealed that the fund now had an even larger share of its assets invested in energy. Perhaps it was partly due to Hunter's outsize returns that month. Whatever the reason, the fact remained that at the beginning of April Amaranth had 34 percent of its capital allocated to energy, and by the end of the month it was 38 percent.

The dramatic energy trading profits—more than $570 million during January, February, and March,[4] and $1.1 billion profit in April[5]—also raised some wariness among Amaranth's other portfolio managers. What kind of risk was Hunter taking for it? Amaranth was supposed to be a multistrategy fund. Its earnings were not supposed to be so volatile. But they were reticent about raising questions. "It was hard to ask about risk when the guy's making money every month," says one portfolio manager who grew concerned.[6]

The executive committee had already decided that Hunter's huge positions had to be cut back, but it didn't really seem to be happening. At least not to the extent they expected. Hunter chafed at directives from energy risk manager Chasman, who demanded that Hunter consult with him prior to initiating major trades. Chasman, for his part, was growing increasingly frustrated with Hunter's responses. As May began, Chasman worried that Hunter was deliberately evading him. He shot off some caustic instant messages.

CHASMAN: Look you need to discuss any potentially big stuff before u do it with me—(1) this is my job and you need to respect it (2) it is in your best interest to have another person who knows the rough structure of the book—i.e. I think you want to know that you have the position you think that you have.

HUNTER: Chasman—believe me we have huge respect for you. We are trying to keep the firm as our main priority.

CHASMAN: So please make sure not to treat me like a mushroom.

The mushroom comment, Chasman later explained, meant that he "did not want to be kept in the dark and fed excrement."[7]

Executives were having trouble monitoring what Hunter's team was doing. And they worried that Hunter was not reducing his holdings to the degree they expected.

Maounis planned to hire someone to expand trading to oil and to help Hunter co-manage the energy team. Hunter recommended Jeff Baird, whom he had worked with at Deutsche Bank. Baird and another former Deutsche Bank trader, Bob Jonke, were oil trading partners at a New York hedge fund. Baird joined Amaranth on May 9 as co-head of the firm's global energy and commodities business.

Maounis hoped that hiring this new oil trader would also be a backdoor way of forcing Hunter to reduce his holdings. Maounis and Rob Jones talked about this in an email exchange a few days before Baird's arrival. Maounis told Jones on May 5 that Baird's arrival would "force BH [Brian Hunter] to get smaller" in his positions, since the firm would need to take some of his capital for the oil desk. Jones agreed. "I think Jeff's arrival will help a lot," he replied.

Jones also thought it would be advantageous for other reasons. "I think they will make each other more productive (like good colleagues should) and, on days like this, we will have a PM [portfolio manager] where we need one: at his desk, doing his duty."[8] It was only a couple of weeks earlier that Jones in a fit of pique had sent daily emails to Hunter demanding that someone be in the office early to give the risk managers timely reports on their trading.

But while Amaranth management wanted Hunter to reduce his holdings, they didn't micromanage it or set firm limits on his total futures, spreads, or options.[9] Chasman later testified that there may have been a few days around the end of April and the beginning of May when Hunter actually reduced his holdings. But overall, he admitted, Hunter's investments just kept growing.[10]

Chasman's risk assessment model calculated Hunter's VAR at the time at around $350 million. But as Vince Kaminski, who developed Enron's risk assessment system, warns, "VAR is only one data point. When you are flying a plane you look at a hundred gauges, not just one blinking light. Nothing replaces thinking, intuition, and discipline."[11]

At the end of May, Amaranth's risk analysis failed spectacularly.

In the first part of the month, Hunter continued to focus on several key strategies. They all revolved around the basic concept that winter prices would be higher than summer prices into the future. He kept his bet on that the March-April spreads would widen, and he gloated when traders such as Bo Collins got burned. On May 10, for example, he told one trader, "God some of these guys on H-J [March-April] is ugly. Poor Bo."[12]

Hunter bet that prices would drop through the summer of 2006 and rise in the upcoming winter. He also continued to invest heavily in a strategy playing off what he expected to be the cold winter of 2007 against a warmer 2010.

In May, as he had done since the start of the year, Hunter purchased NYMEX futures contracts for the winter heating season, especially January, and he shorted the November 2006 contracts. Day after day he dominated trading in those contracts. Hunter's holdings that month were so enormous they equaled what all other traders had held in each of the previous three years.[13] And his positions in surrounding months were huge as well.

Hunter had reached his goal—he was the number one trader of natural gas.[14] He was at the top of his game. But he was playing in dangerous waters.

His massive trading was driving prices way out of line with historical norms. In May 2002, 2003, and 2004, for example, the difference between November and January prices had hovered around 25 cents; in 2005 it only rose to slightly over 50 cents. But now the November-January spreads were up near $2.00. In a similar vein, in the previous four years the difference between October and January contracts had always been less than $1.00. But now it was near $3.00.

Another late season of severe hurricanes this year might spike those prices higher and make Hunter a fortune. It seemed a real possibility—on May 22 the National Weather Service issued a warning that a "very active hurricane season" loomed. It predicted as many as eight to ten hurricanes in the North Atlantic, instead of the average six. The chance of an above-average hurricane season was said to be 80 percent. Hunter could maintain his holdings and hope for some disaster to strike production or shipments of gas. That was one way things could play out. But if the storms or some other catastrophe to curtail production or gas deliveries didn't happen, Hunter was in trouble.

Maybe he could keep adding to his holdings, forcing prices his way, putting pressure on other traders who bet against him. He could squeeze traders who bet prices would fall. If he invested enough money, many would have to close out of their holdings by buying. That would even help him.

His only other option, as one trader put it, was "to start puking it out"—getting out of the holdings in bits and pieces.

Around the middle of May, Hunter tried to sell off some of his gas holdings, according to an Amaranth note to its investors. But he couldn't find buyers, at least not at the high prices he had helped create.[15] Around the same time, natural gas producers started selling their future supplies. Both events started to push down prices.

Another trader sent Hunter an instant message on May 12 that said, "Producers relentless." "No kidding," he replied, "it's unreal." "There is a ton of producer selling," he went on. "Damn," his friend said. "Hahaha, it will end," Hunter reassured him. "They are always out in spring and winter selling away."[16]

Shane Lee later recalled, "We saw an amount of producer hedging that we had not ever remembered seeing since about 2001. I think the market in general had outsized itself for that type of event, us included."[17] By the end of the month, a number of other large traders had also started selling futures contracts while prices were high.

Producers selling, other traders selling, Amaranth trying to sell—all this started causing prices to drop. During the last week in May, natural gas prices fell dramatically. The November-January spread, which had been at $2.15, tumbled to $1.73.[18] For Hunter that was an ominous sign of things to come.

Prices of other key Amaranth holdings also bombed. The March-April spreads for several years out fell. And the firm was particularly hurt on Hunter's bet that calendar year 2007 contracts would rise.[19]

Clearly other traders did not see the situation as Hunter did. "It was naïve to think that they could get out of the market with a size of 100,000 positions," one trader told Senate investigators.[20]

In instant messages, Hunter expressed his agitation. On May 24, he lamented to one trader about the price drops, "Hearing it[']s sort of carnage out there."

A couple of hours later, he told another trader, "I think this last week has made people give back a lot." Certain spreads, he said, "obliterated me." "We are still up this month, but were up really big earlier."[21]

The market chatter was that Bo Collins at MotherRock, as well as Deutsche Bank and J. P. Morgan, had lost money. "I heard MotherRock, JPM and DB got really nutted," he wrote.

The next day was absolutely bleak for Hunter. He wrote a friend, "You around[?] I could use a [pep] talk. getting killed today. been ok until today. but today is a mess."[22]

If Hunter tried to sell off a large part of his energy holdings as prices were falling, he would lose even more money. But to keep what he had, the firm needed to cough up more cash to meet increasing margin calls triggered by the market's volatility.

Amaranth emptied its reserves and halted its private placement loan program to companies. But that wasn't enough. A sense of panic gripped the company as people scrambled to raise the capital that would keep the firm afloat.

Executives decided to jettison other portfolios. "They needed the cash. They had to draw down any liquid portfolios in the firm to pay," a former Amaranth employee recalls.[23]

Frantically the firm began to sell holdings it could easily convert into money, such as stocks and bonds, despite widespread grumbling. Some portfolio managers axed as much as 25 percent of their holdings. And when that didn't raise enough money, some slashed as much as 50 percent. There was plenty of angst at Amaranth about the sell-off.

"You make your money off your position, not theirs, and now you have to sell it. It hurts," says one former employee.

Unloading portfolios under such pressure meant losses for other traders and portfolio managers. It was exactly what had happened to Nick Maounis at Paloma. Executives talked about how to compensate these traders for their losses. They considered creating paper portfolios reflecting the holdings traders sold. They could follow how well these did, calculate the profits they could have made, in order to properly pay the traders at the end of the year. But the plan was never implemented.

Amaranth officials also met with a number of banks to liquidate other holdings at fire-sale prices.[24]

The last two weeks in May were catastrophic for the firm. Their energy portfolio was in crisis. It was the worst month in the firm's history, ending with Amaranth losing more than $1.1 billion.[25] The value-at-risk calculations had predicted a worst-case loss of only $350 million. For a time, it seemed that the implosion had come.

But it didn't. Not then. They managed to scramble and meet all the margin calls. A sort of black celebratory atmosphere permeated throughout the firm.

Even though the fund was down almost 12 percent in May, it was still up more than 15 percent for 2006 because it had done well earlier in the year, especially after Hunter's billion-dollar windfall in April.

Within the office, people hoped the energy traders were unloading their positions, getting rid of some risk. Since the firm still showed a profit for the year, why not just coast until December? they half-jokingly asked one another.

In addition to the relief and hope, there was also anger. Until May, Amaranth executives could have tried to claim ignorance about the risks of Hunter's holdings, say former employees. They had made investors enormous profits. Hunter had argued that his trades were well hedged—that his book, because it was so concentrated in spreads, was much less risky than if it were primarily in outright monthly contracts.

But that all changed after the loss in May. It was now clear there was much more risk than they had thought. Whatever belief Hunter's team had held that its holdings would constantly and consistently profit, whatever illusions management had had about Hunter's invincibility, were now shattered.

"In May it became a moral issue because now they knew," argues one former employee. "They knew it wasn't what they thought it was in terms of risk."

Portfolio managers at Amaranth, who received daily profit-and-loss statements, were deeply concerned. They grumbled that Hunter's positions were still too big. Executives sent emails trying to calm them down, assuring them the firm would reduce its natural gas positions when it was more opportune.

Maounis focused on the risk of Hunter's energy trades. He called together his executive committee, which included several senior traders along with COO Charles Winkler and Rob Jones. What should they do?

They agreed the energy book needed to be cut back, way back. But how? And when?

They looked at Hunter's portfolio, and debated how liquid it was and the risk inherent in his positions. They started what would become weekly meetings, considering actions to take and how to direct Hunter and his team.

"We thought about pulling the trigger and taking the loss," said one trader. "We had many discussions about it. We figured we could get out for maybe a billion dollars. But we decided to ride it out and see if the market would come around."[26]

"They go, 'Okay, we've got to get out of this trade,'" says a former Amaranth employee. "But then they're like, 'Oh shit, if we try to get out of this, we can't, unless we're willing to take a serious hit, a billion dollars or more.'"[27]

"You look like a rock star," says another. "Then suddenly one day you realize you've got a problem. What do you do? Do you 'fess up and take the medicine, or do you do what they did—let it ride?"[28]

Another $1 billion loss in order to immediately cut down Hunter's book—how would investors react to that?

Instead the executive committee rolled the dice with investors' money and decided to see what would happen. No one seemed to object. It was a fateful decision.

Amaranth's executives were convinced its investors wouldn't stick with the firm through more volatility and massive losses, unlike John Arnold's investors. Its large base of funds of funds was fast money, quick to pull out at signs of trouble.

Maounis decided to separate out energy trading from the rest of the firm. Investors who still had an appetite for its volatility, risks, and potentially huge profits could put their money in it. For clients who didn't have the stomach for this, there would be the multistrategy fund. But this would take some time to arrange.

Meanwhile, Hunter was given a firmer mandate: reduce his positions by the end of summer. Maounis still believed that Hunter was the best person to oversee this, even after his reticence to get out of his holdings in April, even after the May loss. Hunter knew his complex trades and had a sense of market liquidity, Maounis thought, and could best plan how and when to unload his positions. Maounis met privately with concerned investors, assuring them Hunter's book would be cut way back.

In the corridors at Amaranth's Greenwich headquarters, worried traders, managers, and back-office personnel looked for and seemed to find some encouraging signs. David Chasman was reassuring, still telling colleagues Hunter's trades couldn't lose.

And oil trader Jeff Baird, who had come on board in May as co-head of commodities, now brought his close friend Bob Jonke over to Amaranth. Initially Baird had hesitated to do so, worried about the portfolio problem Hunter had in May. But a month later Jonke joined Amaranth. If Baird, an experienced trader, had brought in his friend, people reasoned, things couldn't be too shaky.

After the horrendous May loss, Maounis seemed to direct his anger more at Rob Jones than at Brian Hunter. Jones' risk assessment team had failed to predict May's terrible losses. Traders were, after all, supposed to press the envelope, take risks, and earn money. But a risk manager's job was to keep them in check. Still, Maounis rejected suggestions he move Jones and Chasman aside, or hire someone else to unload Hunter's holdings. *Wait till it's done. Then we'll see.*

While all this was going on, the treasurer's department, under Artie DiRocco, was focusing its concern on making sure there was sufficient money to meet margin calls. If not, the firm would go belly up. There was some cash on hand, but would it be enough if there was a next time?

DiRocco's group relied on the firm's risk reports to determine how much to keep in reserve. But given the carnage in May, when actual losses had been nearly triple the risk assessment group's worst-case estimate, the treasurer's division no longer put any credence in the risk analysis figures. Though the latest worst-case scenario projected a maximum loss of $1 billion, the treasurer's department decided to set aside almost $3.5 billion in cash reserves.

They also brought in-house the complex program used by NYMEX to compute margin requirements. Amaranth officials wanted to know what NYMEX would require if the market moved in certain ways. The risk analysis team didn't think too much of the new program, convinced they understood potential market shifts.

In the May update to investors, Maounis called that month's catastrophe "a humbling experience that led us to recalibrate how we assess risk in this business." But he still argued that the firm's gas investments would make money. "We believe certain spread relationships involving natural gas remain disconnected from their fundamental value drivers." Therefore, Amaranth intended to remain invested in them.

In Calgary, Hunter had no thought of major downsizing yet, especially when it came to his wager that winter prices would be higher than summer. He knew market sentiment was against him. If he tried to unload his holdings, he would lose money. He could have just waited to see what would happen, and management could have reined in his trading but Hunter had a different plan. He would increase his positions. That would prop up his holdings, give him time. Perhaps in the process he could squeeze out some traders positioned against him. Then the market might turn in his favor. Or some event, a hurricane perhaps, might help him out. Despite any misgivings executives might have had, it seems Hunter was allowed to plow back into the market.

On May 26, the same day Amaranth was selling off holdings in Greenwich to meet margin calls, Hunter made a crucial decision: he would take on more of the "widow maker." He was already invested in the March-April 2008 spread. On May 26, he also bet heavily that the price of the 2007 March-April spread would widen.[29]

He dove back into trading, buying and selling thousands of contracts. He was responsible for doing half the trades in these March and April NYMEX contracts. He was investing in the "widow maker" when it was already at a high price, close to $1.50, well above the $1 it had usually traded at or below in the past.[30]

At the end of Hunter's May 26 trading spree, the price of the spread had increased by another 25 cents, the largest one-day increase that year. Traders, seeing the heavy trading, connected it to the jump in price. Senate investigators later concluded the price spread increased significantly as a direct result of Amaranth's trading.[31]

If Hunter's trading helped drive up the price of the spread, it also meant he was such a large part of the market that he couldn't get out of his positions without moving prices against him. So over the next months, if prices started to move against him—for example, winter prices falling or summer prices increasing—he simply bought or sold more to keep them in his favor.

Although Amaranth executives had promised investors they would reduce natural gas holdings after the May losses, it never happened. From the end of March to the middle of September natural gas positions increased, Chasman later admitted.[32]

"Part of the reason his position got so big was that he had to have the price improve, go his way, and so he had to push on it harder," explains a trader.[33]

In other words, Hunter was creating his own storm system.

Well after the computers were shut down and the doors closed on the NYMEX trading floor May 26, Hunter and a colleague analyzed and debated what they had done. Long into that night, they sent each other worried emails about whether or not they made the right play. How was the market going to react on the March-April spread?

Around 10:40 p.m., Hunter messaged Shane Lee: "Getting nervous again." He asked Lee if they could deal with any further price problems the following Monday by buying more of the March-April spread.[34]

"Not sure yet," answered Lee. "Need to clear my head a little with some sleep. I am pretty banged up from this week. I know we did the right thing today. Just don't know if it bought us time or if we were right and all of this is symptomatic of mispriced Q1 [first quarter]."

He continued. "I think we could still head down. We have to be honest to ourselves about it. Take some time to rest your brain. I have been through this before and can tell you that you will only hurt yourself by thinking about it too much without decent rest. The answer should be simple to us by Sunday, I think."

They had another worry too: would John Arnold, with his huge holdings and positions, wreak additional havoc on them? On May 26 Hunter had not only increased his March-April position but also substantially added to his short position of July contracts. He was betting prices would fall in the next few weeks as the contract went to expiration. Amaranth now was short more than 40,000 July contracts, having increased its position that day by about 10,000 contracts.[35]

Hunter and his colleagues believed Arnold was also betting on lower July prices, which in and of itself was good news. But they fretted that if things did not go as they hoped and there was even a slight increase in prices, Arnold would be in trouble. In that case, he could be forced to buy heavily to cancel his holdings. This would drive prices up even more.

They were particularly concerned about a replay of what they thought had happened back in December 2003 when Hunter lost money at Deutsche Bank. He and his colleagues blamed Arnold, if not for causing the sudden spike in prices then, at least for exacerbating it.

Back then, they believed, Arnold had had significant short holdings, as did Hunter. When prices suddenly spiked after Thanksgiving and into December, Arnold was in trouble. It was a short squeeze, and Arnold had to buy heavily to unwind his positions. Many traders felt that Arnold's trading had pushed prices up more than the fundamentals called for.

"One thing that worries me is that if the fronts go up, does John [Arnold] blow up?" Lee said now, reflecting his belief that Arnold would be seriously hurt if summer prices rose. Lee added that some of Arnold's holdings were already causing him problems, that they were "getting crazy to deal with the pain."

Then he warned Hunter that if Arnold was squeezed out of his holdings, as they believed he had been three years before, Amaranth could suffer. "He caused Dec 2003 . . . does he cause May 2006?"

Lee cautioned, "My gut tells me we just capitulated. But that is only as long as another big deal comes through. All we can do in the short term is pick at scabs in the market and stay ahead of John [Arnold]."

Then he quipped, "Just promise me if things go bad, I can at least be your Bentley driver. My kids will need to eat."

As May came to a close, the firm was still heavily invested in energy, despite that month's losses and growing concerns in Greenwich about what was happening in Calgary. In fact, partly due to the sale of holdings in other portfolios to bail Hunter out, energy was an even bigger focus for Amaranth. At the start of May, it had 38 percent of assets invested in energy. By May 31 that had grown to 50 percent.[36]

Hunter was trading financial instruments worth tens of billions of dollars. Based on Hunter's holdings on the last day of that month, one economics professor calculated that Hunter's long and short positions had a notional or face value of $34 billion.[37] If things went his way, he stood to make a fortune. But if not . . .

Traders quickly learned about Amaranth's devastating May losses. Many were first alerted to the firm's problems by the news that Amaranth was having a fire sale of its equity holdings. Stock traders heard "that Amaranth was liquidating equity portfolios to raise cash to pay for their energy portfolio," says a hedge fund manager, and word was relayed to energy traders.[38]

Some traders had gleaned information about Hunter's positions through their own trading with him and market rumors. But they soon had a more exact account of what had happened and the extent of Hunter's holdings. Maounis sent his investors a monthly report revealing exactly how much Amaranth had lost in May and how much of the firm's capital was devoted to energy, along with an assurance that Hunter would be drastically cutting back. These were the signals many in the energy-trading community had been waiting for.

"The party was about to end," as one trader explains, and that created an opportunity for others. Once they saw Hunter's May losses, says the trader, "it gave them a little more moxie to take on some of the trades."[39]

John Arnold and Bo Collins, along with a number of other large traders, had believed for a long time that winter prices and the March-April spread were way too high and that Hunter's trading was responsible. But they had stayed out of the way of Hunter's freight train. Now that he was under pressure to reduce his positions, they expected him to unload. Then prices would collapse. Arnold and Collins planned to invest on that belief. Others did too.

But the market had a nasty surprise in store. Hunter didn't seem to be off-loading his positions. Instead he was stocking up on more of the same. First came Hunter's May 26 buying spree. Then he continued buying over the next few weeks. As a result, the traders who had tiptoed back into selling the March-April spread were hurt. "I know several traders who tried to start taking on his position after May. Most got socked in the end," says Foster Smith, an energy trader who then headed up North American gas and power trading at Deutsche Bank. "They said, 'Shit, I'm wrong. I have to get out again.' "[40]

"I think what threw everyone off a little was Brian was able to stay in the position as long as he did. And then he started adding to it as though it were going to some completely new level," says a trader who shorted the March-April spread. "That's when we started seeing some blood in the water."[41]

That was when John Arnold, who had stayed away from trading against Hunter for more than a year, and Bo Collins, who had only nibbled on March-April trades in the weeks before Amaranth's May debacle, made their move.

May was "the tipping point for some and maybe in particular Centaurus, to say, 'Hey, we smell some weakness here, and next time he gets in trouble he won't be able to get out,' " explains a trader friendly with both Hunter and Arnold.[42]

While other players reversed themselves after seeing Hunter back again buying the March-April spread in late May and early June, Arnold and Collins did not. They stayed with their investments, betting against Hunter. "Maybe everyone did get out except Centaurus. They kept that on and when they started, it was all over," says a trader who knows Arnold. "It was like a game of poker—how many chips do you have?"[43]

"Whoever could stay in the game the longest would likely win," explains another trader. And John Arnold, whose investors were loyal to him while he rode through heavy losses, was determined to be the last one standing.[44]

Meanwhile, throughout June worried investors pressed Maounis and other Amaranth executives to explain what had happened.

San Diego pension fund managers found out about Amaranth's May losses on June 2.[45] Five days later, SDCERA's investment consultants, Rocaton, questioned Maounis, Jones, and Hunter, who attributed the firm's losses to Amaranth's attempt to get out of holdings and take profits. Amaranth couldn't realize gains, they explained, because market liquidity had dried up. It was, they said, an "unprecedented" situation. And they reassured the pension consultants that such unforeseen circumstances were now incorporated into their risk models. The firm was protected from a recurrence. They emphasized they were drastically cutting their energy risk exposure.

Rocaton discussed all this with SDCERA on June 13, three days before the quarterly deadline for the pension fund to withdraw money from the hedge fund. SDCERA officials were satisfied with these answers and those they had received earlier directly from Amaranth. They didn't withdraw their money.[46]

Throughout June, Amaranth executives met with investors, including the three funds of funds that invested money for the New Jersey state pension plan, to explain the May losses. In these sessions too Amaranth indicated that it intended to reduce its energy exposure.[47] Hunter flew to Greenwich two weeks in a row to join Maounis and others at fifteen to twenty-five of these meetings.[48]

Not all investors were reassured. The New York–based Blackstone Group's fund of funds unit was very concerned about Amaranth's volatility and its risk management. If there were not a problem, the firm wouldn't have lost so much in a month, they told Amaranth employees when pulling out their investment.[49]

By July, investors, worried by the May losses, had pulled $400 million from the hedge fund.[50]

Over the next couple of months, Amaranth executives tried to rein in the Calgary team by bringing them to Greenwich for days at a time. Some spent most of June, July, and August in Connecticut.[51]

Just as at Deutsche Bank three years previously, Hunter was seated on the trading desk, instructed to unwind his holdings and watched by his bosses. The energy team was situated directly in front of Jones' glass-walled office, where Jones had the flashing numbers of real-time ICE trading and Amaranth's portfolio projected on his wall.

"There was a view that it would be helpful during certain periods of time to have Brian and, later, certain members of his team there, sitting right outside Nick and Rob's office," Amaranth's investor relations executive said later.[52]

It was the best way to reduce the risk and the size of the energy holdings, COO Winkler later noted. "Rob and Nick felt that we wanted the whole team together. It was a big position, it was a big job, and we thought having everybody together and making sure it got done would be the best way to have it at that time."[53]

As June rolled on, however, the previous month's crisis was soon in Hunter's rearview mirror. He started to rake in profits again. And Amaranth's investments in energy continued to grow, in part because Hunter made money. From 50 percent of the firm's assets at the end of May, the amount in energy swelled to 56 percent by the end of June.[54]

In particular, Hunter's holdings of both the March-April spread and other winter and summer contracts increased dramatically throughout June. He added 13,000 January contracts and doubled his bets that August prices would drop. He went from shorting close to 40,000 November contracts to shorting more than 55,000. By the end of June, his holdings of upcoming summer and winter positions were the largest yet. His buying on two specific June days of the March-April spreads spiked prices on those days and kept them high for many days after that.[55]

Hunter was successful again in June—thanks to his huge trades he was moving prices in his favor, and the firm was up about 6 percent that month, with Hunter credited with earning more than three-fourths of that.[56] As a result, notes an exasperated former employee, "the top guys forgot about reducing the size of his holdings."

Maounis was certainly happy to tell investors in his monthly update that "our energy business was a strong performer in June, predominantly driven by a widening of certain seasonal spreads in natural gas." But the reality was that with key market players arrayed against him and nothing on the horizon to warrant the high winter prices, Hunter faced significant losses if he tried to reduce his holdings.

John Arnold and Bo Collins did not think Amaranth's management would continue for long pouring money into Hunter's positions, and word of this soon reached Hunter through broker and trader chatter.

Hunter was very concerned about protecting the high prices until some outside event, such as a late fall hurricane, came along to support them. Then he might have a chance to get out of his holdings, maybe even make some money. Meanwhile, anyone shorting the March-April spread was a threat to him. So Hunter decided to go on the offensive and let the market know he was still a player. "I took some of those today," he told a trader, "the H/J [March-April]."[57] Brokers and traders in turn relayed rumors of Brian aggressively buying those spreads and chattered that Hunter was specifically targeting Arnold with his trades—that he planned to "bury Arnold on a trade." There was also talk about him "blowing Collins out of the water."[58]

One trader remembers a broker calling, ostensibly on Hunter's instructions. Hunter planned on "buying the March-April spread until it reached $2," the broker said, urging the other trader to buy in.[59] It's unclear if the call really was made on Hunter's orders or if it was just a broker stirring the pot to increase business. But traders clearly saw a lot of money piling into the March-April spread, and they believed it could only be Hunter.

Hunter fretted that too many traders were betting against him, expecting winter prices to go down. In instant messages to other traders, he complained about the "hatred of January" and people "laying waste to v/f [October-January]."

He grumbled to another trader on June 13 that "it's messy all around." People were offering low prices for the October-January spread, he complained. "That's the problem." They were "trying to crush it every day." And he asked, "Why all the selling?" Hunter offered his own explanation: "Someone was trying to force it."[60]

A few days later, Shane Lee was stunned at the hostility from traders when he was bidding higher for more of the October-January spread. "Some guy went ballistic on me," he told Hunter. "You wouldn't believe all the anger messages I got." Hunter was surprised. "Really? That's nuts. What did they say?" Lee replied, "That we were gonna get our faces ripped off." Hunter answered, "Winter hate, it's crazy."[61]

In the first half of June, as Hunter started buying the March-April 2007 spread, its price bounced up and down about 25 cents. There was too much selling by traders such as Arnold and Collins to keep prices up consistently. Hunter decided to do some dramatic trading.

On June 14 and 15 he bought huge amounts of March contracts and sold the April contracts. On June 14 alone he was responsible for more than half the volume of NYMEX futures for March and April. He traded intensively on ICE as well. He continued the same frenetic trading the next day.[62] Suddenly the price difference between the two months doubled to 51 cents.

Hunter bragged to a friend that he was the cause. He was teaching other traders not to bet against him. "That was my doing today," he asserted. "People were getting out of control on H/J [March-April] selling. Market needed a settlement lesson. Those H/J's [March-April spreads] are scary."

His friend joked, "You are evil." Then he added, "In a nice way."[63]

Hunter gloated to Shane Lee that Arnold was hurting, along with another major gas trader, T. Boone Pickens.

HUNTER: November-January doing great today.
LEE: Yep, u were right. H/J [March-April] explosion too, market very, very, very upset today.
HUNTER: You think people are hurting?

LEE: Yes. Think about how Boone's last 2 days are going . . . 250 million.

HUNTER: Good point. Yeah. And Arnold.

LEE: Arnold got ripped for 60 cents front to back yesterday.
Boone will probably have to get on MSNBC today.

HUNTER: Ha, ha.[64]

Arnold may have been hurting, but again his investors were loyal. He had had terrific returns in previous years. Now they were willing to stay with him through a significant drawdown.

Bo Collins, at the smaller hedge fund MotherRock, was also bleeding heavily. But his investors were much more skittish.

Collins had put on a complicated structure of tens of thousands of options that replicated shorting the March-April spread. Looking at supply fundamentals, he believed the March call options were priced too high. So he had options positions that would pay off if the March gas price fell. To protect himself, he bought futures contracts. If his options lost value, he could continue to protect them by buying more futures. He calculated he could only lose money if March contract prices or the March-April spread went higher than they had been after the hurricanes. But there didn't seem to be anything on the horizon to justify that.

It was a big position that could have doubled his firm's capital if prices moved in line with his view of fundamentals. But instead there was an unprecedented run-up in the March-April spread price. And there was something even more troubling: Hunter was buying the expensive March options that Collins was shorting.

Hunter was protecting his holdings in two ways. He was buying the March-April spread, which kept increasing in price as he did so. And he was buying the March call options. Hunter's massive trading of both the spread and the options drastically hurt Collins. And Hunter had a good idea he was doing just that. He knew some of Collins' positions because the two traded options with each other through a broker. And exchange floor traders were also talking up the battle going on between Hunter and Collins.

Carol Coale was in charge of equities at MotherRock. An astute researcher, she had been the first Wall Street analyst to raise questions about Enron's finances years before, when she worked at a major brokerage firm. While Hunter was ripping into Collins' positions, she was on vacation in the Caribbean. She tried reaching Collins in the office several times while she was away, but couldn't. She knew something was wrong at MotherRock. She returned home to Houston and hopped on a plane to New York.

That night at dinner, Collins gave her some devastating news: MotherRock had lost 25 percent of its assets that month. And one of the firm's largest investors, who accounted for about one-fifth of its assets, was planning to pull out. Collins was struggling to meet margin calls and stay open.

As July rolled in, Hunter clearly seemed back in the game. He had made money again in June. While virtually all the other portfolios at the firm had seen losses, Hunter's was up and the firm had netted more than half a billion dollars. Maybe things were okay.

The *Wall Street Journal* sent a reporter to Calgary in July for a second interview with Hunter. They wanted a feature on the hotshot trader everyone was talking up, the guy who had scored such a huge bonus after the hurricanes. The reporter sat with Hunter in his office, watching him trade, and started drafting a glowing piece about him.

Hunter made plans to host Maounis and other colleagues from Greenwich during the first two weeks of July at the annual Calgary Stampede. The entire city focused on the ten-day event, when more than a million visitors descended on Calgary, including the prime minister, who donned cowboy gear. Movie stars such as Samuel Jackson and Josh Hartnett were seen strolling through the streets.

The Calgary Stampede was where the cowboy spirit of the city met the energy industry's constant exploration for new business. Cowboys provided the events: bull riding, steer wrestling, roping calves. Singers, comedians, and dancers entertained on the main stage. Energy companies, financial institutions, and money managers hosted private parties at the rodeo and held pancake breakfasts. There were cocktail parties and dinners at the best restaurants.

Nick Maounis and Rob Jones, who had never been to Calgary, decided to make their first trip that July, along with several other Amaranth people, including Charles Winkler. Hunter entertained potential clients (including executives of the Alberta provincial pension fund) and industry colleagues at a cowboy bar, reserving a private area on the second floor overlooking the dance floor to serve drinks and food.

If Maounis was nervous about the firm's May problems or concerned about Hunter's ability to downsize without more losses, he didn't show it. He enjoyed the parties and events. On Saturday, Hunter, Maounis, Jones, and Winkler donned cowboy hats and went off to watch the rodeo.

Stampede was always a busy time for Hunter, who was courted by brokers seeking commissions from his massive trades.

"When Brian Hunter came into the room, it was like Mick Jagger had walked in," says a former hedge fund owner. "He had a gaggle of people around him saying, 'Let me take you to dinner,' or 'I want to take you out.' Or they'd say, 'I'm flying to Vegas this weekend and I want to take you on my jet.' "[65]

For a guy barely thirty-two years old who had had a humble childhood in the farmlands nearby, it was a heady experience.

Hunter's huge trading of the March-April spread was counteracting the selling of traders such as Collins and Arnold. But he couldn't control the weather. And in mid-July Hunter had a nasty surprise.

A record-breaking heat wave hit the United States. From California to New York, temperatures soared above 100 degrees for days and even weeks at a time. Hundreds of deaths were blamed on the heat. Fargo, North Dakota, hit 100, breaking a record that had stood since 1929. It got so hot that power cables were destroyed, sending portions of Chicago and New York City into darkness.

Electricity consumption skyrocketed, shattering records, as everyone turned their air conditioners up high. For the first time during summer, natural gas was taken out of storage to meet the extraordinary demand.

Hunter was burned by the hot temperatures. It caused a spike in the price of summer natural gas contracts, which Hunter had heavily shorted. The price of the August contract began to rise quickly, jumping more than $1 in the week ending July 26. The September contract jumped more than 75 cents.[66] But Hunter had begun the month of July short more than 40,000 August contracts and an equal number of September contracts, betting prices would fall. By July 18 he had doubled that bet on September contracts just as prices started to rise sharply.[67]

Near midnight on Thursday, July 27, Shane Lee and Hunter agonized over what to do.

Lee instant-messaged Hunter, "90 percent of people I talked to got killed. No one saw this coming. If the market is really starting to believe we may not fill [have a lot of storage] why the hell is h/j [March-April] only $2.00. Fricken deviant market."[68]

And once again, as they had in May, they worried that John Arnold, who they believed was shorting the summer months too, would drive prices against them. "I would be quite concerned about centy [Centaurus] in this move. Don't know how many bullets he has left. I guarantee he hasn't been as protected as us," Lee messaged Hunter.

On Saturday, July 29, Hunter was asked by another Amaranth energy trader, Brad Basarowich, whether he thought traders were targeting them or just buying because they too were in trouble. "U think people are out to get us?" Basarowich messaged. He told Hunter that his view was "they have the same position that is killing them too and they are bailing like rats 'cause they are getting killed."

Hunter agreed: "I think the same." If he could just keep his positions on, he would be shown to be right, Hunter believed. He complained to Basarowich he was being pressured to cut them down. "We don't have time. That is the problem. Other groups and investors are all over us to get smaller."[69]

Still, Hunter didn't reduce his holdings in July. At the end of the month his stake in the March-April 2007 spread nearly doubled over the course of a few days.[70] Hunter also held an extraordinary 80,000 contracts for the upcoming January. The amount of gas it represented was nearly equal to what all U.S. residential consumers actually used that January.[71]

For Bo Collins, what was most important about Hunter's activities that July was the money Hunter invested in March-April positions. Ultimately that money put Collins out of business.

With prices rising on the summer holdings he had shorted, and with only modest hikes to his winter positions, Hunter made a dramatic decision: he would go all out on the "widow maker." He would benefit if the spread increased, even if it was caused by his buying. And if he inflicted more pain on Collins, Arnold, and any others who were arrayed against him, perhaps more traders would join his bandwagon.

On July 31 Hunter spent the day buying March swaps and contracts and selling April. He traded on NYMEX and on ICE. He was by far the largest trader of the spread that day.[72] As Hunter pounded the March-April spread, the difference in price between the two months widened and widened, by the end of that day increasing an extraordinary 72 cents to over $2.50—the widest it had been all year.

For Bo Collins, the impact was devastating. His firm was down another 25 percent. His margin calls increased. MotherRock was a new firm with only a one-year track record, and investors were already panicked by the volatility in the gas market. When MotherRock started hemorrhaging money, its investors bolted.

On August 3, Collins sent a letter to his investors that said, "We are in the process of developing a detailed plan for winding down the fund."

A hedge fund analyst wrote to a colleague a few days later, "Bo is done, Monday blew them up. Market going nuts with Amaranth the featured FU [fuck you] player. They took it to MotherRock on Monday in the h/j [March-April] spread."[73]

Late in the day on July 31, Hunter received an instant message from another trader. "Brian, u busy. What the hell is going on out there. Rumour is you are getting even more rich!!!"

HUNTER: Really, why is that?

TRADER: Let's see I heard March April swap spread you made a killing. Some other swap spread too. Dec/Mar I think. So, according to the market you are brilliant!!!!!!! Can do no wrong. Ever!⁷⁴

But the reality was that Hunter lost money in July, and it cost him several hundred million dollars to trade the options and spread positions that killed off MotherRock. The way he pressed the option positions in particular, say traders who watched it happen, indicated that he had been targeting Collins. "There's no doubt in my mind that's absolutely what he did," says Foster Smith, then at Deutsche Bank and who earlier had worked with Collins at El Paso. Smith later went to head up J. P. Morgan's North American gas and power trading. "The irony of it," Smith explains, "is that for the one week in which he basically took Bo out, the amount of positions he had to put on to do that ultimately led to his undoing. It was almost like he threw a boomerang out there and it took out a large adversary. But it ended up coming around and taking his own head off too."⁷⁵

PUMP AND DUMP

Brian Hunter was in trouble.

Nothing on the horizon seemed likely to spark a major up-turn in the price of his huge winter holdings. And the July heat wave that had driven up summer prices lost him money. Despite his profits from the rise in the March-April spread price, he was down in July.

Almost every other investment strategy in the firm was profit-able that month. But Hunter was investing more than half the firm's capital, so Amaranth overall was down about 0.5 percent. It had been a roller-coaster ride for the firm over the past several months: up $1 billion in April, down $1 billion in May, up in June, now down in July.

Maounis still rejected suggestions he bring in someone with no vested interest in the energy book to downsize it. He still believed Hunter was the best person to unbundle his holdings. In the firm update for July, Maounis promised investors that "we are targeting a smaller allocation for natural gas in the future." But in the mean-time, "we believe opportunities in the natural gas market remain attractive and continue to maintain positions where we believe fun-damentals are disconnected with current prices."[1]

Maounis' assurances failed to soothe some of Amaranth's ner-vous investors. Representatives of the San Diego pension fund's consultants, Rocaton, held a conference call with Maounis, Winkler, Jones, Hunter, and others on August 10. Amaranth executives as-sured them that after the May losses, the firm had reevaluated the dangers of energy investing. Now the company understood how volatile and illiquid energy investments could really be and was cutting back on them, according to Rocaton.[2]

Four days later, when San Diego County pension officials heard about MotherRock's collapse, one of them contacted Amaranth's investor relations. Don't worry, she was told, Amaranth was adequately protected by hedging strategies. And the firm had a large risk management team that evaluated the energy portfolio under many dire scenarios. Amaranth's investor relations officials stressed that the fund planned further significant reductions in natural gas holdings.[3]

Other investors grew concerned when they learned in early August that despite the May losses and the extreme volatility in the natural gas market, Amaranth's gas allocations were more than half its holdings. Funds of funds, including New York–based Arden Asset Management, Washington–based Rock Creek Group, and New York–based Goldman Sachs Asset Management, called the firm or met with Rob Jones to ask why so much money was invested in natural gas. Arden went so far as to start the process to get its money back. Goldman Sachs and Rock Creek took steps toward reducing their investments.[4]

As August began, Hunter seemed to catch a break. A tropical storm developed, and there was speculation it might gain strength and enter the Gulf of Mexico, threatening oil and gas production. The winter futures contracts—November through March, which Hunter was betting heavily would increase—rose an average of 75 cents to $10.95 per MMBtu.[5] Things looked promising—from Hunter's point of view. Tropical Storm Chris had top sustained winds of sixty-five miles per hour as it passed north of Puerto Rico on August 2, and forecasters warned that it could become the first hurricane of the 2006 Atlantic season. Within forty-eight hours, though, Chris lost steam as it pushed across the eastern Caribbean, and it never developed into a serious threat to energy supplies—good news for the people who might have been in its path, but not so good for Brian Hunter.

But then on August 8, Hunter got another break. The National Weather Service issued an updated forecast about the hurricane season, reiterating its prediction of an abnormally large number of storms. Even though that year's three named storms so far "may pale in comparison to the record nine storms that formed through early August 2005," Conrad Lautenbacher, director of the National Oceanic and Atmospheric Administration, which runs the National Weather Service, warned, "conditions will be favorable for above-normal activity for the rest of this season."[6]

The hurricane season forecast maintained the value of Hunter's winter holdings and provided him with a valuable opportunity to start unwinding them. "They should have unloaded as fast as they could," says an energy trader. "That was their window."[7]

But Hunter didn't. He was too big.

Gas supplies were plentiful. Traders didn't buy into the warning from the National Weather Service. Experienced traders believed the fundamentals dictated lower prices. On August 2 the average price of winter 2007 contracts was $10.95. By August 16 it had fallen to $10.48.

Traders, especially John Arnold, sniffed blood.

"When that hurricane hype blew through, the spread started to collapse, and I think that's when the market kind of realized, 'We've got a big fish trapped in a small hole right now,'" says commodities trader Marc Chamberlin. "They knew Amaranth's positions were that big."[8]

From late April through mid-August, Amaranth held a total of more than 100,000 contracts, more than 40 percent of all contracts on NYMEX during this time. This was equal to almost one-fourth of all the gas used by residential customers in all of 2006.[9]

Hunter's winter contracts weren't the only investment that became the focus of other traders' attention. They were aware that for months Hunter had heavily bought the March-April spread at prices well over $2. That spread had topped $2.50 in July and hovered between $2.25 and $2.50 in the first half of August. If prices collapsed, coming back in line with supply and demand, Amaranth would be in trouble.

The sharks were starting to circle their prey.

"When Hunter moved into that March-April spread, the trend

was in his favor," notes an energy trader. The price had been climb-
ing. It rose even higher as he bought huge amounts of the spread.
But he "started pushing it so far, to the point where he maybe realized like, 'Hey, I may have taken a few people out.' He was feeling
pretty good about himself. But, I think, he had pushed it so far north
of $2 that the likes of a John Arnold and others who had been in the
market for a long time . . . knew he was basically paying too much."[10]

As August wore on, Hunter's problems began to intensify.

Amaranth's margin requirements were rising. On August 10,
Amaranth handed over $1.3 billion to J. P. Morgan Futures Inc., its
clearing broker. Six days later, its margin requirement rose to an
alarming $2 billion. "I don't understand this huge increase in margin
at JPMU [J. P. Morgan Futures]," Hunter wrote to an Amaranth
operations staffer that August day. "Last Thursday it was 1.3 and
today is almost 2 billion."[11]

The increased margins were in part a function of prices turning
against him. But his decision to shift holdings between NYMEX
and ICE affected his margin requirements too. Hunter thought
he was reducing his overall risk by the moves. But regardless of
whether that was the case, some of these moves forced him to pay
more collateral. Margins are based on the holdings on a particular
exchange. So even when Hunter took offsetting positions on another exchange, they weren't counted as such for margin purposes.[12]

Hunter was also moving holdings around to avoid scrutiny from
NYMEX. Virtually every month in 2006 he had exceeded NYMEX
accountability levels, triggering a review. As previously noted, generally NYMEX officials responded by just raising accountability
levels for Amaranth. Exchanges make money from trading, so they
are not eager to curb it. But while accountability levels were one
thing, violating the strict limits on trading in the last three days of a
contract was another. When Hunter violated those position limits,
NYMEX came down harder. In March it sent Amaranth a warning
letter about the size of its activity in the next-to-last trading day for
the February contract. At the end of May, NYMEX told Amaranth
to limit its trading for the final days of the June contract. When

Amaranth did not heed its instructions, NYMEX sent it another warning for violating position limits for the June contracts. A third strike could mean fines or prohibitions on trading.

At the beginning of August, NYMEX officials had a number of questions for Amaranth's traders. They sent the firm a letter on August 2 demanding to know why Amaranth had heavily traded the expiring May contract in the last four minutes of its settlement day.[13] And they wanted to know why Amaranth now held as much as 51 percent of the expiring September futures contract. On August 8, a NYMEX official spoke to Amaranth's compliance officer. He said the exchange could accept a trader holding one-third of a month's contracts, but not half. The exchange wanted Amaranth to reduce its positions.

The following day NYMEX staff had two conference calls with Amaranth executives to relay their concerns. They stressed that Amaranth had to lighten up its September holdings, but not by shifting them into October positions. Those were also too large.

On August 10, NYMEX officials called Amaranth again, emphasizing their concern that the fund's October holdings were too large and needed to be reduced immediately.

Hunter responded by cutting back his positions on the regulated NYMEX exchange. But he just moved them to ICE, where there were no trading limits. Hunter downsized on NYMEX and increased holdings on ICE to comply with NYMEX limits. He acknowledged this when, for example, he thanked a trader for shifting a trade from NYMEX to ICE. "We have exchange limits," he explained to him. "On NYMEX not on ICE. They settle the same. But NYMEX sends out warning letter. Which is bad for fund."[14]

J. P. Morgan Futures, Amaranth's clearing broker, which would be on the hook if anything went wrong with its exchange trades, was increasingly worried. It was jolted by an August 22 analysis warning that Amaranth could lose $2.9 billion in the event the market turned ugly. That was double what its potential loss had been calculated at in early July. Clearing broker officials scrambled to set up a senior-level meeting between the firms to discuss the situation.[15]

With prices turning against him, risk soaring, margins increasing, and the weather not cooperating, Hunter was facing a perfect storm. "Feels like a game of chicken right now," Shane Lee told Hunter in a late-night email on August 22. What about all Hunter's March-April spread trades? wondered Lee. Could they be sold now? "Do u think u can get off your March/April?"[16]

But it was beginning to be too late for that.

By the end of August many traders, not just John Arnold, believed the summer-winter spreads were way out of whack with fundamentals, and they had gotten wind of Amaranth's bind. Even companies that didn't generally engage in speculation as an end-game itself, such as utilities, who only traded to hedge their physical gas costs, now jumped into the fray.

"When someone's doing that much in one trade, one strategy, people start to talk about it," says a trader who watched events unfold that summer. "Amaranth was doing a lot of over-the-counter trading with counterparties. And the brokers talk. People started to get wind of it and said, 'My God, the spread is moving.' They asked, 'Why is it moving that fast?' It's a relatively small market. And people started sensing Amaranth was the bully on the street and they had never gotten out. And when they pushed it so far, people said, 'We've got to put that trade on.' The market collectively said, 'It's not priced properly.' And that's what started the cascade. Even the likes of utilities will put that trade on at that level because it's so obviously overdone."[17]

As August drew to a close, things looked bleak for Hunter. He held enormous holdings of summer and winter contracts. There was little sign of anything to justify spiking winter prices. All through the spring and into the summer, he had rolled his short holdings from one month into the next. But now he was running out of summer months. He would have to trade out of his positions soon. Hurricane season was almost over and gas supplies were plentiful; the summer-winter spreads were poised for a collapse. What could he do to unwind his holdings?

He had a limited number of moves available. His bet that winter prices would be higher than summer ones were concentrated in a few investment strategies. By the third week in August, he held enormous positions of the March-April spreads, particularly for 2007, but also for several years into the future. He held tens of thousands of January 2007 contracts. His November-January spread had been shifted into October-January spreads. His summer holdings had all been rolled into September contracts. He was betting heavily that September and October contracts would drop in price.

By August 21 there was only a week left of trading on the September contract. By that point Hunter had shorted more than 150,000 September and October 2007 contracts combined and faced enormous losses if prices moved against him. Even a move of just 10 cents on 150,000 contracts could lose Hunter $150 million.

As the final period for trading the September contract approached, Hunter decided to let many of his contracts expire on their last trading day. But how could he do that profitably?

Hunter ran a chancy play. On virtually every day that week, he added to his bet that the September price would drop, nearly doubling his overall position. On August 28 alone, he was responsible for one-fourth of the September contracts shorted that day. As Hunter engaged in massive trading that week, the price of the September contract moved in his favor, dropping from nearly $8 to $7.[18]

At the same time as he was shorting more September contracts, Hunter decided to try another tack. He bet that the difference in price between October and September contracts would widen. Although he was short massive amounts of contracts in both months, he positioned himself to benefit if September prices fell faster than October's, and the price difference between them increased.

Typically September and October prices were only 7 or 8 cents apart. Earlier that summer the spread had bounced around more than in prior years. But by the last trading week of August it was back to its more normal range. Then on August 28, when Hunter shorted tens of thousands of September contracts, the September-October spread price widened to 34 cents, also to his benefit.[19]

That day, in a glass office tower in Houston, John Arnold and his

204 | BARBARA T. DREYFUSS

gas traders at Centaurus puzzled over this sudden spike in the September-October spread. These prices didn't make sense. They believed that the difference between September and October contracts would narrow, and that September contract prices were out of line with physical gas prices and were likely to rise.

The next day, August 29, was the last trading day for the September contract. John Arnold was ready to trade on his view that the September-October price spread would fall and September contract prices would increase. It was the opposite of what Brian Hunter hoped to see that day. The battle lines between the two leading natural gas traders were set.

Watching from the sidelines that morning, officials at NYMEX pondered Hunter's plans for the day. They worried that he held large numbers of expiring contracts and that his trading that day might affect prices. They remembered previous months when he had traded heavily during the close.

At about 11:00 a.m. NYMEX personnel called Amaranth's compliance officer, Michael Carrieri. They told Carrieri they expected the firm to trade "in an orderly manner" throughout the day, especially in the last half hour. In fact, they said, they didn't want Amaranth to do any large volume of trading in the last thirty minutes.[20] With such a strong directive from NYMEX, Hunter intended to do the bulk of his trading before then.

Hunter and his team were down in Greenwich that day, Amaranth executives watching them closely. Rob Jones came out from his glass-walled office to sit directly behind Hunter on the trading floor, monitoring his trades. Other people in the office walked by and remarked how unusual it was for Jones to be out there on the trading floor. Something must be going on.

As trading began, the September-October spread was 36 cents. Within fifteen minutes it started to move. Before noon the difference in price between these two months had risen to 50 cents—good news for Hunter. Amaranth was heavily selling September contracts, hoping the price would fall. A large part of what Amaranth sold was being purchased by Centaurus. And as the day's trading wore on, with Amaranth and Centaurus trading against each other, Hunter seemed to get the upper hand, with the September contract dipping down a dime or more from where it had opened.

At about 1:15 p.m., with an hour and fifteen minutes left to the trading day and forty-five minutes before the settlement period, Amaranth traders stopped trading on NYMEX and, shortly after, on ICE. On ICE, where most of their trading had taken place, they had accounted for fully 45 percent of the volume of trading on September contracts so far that day. And they were satisfied with the level of September and October gas contract prices, as the spread was still around 40 cents.[21]

But John Arnold didn't have to stop. And now he made his move.

"Picture an epic tank battle in World War II," says a trader. "Suddenly the German tanks stop shooting . . . that's when you go and crush them."

At about 1:40 p.m., the price of September gas contracts started to rise. And it kept going. In the last forty-five minutes of trading that day, Centaurus bought 13,000 September gas contracts. For a time Centaurus was buying as much as all other traders combined, on both ICE and NYMEX.

In Greenwich, Hunter, with Jones behind him, stared grimly at his computer screen as he watched the price of September contracts jump 60 cents during the last hour of trading. The price difference between the September and October contracts, which Hunter hoped would widen, shriveled.

Hunter was furious. Right after the close of trading, he shot off an instant message to another trader complaining that someone had been manipulating prices in the last half hour.

"Classic pump and dump," he messaged. "Boy I bet you see some CFTC inquiries for the last two days. That was manipulated."[22] Hunter didn't know for sure at the time who was behind the huge buying spree. But he strongly suspected Arnold.

In less than an hour, Amaranth lost nearly $600 million.[23] It was a disaster.

Few people at Amaranth were immediately aware of what had transpired during those minutes leading up to the close on August 29, when Hunter stopped trading but John Arnold didn't. Even some of the other energy traders at Amaranth were too busy at the time overseeing their own investments to know what had hit Hunter's natural gas portfolio.

But they soon found out. And so did back-office staff as they completed their daily calculation of profit and loss. Word started to spread that $600 million was gone.

Initially, people in the firm hoped that it would be like other days when investments had soured, and they would recoup their losses quickly. True, the volatility in the firm's profits and losses over the past six months was scary, and the August losses were of concern. But the firm had managed to get through even worse in May—although that had occurred over several days, not over minutes.

This time, though, it was different.

Amaranth hadn't reduced its risks after the May debacle, hadn't sold off any large portion of its energy holdings. Hunter's trading had largely propped up prices. And now many other traders knew it. There were few takers for Hunter's positions at prices that would make him money. Many believed winter prices were way overblown. They were surprised that Maounis had allowed Hunter to keep such huge positions for so long. Now, once the news of his August losses made it into the marketplace, traders would know Hunter was trapped. There would be no way now for Hunter to continue pulling off the huge trades that had kept him afloat.

Hunter's margin requirements would soar. He would have to unwind his holdings.

Over the next hours and days, more employees heard the news. From then on, those who had access to the profit-and-loss statements on the computer checked them daily. Those who didn't prevailed on those with access to share the news. At times, Hunter would make back a little of his losses, and hopes would rise a bit.

Some portfolio managers and traders were panicked, convinced the company would never be able to come out of the crisis. Others were angry. A few just hoped that Maounis would treat them right on the way out.

Maounis and Jones were furious at Hunter. They held tense closed-door meetings with their star trader. Shouting, they issued their demands: Hunter and his team could not go back to Calgary but had to stay in Greenwich and make things right. They needed to figure out what was happening in the market and unwind as much of the natural gas holdings as quickly and favorably as they could.

Hunter and his team parked themselves in a hotel twenty minutes away and worked late nights, thrashing over the trades they had done, the trades they still needed to do, and the state of the market.

Rumors flew through the firm that someone at Amaranth or its clearing broker had leaked details of Hunter's holdings. How else could someone have traded so precisely against him during the August 29 close? At Amaranth, the hunt for the villain was on.

Jones complained to John Hogan, head of credit at J. P. Morgan Futures Inc., that someone there might have leaked information to outsiders concerning the fund's natural gas positions.[24] Hogan called a compliance officer at his firm and asked for an investigation into the possibility that someone had breached client confidentiality. And on August 30 Amaranth sent a letter to NYMEX claiming it was the victim of market manipulation and demanding an inquiry. Amaranth had abided by NYMEX's request not to execute large orders in the last half hour of trading, executives wrote, but "it is apparent to us that certain market participants are not trading in a responsible manner." It asked NYMEX to "immediately initiate an investigation into the trades and traders that caused yesterday's artificial price spike." The manipulated price, it argued, harmed "all natural gas market participants, including consumers whose cost of natural gas most certainly will be tied to yesterday's inflated settlement price."[25] Eventually NYMEX and others would look into trading during the close that day. But they took no action. Even if they had, the price moves on August 29 were already disastrous for Amaranth.

Because of Hunter's large profits earlier in the month, Amaranth still finished August with a net gain overall of just over $600 million.

But the huge loss of August 29 had a dramatic impact. Because of it, and the volatility in gas prices, the firm's margin requirement soared. On August 30 it was nearly $1 billion. The following day, August 31, the margin requirement climbed to more than $2.5 billion.[26]

On September 1, more bad news hit Hunter. Hurricane experts at Colorado State University revised downward earlier forecasts of significant upcoming storm activity. Only five hurricanes would form in the Atlantic this season, predicted the storm-forecasting team at the school, instead of the seven previously expected.

It got even worse. Meteorologists were forecasting a mild winter, not the severe one Hunter was counting on.

The forecasts confirmed the belief of many traders that the difference in price between the March and April contracts was overblown, and the March-April spread continued collapsing. Between August 25 and September 1, it dropped 44 cents, to $2.05.[27]

It had been as high as $2.50 on July 31, when Hunter's buying spree put MotherRock out of business. Hunter's huge purchases that day, at such a high price, were a tipping point for him in September. "That very position that he added was most problematic to get out of and cost him really everything in the end," says a fellow energy trader.[28]

The hammering to its energy positions was disastrous for Amaranth, overshadowing whatever gains and losses occurred in other parts of the firm. There was some cash available, and at first Amaranth was able to raise more from its prime brokers, using the firm's assets as collateral. But as the troubles mounted, that changed.

It quickly became apparent that John Arnold was not the only one trading against Amaranth. It seemed that every energy trader was aware of what was going on, and kept beating down winter prices.

"Too many people in the market knew we were in trouble," says a former Amaranth employee.[29] Shane Lee later said traders at other firms were telling him precisely how much the fund's daily losses or gains were.[30]

Traders had Hunter in what they dubbed a "spiral of death."

Over the next several days, the value of all Amaranth's key natural gas holdings plunged further. Hunter could no longer prop them up.

"Amaranth was dealing with an extremely big problem with their cash," Shane Lee later explained. "And it was a decision whether to get rid of part of the position and see if the company could remain solvent or get rid of all of the positions so that there was no question that the company was solvent."[31]

Amaranth needed to reduce its risk quickly. Selling when prices of its holdings were already depressed would only exacerbate losses. So the company scrambled to try to acquire some countervailing holdings.

Ironically, it turned to Bo Collins' portfolio of holdings that were short the March-April spread. When Collins folded in August, his clearing broker, ABN Amro, which had guaranteed his holdings, gained possession of them. Now Amaranth executives hoped these short positions could offset some of their firm's holdings. They were surprised at how small Collins' investments were, compared with theirs. Nonetheless, they bought them from ABN Amro on September 5. But the positions did little to stem Amaranth's slide.

Hunter and his associates began to face the possibility that catastrophe loomed.

"We've all got friends here," Hunter said at one point to Donohoe. "We need to do our best to get out of this mess."[32]

He turned to Lee for advice, messaging him on September 7, "How do you really feel about this? Is winter . . . going to get obliterated?"

Lee responded that it was wrong for winter prices to collapse but that they would unless there was some big event that changed traders' views. "Zero fundamental reason for winter to get smashed," he messaged Hunter. "Dude it[']s stupid. They sell it with impunity until a catalyst makes them pay the piper. No catalyst in Sept. without a hurricane."

And without a storm, Shane Lee warned, the result could be cataclysmic for Amaranth. "The question is not what we think, Brian. The question is whether we can weather this as a company."

Ten minutes later, he sent Hunter a more detailed view of their choices. None of them were attractive. They could get out of their holdings, losing $300 million to $1 billion. Or they could spend more to prop up prices. Or they could let the market take its course.

"There is no catalyst now," he told Hunter. "That's the problem. You exit this size without one . . . and we got a big problem."[33]

By the next day, September 8, the March-April spread had dropped to $1.90.[34] Amaranth's margin call exceeded $3.25 billion. The firm scrambled to meet the demand. It liquidated bonds, stocks, and other holdings, managing to meet the requirements. But Amaranth was fighting for its survival.

As September wore on, its situation grew increasingly dire. Despite Maounis' constant promises to reduce Amaranth's natural gas holdings, Hunter's investments were larger on the fifteenth of September than they were on the thirty-first of March.[35]

On Thursday, September 14, the March-April spread dropped to $1.55. On that day alone, Amaranth lost $560 million.

It wasn't just the "widow maker" spread that was collapsing; they all were. The price of the 2007 summer-winter spread (the difference between the average of all the winter months and the average of the summer contracts) was sinking. It was $1.99 on August 31. By September 14 it had fallen to $1.16.[36]

Prices of Amaranth's holdings were in free fall.

John Arnold believed they would fall further.

Around that time a report from a well-regarded energy consulting firm, PIRA Energy Group, was released, predicting low winter prices for natural gas. Although he didn't think too highly of the firm that put the report out, Arnold knew that other investors took it seriously and would be guided by PIRA's analysis. He also knew storage levels of gas were the highest they had ever been. And there was now little threat of near-term weather disruptions.

He was already getting calls directly from other traders who were desperate to sell their winter holdings. That would only increase. He expected a further drop in winter prices. It would mean the March-April spread would tank too.[37] And if that happened, given Arnold's heavy betting that it would, he stood to win big.

Amaranth was starting to capsize. The firm's cash was draining away as it struggled to meet margin calls. It continued to sell stocks, bonds, loans—whatever holdings were easily converted into ready money. But as news of Amaranth's financial situation spilled out, its prime brokers started closing the spigot. Some even refused to give Amaranth the cash they were holding for it.

Amaranth's executives began to fear they couldn't meet their margin calls. If that happened, J. P. Morgan Futures, its clearing broker, could halt Amaranth's trading altogether and seize the margin funds. That would trigger a cascade of other defaults and seizures.

The scene in Amaranth's office was growing chaotic. Representatives of prime brokers were showing up, insisting on meetings with Maounis and other executives to discuss Amaranth's financial situation. Others were calling. Investors were on the phone, demanding their money back.

Thursday night, September 14, a handful of men drove down Taconic Road in Greenwich, Connecticut, and turned onto Andrews Farm Road. Passing next to the guardhouse and through the security gate, they arrived at Nick Maounis' house. The members of Amaranth's executive committee were meeting to figure out how to save the firm.

Inside Maounis' Georgian-style mansion, they debated their choices, which were limited. Amaranth was hemorrhaging cash. The value of its gas positions was going through the floor. If prices continued to collapse, they might not be able to find any more cash to meet margin calls. They decided Amaranth had to jettison its natural gas holdings immediately.[38] The rest of the firm, they hoped, could still be kept afloat.

It was near midday on a rainy and gloomy Friday, September 15, when Nick Maounis picked up the phone for a call he had never expected he would make. It was just a year since Hunter had electrified Wall Street with his trading success.

212 | BARBARA T. DREYFUSS

With that call, Maounis unleashed a tempest. For the remainder of what would become a sleepless, chaotic weekend, Amaranth officials engaged in a desperate, last-ditch attempt to save the firm. They figured they had until Monday morning, when the markets reopened and traders would continue their devastating attack on Amaranth's energy holdings.

13

$6 BILLION SQUEEZE

Three and a half days to salvage what had been a $9.6 billion firm.[1]

Maounis dialed a friend, Howard Wietschner, a managing director at Goldman Sachs, whom he had known for more than eleven years. Maounis began by saying he wanted to discuss market speculation and rumors about Amaranth's crisis. There were problems, he admitted. But, he told Wietschner, Amaranth's problems were an opportunity for Goldman. It could now buy the firm's energy book.[2]

Wietschner wasn't surprised to hear from Maounis. He handled Goldman's relationships with hedge funds such as Amaranth, providing them whatever services they needed, and he kept in close contact with his clients. Word had already reached him about Amaranth's substantial natural gas losses, and he knew its executives were under tremendous stress as they struggled to save the company.[3]

Over the next few hours, Wietschner and other Goldman executives debated with Maounis and Rob Jones the pros and cons of taking over some of Amaranth's energy holdings. The problem, Amaranth executives contended, was not that Amaranth had bet wrong in energy markets, but that other traders had attacked their firm, artificially depressing the value of their holdings. Amaranth had a liquidity crisis as a result and just needed cash.[4]

Maounis maneuvered, looking for the most appealing pitch to Goldman. Goldman could make some quick money by taking over Amaranth's energy holdings, he told its executives. The assumptions behind the energy holdings were still valid, he argued. They reflected a correct analysis of fundamentals. If Goldman, with its large amounts of cash and holdings, took Amaranth's positions, it could wait out the storm, and profit.[5]

After back-and-forth discussions between Amaranth and Goldman personnel during the day, Rob Jones emailed Wietschner around 5:30 p.m. He listed the trades Amaranth wanted to transfer to Goldman. Details on who would work out the nitty-gritty would come later, he added.

Amaranth's investment losses had now risen to more than $2 billion since the last week in August.[6]

At Amaranth, anger at Hunter grew. Portfolio managers and traders had a lot of their bonus money invested in the firm, and it was Hunter who was responsible. The firm was teetering. Tension filled the corridors. Senior executives talked about hiring security for Hunter. They worried that other employees would go after him.[7]

By September 15, the March-April spread was down an additional 40 cents, to $1.15. The 2007 winter-summer spread closed at 73 cents, down from $1.16 the day before.

But that wasn't the worst of it. The days of crushing margin calls had largely wiped out Amaranth's ready cash. It could cover its current margin call, but that was it. It would have to replenish its margin account if prices continued their downward spiral the following week. It needed to jettison the energy portfolio that weekend.

Despite his vigorous pitch to Goldman, Maounis wasn't pinning his hopes solely on that investment bank. He decided he had to play the field.

Usually a firm in trouble tries to sell its positions quietly, to avoid other traders taking advantage of its plight. But word of its problems spread as desperate executives at Amaranth shopped its portfolio to a number of other banks and traders.

Over the weekend, Amaranth executives met or spoke with officials of J. P. Morgan, Goldman Sachs, and Merrill Lynch as the firm frantically tried to off-load its energy holdings.

Company executives, back-office employees, traders settled in for a long, brutal weekend. Food was ordered in. Energy traders from Amaranth struggled to determine a fair value for their holdings.

Some of the Amaranth support staff went home to shower and rest for a couple of hours before coming back to pull all-nighters. And the game room, where employees had gathered for birthday parties and Ping-Pong tournaments, had couches where people could rest. Maounis, Jones, and Winkler had couches in their offices if they needed to take a break. Mostly they stayed up, straining far into the night to put together a deal.[8]

Hunter strongly suspected Arnold had been behind the trading spike on August 29 that had started his collapse, and he believed Arnold was still trading heavily against him. The buzz was that Arnold had made a bundle.

Nonetheless, Hunter needed Arnold. On Friday, September 15, he tried to contact Arnold to offer to sell him his March-April spread holdings.

Arnold, who was out of the office, didn't reply.[9]

That same day, NYMEX officials visited JPMorgan Chase's offices to discuss Amaranth. Hogan of J. P. Morgan Futures, the clearing broker, called to check in on Amaranth and learned it had lost more again that day.

Around 7:30 p.m. on Friday, Wietschner, Goldman's point man for its negotiations with Amaranth, and other executives brought into the talks Elisha Wiesel, who headed Goldman's commodity strategies. Wiesel agreed to evaluate Amaranth's energy book so that Goldman could decide whether to bid on it and what its offer would be if it decided to make one.

About eleven o'clock that night, Wiesel emailed a senior Goldman executive. Taking on Amaranth's holdings would be a huge move for Goldman, dwarfing the combined risk of all the other energy positions Goldman held at the time.[10]

The next morning, Hogan emailed colleagues, including the heads of JPMorgan Chase's investment bank, to give them an update on Amaranth.[11] "They are sucking wind big time and have lost over 22% (roughly $2 bio [billion]) in the last two weeks on the unwinding of their nat gas spread trade," he reported. Although Amaranth was still up for the year and had $1 billion in cash on its balance sheet, he said, Amaranth executives were nervous and were trying to sell other holdings to raise an additional $1 billion in cash.

But Hogan wasn't optimistic.

"My view is it's potentially worse than they think," Hogan wrote. "If the markets should have a hiccup next week I think they could be in trouble as the $1 bio [billion] won't be enough to meet all their potential margin calls. I think we should call Maounis . . . and proactively help them sell assets to raise cash as quietly as possible. I do believe they are being more open to us than anyone else at this point and are worried others may find out and pull the plug."

One of the heads of the investment bank responded, "Let's absolutely keep a close eye on this but keep a level head."

Within an hour, Hogan reported a talk he had had with Winkler. There might be a way the investment bank could make money off Amaranth's troubles, Hogan said. "They are all hunkered down in their office in Greenwich. I asked if we could be of help as they worked through their issues. He asked if we would lend them money against their illiquid credit book." But Hogan told Amaranth he needed to see its entire portfolio before JPMorgan would consider lending it even a nickel.

Around 2:00 p.m. Saturday, Amaranth officials suggested that Hogan bring his colleagues to Greenwich to help them figure out how to raise cash. Hogan assembled a risk management team, including credit and legal people from J. P. Morgan Futures Inc. The members arranged to meet the next day, Sunday, in the lobby of the Amaranth building at 12:45 p.m. for a briefing and to map their own game plan before they went in to speak with the hedge fund executives.

Early Saturday evening Hunter swallowed his pride and sent another email to Arnold expanding on his offer of the previous day. He told Arnold that if he didn't want Amaranth's "widow maker" spreads, there were others he could buy.

Desperate to sell off his holdings, Hunter offered Arnold a string of alternative deals. "If H/J [March-April] doesn't fit as well," he pleaded in a message, "I can do V6-J7," referring to the

October 2006–April 2007 spread. He offered Arnold November-March trades and some others.

"Sorry for the hassle," he ended the email. "Cheers."[12]

There was still no answer from Arnold.

Amaranth's executives continued their discussions with Goldman Sachs throughout Saturday. Later in the day, Goldman officials told Amaranth they had reservations about the size and makeup of the portfolio. These were risky positions, they pointed out. They would take over the energy book they were reviewing, paying the dramatically lower prices of the past Friday—but only if they were paid a concession fee to do so. After all, prices might continue to plummet even further and Goldman would lose money on the holdings.

Their price: a breathtaking $1.7 billion.

Paying the blood money would mean further losses for Amaranth, but executives didn't think they had a choice. They had to unload the natural gas book. They couldn't wait to see whether it continued to crash, causing them even greater losses.[13]

But Amaranth did not have $1.7 billion in cash to give Goldman. It only had about $700 million in various accounts. The rest would have to come from selling other investment holdings and from the cash Amaranth had on deposit in its margin account at J. P. Morgan Futures for its natural gas holdings.[14]

Goldman wasn't the only player in this game. While Goldman put out its concession fee demand and Hunter tried to reach Arnold, Amaranth also began serious discussions with Merrill Lynch. The two firms discussed a significant purchase of three years' worth of Amaranth's March-April spread holdings.

Merrill made Amaranth a juicy offer. It would take one-quarter of Amaranth's gas positions if Amaranth paid it $300 million, a proportionately smaller fee than the Goldman offer. But it was a one-time bid that would no longer be valid after Saturday night.

Amaranth executives jumped at it; at eleven o'clock Saturday night Hunter and a Merrill Lynch representative worked out how they were going to finalize the trade once the markets opened on Monday.

"Obviously a pretty big one for Merrill, and I would like to keep out of the broker market as well," Merrill Lynch's Michael Hoss emailed Hunter, indicating he hoped to keep news of Amaranth's selling as quiet as possible. He feared that if brokers got wind of it, the market would be certain about Amaranth's desperate straits and would drive prices down further. Merrill's new holdings would be hurt too. "I agree that it is probably better to clear it through ICE," said Hunter.[15]

Goldman Sachs was unaware of what Amaranth was doing with Merrill until Sunday morning. Jones called Goldman's Wietschner, then followed up quickly with an email, surprising him with the news that Amaranth had just traded away some of the holdings it had offered Goldman. It was a much better deal for Amaranth, Jones explained, than what Goldman was offering. So the firm had a fiduciary responsibility to its investors to accept it.[16]

Amaranth executives believed the Goldman people would be pleased that Amaranth had reduced its energy book, since they had been complaining about its size and the risk it represented. With some of that risk traded away now, Amaranth expected Goldman to reduce the money it was demanding Amaranth hand over to sweeten the deal.

Not so. "I know that we did not say, 'Hey, Amaranth, you're right, thank God you sold some of it, let's bring the price in,'" Goldman's Wiesel later recalled. In fact, the Goldman team was furious to learn that Amaranth was negotiating simultaneously with other firms.

"They were behaving in such a manner as to suggest that they were broadcasting to the market what they were doing," said Wiesel, "which inherently made the position more risky."

Goldman feared that if word was out about Amaranth's fire sale, other traders would capitalize on it. In that case, Goldman would lose money if it tried to unload anything it bought from Amaranth.[17]

The frustrated Goldman team decided to evaluate some more, continue negotiations with Maounis, and ask Hunter to confirm that they were all negotiating over the same investments.

While Amaranth and Goldman continued to discuss the matter, Hunter got an email from Arnold about the trade offers. It was a little past nine on Sunday morning.

Arnold's response was devastating. He blasted Hunter for offering the trades around town, because now if Arnold were to buy them, other traders would know and likely go after his positions. "You have shopped this position to at least one other counterparty who will be a seller first thing Monday morning if I were to buy the book," he lectured his rival.

He stressed that industry fundamentals did not support the high prices embedded in Amaranth's trades. He cited the PIRA Energy report predicting very low winter prices, saying that investors listened to their advice. Arnold also told Hunter that the level of gas in storage would soon be at an all-time high.

Betting on the March-April spread widening had paid off only once in the previous ten years, he noted, yet traders had loaded up on it recently. Now, with prices in free fall, these traders "will probably try to be spitting out on Monday." Market psychology was clearly against Hunter's high-priced positions.

In fact, he chided Hunter, prices were still as high as they were only because of Amaranth's huge holdings.

"Even though that spread has collapsed over the past two weeks, the only reason it's still greater than $1 is because of your position," he wrote. "Historically, that spread would be well below $1 at this point given the scenario."

Then Arnold made his offer. He wanted stunning discounts. He offered only 45 cents to 60 cents for the March-April 2007 spread—less than half its Friday closing price of $1.15. And, he said, he would pay only $1 to $1.20 for later-year spreads, which on Friday had closed at double that price.

"Please advise whether you want me to prepare a firm bid with these types of numbers or if the prices are too low," he wrote.[18]

Ten minutes later, a humbled Hunter responded. "I understand where you are coming from. Let me think about the indications for a moment."[19]

Hunter and his colleagues knew Arnold was trying to cash in on their distress, but their situation was dire. Shane Lee estimated that if they took the offer, their losses on these positions would be in the range of $600 million to $800 million. Still, Hunter wanted the deal.[20]

But Amaranth's executives had already spent almost two days negotiating with Goldman Sachs for the major portion of the natural gas book, not bits and pieces. They wanted to jettison as much of the natural gas book at one time as they could.

All that Sunday, Amaranth continued its negotiations with Goldman. They discussed how to transfer the positions, the margin requirements, and agreements that Amaranth would not trade against Goldman on these energy positions.

Sunday afternoon, J. P. Morgan representatives, led by Hogan, showed up. They met with Amaranth's management team to discuss the increasing risk to the firm's investments and its cash on hand. DiRocco updated them on the losses the firm had incurred Friday and the fund's liquidity position. Jones told Hogan that they were negotiating with Goldman Sachs on the sale of the energy book.

Jim Greenberg, in charge of facilitating J. P. Morgan's business relationship with Amaranth, was also walking through Amaranth's offices Sunday. Greenberg was a longtime friend of Winkler's; Winkler had been at Greenberg's wedding five years before. But now the relationship between the two grew tense.[21] Greenberg, according to Winkler, said that J. P. Morgan was angry that Amaranth had approached its rival Goldman Sachs to take its energy book. Instead, he said, they should have offered it to J. P. Morgan.

At 7:00 p.m. Sunday, the J. P. Morgan risk team held a conference call with Jamie Dimon, JPMorgan Chase's chief executive officer, to discuss Amaranth's situation. The team debated several choices, including letting Goldman Sachs take Amaranth's energy book or bidding for it themselves. If Morgan wanted to make its own bid, it would need its own evaluation of exactly what holdings Amaranth had.[22]

Sunday wore on. The strain showed. Executives were exhausted, stressed. Jones seemed to be taking it the worst. He was gray and blotchy, run-down—a broken man.[23]

At 10:13 p.m. Amaranth board member Manos Vourkoutiotis, who was in the office, emailed Maounis, who was in another room, to join him.[24] They were about to get another bid from Goldman. Two minutes later, the call came in. Vourkoutiotis, along with Maounis and Jones, listened as Wietschner spelled out Goldman's new offer—which was for Amaranth to pay them even more tribute money to take on the energy investments.

Despite the fact that Amaranth had already sold off part of its holdings to Merrill Lynch, Goldman now wanted $1.85 billion— $150 million more than previously mentioned—to take the remaining energy holdings off Amaranth's hands.[25]

After receiving Goldman's offer, Maounis, Jones, and others huddled, weighing it, discussing its ramifications. They notified J. P. Morgan's Hogan that they had an offer from Goldman Sachs. Soon after, Hogan told DiRocco that J. P. Morgan was interested in analyzing Goldman Sachs' bid in order to determine if it wanted to make a similar offer.

J. P. Morgan sent its two top energy derivative traders, George "Beau" Taylor and Parker Drew, to Greenwich to evaluate Amaranth's energy investments. The two were moved from room to room. Finally they were settled in a small office near the main lobby. Just after midnight they received an Excel spreadsheet with the same trades that Goldman Sachs had bid on. They opened the spreadsheet, took out a paper with a listing of the previous Friday's closing prices of natural gas futures contracts, and started to calculate the value of the holdings and its risks.[26]

At the same time, the Goldman team was waiting for an answer from Amaranth on its $1.85 billion concession fee demand. Goldman's Elisha Wiesel, who had spent the day discussing Amaranth's gas positions with Hunter, emailed Howard Wietschner of Goldman, asking, "Any word back from Nick yet?"

Three minutes later Wietschner emailed back, "He's just calling me now. We are hit."

"That sounds great," Wietschner told Maounis. Soon after, he triumphantly emailed three Goldman executives that Amaranth "hit our bid."[27]

Amaranth had found a buyer for much of its natural gas holdings.

It would be expensive, and the company would be transformed into a different entity, but the Amaranth team could finally see a way out of the mess. There was a sense of relief that it would finally jettison its energy holdings. Perhaps there was still a chance to save the rest of the firm.

Soon after Maounis agreed to the deal, Wiesel emailed a list of thirty-nine trades to Hunter, asking if they accurately reflected the positions the two firms were discussing. An hour later, Hunter confirmed they did. Discussions on the details continued into the night.

But J. P. Morgan still wasn't out of the picture.

Ensconced in the small office, J. P. Morgan's Taylor and his colleague finished their analysis of Amaranth's energy holdings at about 2:00 a.m. The two traders concluded that an appropriate concession payment, given the risks inherent in the energy investments, was actually less than Amaranth was willing to pay, only $1.6 billion.[28] Word never got to Amaranth, however. There was no offer from J. P. Morgan.

As Sunday morphed into the early hours of Monday, few in Amaranth's Greenwich headquarters got much sleep. Hunter and Wiesel went through the mechanics of the trades, and other discussions took place between the risk management people at Goldman and Amaranth.

The market opening still loomed. Amaranth executives were eager to wrap up as much as possible so that the deal could get done quickly on Monday, before their energy holdings lost more value.

But Amaranth executives were wondering whether there might be an offer still coming from J. P. Morgan. At 7:40 a.m. on Monday, Jones emailed Winkler asking if he had heard anything yet from J. P. Morgan. He hadn't.[29]

Two hours later Amaranth treasurer DiRocco confirmed to J. P. Morgan's Hogan that Amaranth had negotiated a deal with

Goldman Sachs. Amaranth would pay Goldman Sachs $1.85 billion to take the trades off its hands.

A conference call was set up for 10:00 a.m. that Monday, September 18, with Goldman Sachs, Amaranth, J. P. Morgan Futures, and NYMEX officials. Maounis, Jones, Winkler, and others called in from Amaranth's Greenwich offices; Wietschner, Wiesel, and others represented Goldman Sachs. Thomas LaSala, NYMEX's chief regulatory officer, listened in, along with a number of J. P. Morgan executives, including John Hogan and lawyer Diane Genova.

Jones and others at Amaranth expected the call to be a mere formality. NYMEX officials asked about the trades being considered. The Goldman Sachs people went through their understanding of how the trade would be done, including settlement and some money issues.

Then it all went sideways.

"YOU'RE DONE"

A disagreement erupted between Amaranth and J. P. Morgan about releasing Amaranth's collateral. Goldman wanted its $1.85 billion concession fee before it would complete the deal to acquire most of Amaranth's energy holdings.[1] But Amaranth had little unencumbered cash on hand. To complete the deal with Goldman, it would need J. P. Morgan to release some of the $2.513 billion in its margin account—funds deposited to back up its energy trades.

J. P. Morgan refused.[2]

"This isn't what we talked about," protested J. P. Morgan's Genova, according to NYMEX's LaSala, referring to releasing the money before the deal was finalized. "This doesn't work."

The call ended. J. P. Morgan had nixed the deal.

Amaranth was facing annihilation. It urgently needed to find a buyer for the energy book. The market had just opened, and already Amaranth was losing heavily.

Word was out that Amaranth was in crisis. It was hard to miss: Amaranth had shopped around its holdings all weekend. Anyone who didn't already know the situation had figured it out by Monday.

Around forty-five minutes after trading began that morning on the NYMEX, Hogan received an email from one of his firm's risk managers, giving a blow-by-blow account of what was happening to Amaranth's holdings. "The market has opened strongly against Amaranth," it said. "The contracts where they are long are dropping in price and the contracts where they are short are going up. I'll have a P&L update in half an hour but so far they have lost close to 600 million in the '06 and '07 contracts alone."[3]

Meanwhile, Jones and other Amaranth executives were in a state of shock. What they thought had been worked out with Morgan about the deal with Goldman was now in limbo. Jones later called it a surreal moment.[4] Everyone had expected J. P. Morgan to say yes.

Soon after hanging up on the conference call, Amaranth's DiRocco was back on the phone with Genova and other J. P. Morgan people.

He exploded. "Why won't you clear these contracts?" he screamed, according to Genova. "Why won't you agree to the terms of our proposed Goldman deal?"

Genova shouted back. "Artie, we are ready, willing, and able to clear risk-reducing contracts in the normal course of business, which means we do not release margin up front. We release margin the day after the contracts clear, assuming that . . . there, in fact, *is* excess margin."

J. P. Morgan's investment bank co-CEO Steven Black got on the phone. The conversation dissolved into a screaming match.[5] Amaranth wanted the money released. J. P. Morgan was saying no.

The deal looked dead, and traders were gunning for Amaranth.

At the end of the day, the March-April spread closed at a devastating 75 cents. When Hunter had started to buy it heavily, it was at $1.50. His enormous purchases, particularly in June and July, helped drive it up as high as $2.50. His buying supported the high prices, but also meant that prices would need to go still higher for him to make a profit. Instead, they had collapsed.

After the conference call broke up Monday morning, Amaranth's executives were frenzied. Their energy holdings were losing value dramatically, the deal with Goldman appeared to be on the rocks, and J. P. Morgan had not made a bid.

The weekend had taken its toll on Maounis. He looked awful—haggard and worn. Usually a neat dresser, he now looked almost shabby. The jovial smile was gone, and he was tense and withdrawn.

That day, the San Diego County Pension Fund sent a letter demanding the withdrawal of its money from Amaranth.

Despite the disagreements at the morning meeting, Goldman Sachs executives continued their discussions with Amaranth over the next several hours. But as the morning wore on, it became apparent to many Goldman Sachs negotiators that they didn't have all the facts they needed to process the deal. They discovered that they did not have a list of the specific trades Amaranth wanted them to take over. They had been given a proxy portfolio, one that merely mirrored the risk of Amaranth's holdings.[6] At the same time, they learned the deal did not involve Amaranth's entire natural gas business. Amaranth would retain extensive holdings.

As they were processing the impact of all this, events took a surprising turn.

Seemingly out of nowhere, another firm appeared on the scene. That morning, as Winkler was preparing for the conference call on the Goldman deal, his assistant took a phone message from his former boss, Ken Griffin, the thirty-seven-year-old head of Citadel. Griffin, whose hedge fund was then managing about $12 billion, had a stunning offer. If Amaranth needed a liquidity line, Citadel would help out.

Griffin had close ties to Amaranth, as Winkler had been his chief operating officer before going to Amaranth. And Griffin knew Maounis from their days as convertible bond traders in the 1990s. He had attended Maounis' Final Four parties. Soon after getting Griffin's message, Winkler called him back. Griffin was direct.

"Charlie, what can we do and how can we help?" he asked.[7]

"It's real simple," replied Winkler. "We need to be able to trade this book, and we need a bridge loan and a couple hundred million to stay in business." Winkler assured Griffin they had the collateral to support the loan. Griffin was supportive.

As Amaranth scrambled between Goldman Sachs and Citadel, prime brokers who held the firm's cash and various investments were calling and coming to the office, seeking assurances they would get paid what they were owed. They were grabbing any cash Amaranth had on deposit with them. Amaranth struggled to get its money from brokers to pay creditors.

In fact, several creditors warned Amaranth that if the firm was still holding natural gas trades on Wednesday, they would not continue extending it credit. They would foreclose and liquidate Amaranth's holdings, which could mean investors would lose everything.[8]

Early that day, Maounis sent out a letter to investors telling them the firm had significant losses and was down in excess of 35 percent for the year. "In an effort to preserve investor capital," the letter said, "we have taken a number of steps, including aggressively reducing our natural gas exposure." He forwarded it to employees as well, and it soon hit the news.

"One of the nation's best-known hedge funds, Amaranth Advisors, said today it stands to lose more than 35 percent of its total value, after a drop in prices for natural gas," *Nightly Business Report*'s Paul Kangas told viewers that day. "Based on the $7.5 billion the company's website says it has under management, that means the loss could be more than $2 billion."

Media reports quickly focused on Hunter (although initial stories referred to him as "Bill" Hunter). CNBC's David Faber said that Hunter might have been behind the losing natural gas trades, while the Associated Press referred to Hunter's appearance in the *Trader Monthly* rankings in 2005, when he was named one of the market's top energy traders.

Throughout the Greenwich headquarters of Amaranth, there was a sense of shock. A hedge fund with total assets of $9.7 billion at its peak just didn't collapse in two weeks, people thought. It was difficult to get much work done, as news reports delved into their normally secretive business. On the trading floor, traders stood to watch the TVs high up on the walls as breathless reporters and commentators broke the news about Amaranth's losses, zeroing in on its huge natural gas investments: *While Amaranth hasn't said it's closing down, its losses far outweigh those of MotherRock . . . That is ridiculous . . . put all his eggs in one basket . . . That is not risk management, that is a coin flip . . . Amaranth has blown up.*

228 | BARBARA T. DREYFUSS

Traders glanced at Hunter as he scrutinized the coverage.

Hunter seemed amused, laughing out loud at the errors report-ers were making. Colleagues standing nearby looked at him in dis-belief and anger.

All day Monday, even as Goldman executives debated the Ama-ranth deal and the news swept through the business press, Hunter and his traders proceeded with the dismantling of their investments, providing reports to Citadel, Goldman, and J. P. Morgan about Am-aranth's immense gas book.

Hunter remained as cool and calm as ever, snickering at inside jokes with his team. Someone picked up a football a broker had given them as a marketing tool months before and they tossed it around the trading floor. He and his team seemed immune to the drama swirling around them.

Their demeanor exasperated others. "They just acted like kids right out of college," recalls an employee who watched them on the trading floor.[9] A trader of a different portfolio sitting nearby finally snapped at them to stop it.

Citadel and Amaranth agreed to a deal, one similar to the agree-ment Goldman Sachs had negotiated with Amaranth. There was a concession payment of $1.85 billion. But there were also two major differences. Instead of the trade being done at Friday's closing prices, Amaranth would absorb two-thirds of the $600 million in trading losses it suffered that Monday.[10] And Citadel was willing to give Am-aranth a bridge loan, tiding it over until the deal was complete and its collateral was freed up. Amaranth's executives believed Citadel— a large and lucrative client of J. P. Morgan and not a competitor like Goldman Sachs—would have an easier time finalizing the deal through J. P. Morgan.

Amaranth was banking that the new arrangement with Citadel would do two things. First, it would eliminate the risk of the natural gas book. Second, it would leave Amaranth with enough capital to allow it to continue operating as a firm.

Late Monday afternoon it appeared that a deal had been final-ized. Maounis called Griffin and asked if they were done.

"You're done," Griffin said.

Now it was time for Amaranth to break the news to Goldman that a deal between the two was off. Around 4:00 p.m., Monday, Maounis called Wietschner. Maounis thanked him for all the effort Goldman Sachs had put into the negotiations. Then he apologized and said Amaranth wasn't making a deal with it after all. It would be going elsewhere.

Finally, the new arrangments seemingly in place, Maounis left the office—after more than three grinding days.

But sometime after 6:30 p.m. Winkler said he received a distressing call.

"Charlie, it's Ken," Griffin said. "You need to call Steve Black or Bill Winters at J. P. Morgan. They tell me that you're not as solvent as you say you are."[11]

"Who are *they*?" demanded Winkler.

"They're Jamie Dimon's lieutenants," Griffin answered, referring to JPMorgan Chase's CEO.

"I'll call them," an angry Winkler said.

Meanwhile, Citadel staff worked through the night on the deal. A meeting was scheduled for the next morning. Amaranth executives were still confident they had an agreement.

Tuesday morning, September 19, Amaranth executives met at the office for a conference call with Citadel. To their surprise, it was not Citadel's Ken Griffin but Dimon who led the call. There was suddenly a new deal on the table. Citadel and J. P. Morgan had teamed up. Amaranth would do the sale with J. P. Morgan, and J. P. Morgan would sell Citadel half the trades.

The previous night Citadel executives had been worried about Amaranth ending up in bankruptcy, even with Citadel's purchase of the energy book. A bankruptcy judge might allow J. P. Morgan, which had lent Amaranth money for its energy deals, to take back Amaranth's assets from firms that had bought them as it was failing. Executives from J. P. Morgan contacted Citadel in the early morning hours and offered to waive their right to such assets, provided Citadel agreed to let J. P. Morgan in on half of Amaranth's energy trades.[12] But now Amaranth had to pay an even larger concession fee: $2.5 billion.[13]

The losses to Amaranth were enormous. The firm had shed more than half its value since the beginning of the year. For the month, its assets were down 65 percent.[14]

Fury swept through Amaranth—fury at company executives and at Hunter. *How could this have happened? How could they have been so ignorant of the risks that Hunter was taking?*

Executives were worried about violence directed at Hunter and his team. An analyst who sat near him on the trading floor wanted extra security. Tension filled the air. So, senior management moved a building security guard upstairs. A gun at his side, he sat quietly in the trading room near the energy traders.

At one point, someone slammed down a stack of papers, making a loud banging sound. The security guard leaped to his feet, eyeing the room. Then, nervously, he took his seat again.

Maounis said little and stayed holed up in his office, trying to deal with investors and creditors and attempting to keep afloat what remained of the firm. Jones, a quiet man at the best of times, was barely able to talk.

"I'm sorry," other employees recall him saying. "I'm sorry."

The energy team and the back-office staff worked late into the night to put together the new deal with J. P. Morgan. Investors besieged the firm with calls and demanded meetings with Maounis, Winkler, and Jones. In the ensuing days, many came to the office, trying to understand what had happened and how bad things were. More demanded the return of their money.

On Tuesday night, Winkler, Amaranth general counsel Karl Wachter, chief financial officer Jim Glynn, and human resources director Stanley Friedman were conferring in an office when an email came across the computer screen. It was a four-sentence note sent out by Maounis to employees. "I want to thank all of you for your years of loyalty and support, especially during this especially difficult time for all of us," it started. "I am quite sure that the Amaranth spirit will live on in all of us as nothing can ever take that away from us." They were horrified by the tone, concerned about how people would interpret Maounis' distraught words. Within an hour, they had drafted their own message, which Friedman sent out, saying that Maounis' email "was not intended to say goodbye" or suggest that the firm was closing.[15]

In an email to investors late Wednesday night, after the sale of the energy book was arranged, Maounis laid out the firm's grim plight. He said that during the week of September 11 the company had experienced "significant" losses in its natural gas derivatives portfolio and had faced "significant" margin calls. To prevent further losses and to reduce the risk of defaulting on the margin calls, Amaranth had transferred its energy position "to a third party at a price that resulted in additional significant losses," Maounis said. What's more, it had sold off positions in the fund's other portfolios. He also reminded investors that it was too late to request money back for the October 31 quarterly redemption date. The deadline had been two days before, September 18.

By then, the price of Hunter's key holdings had collapsed completely. The 2007 summer-winter spread was down 75 percent from three weeks earlier. The March-April 2007 spread had sunk by two-thirds.

Soon after clinching the deal with J. P. Morgan, Maounis gathered about three hundred employees in the glass-walled trading room. Crowding in, staffers perched on the desks, in front of the rows of computer monitors. They pushed aside headphones and oversized keyboards and dangled their legs over the individualized air-conditioning units under each desk that had once cooled overheated traders. There wasn't much use for them now.

Speaking softly in the packed room, Maounis acknowledged the obvious: the firm had incurred devastating losses. The energy book had been sold, he said, trying to sound hopeful. He was pursuing various options, he told them, trying to keep the firm afloat.

Then Maounis choked up. He didn't know exactly what the new firm would look like, he said, but his goal was to keep going. He appreciated all the work they'd done.

There were no questions from the staff.

People felt "a lot of desire to be there, be supportive, to work with Nick and to make it happen," says one employee who attended the meeting. "No one shouted out, 'How did you let this happen?'" But the speech stirred plenty of confusion among employees. Should they keep working? Should they liquidate positions? Should they continue to trade? Traders and portfolio managers asked whether special agreements with Maounis—such as signing bonuses—would be honored.

Maounis was looking for a white knight to step in and buy the company. That week he started serious discussions with Citigroup Alternative Investments, which wanted to build its internal hedge fund operations. It was considering taking over large chunks of the fund's infrastructure, including its technology and accounting operations, as well as some of its trading teams.

But Citigroup had a key demand for any such deal, says an executive with knowledge of the negotiations: Maounis couldn't be part of it.

By that point, Maounis was meeting virtually nonstop with lawyers, including prominent attorney David Boies, who had represented Al Gore in the disputed presidential election challenge in Florida in 2000. On Friday of that week, September 22, Maounis held a conference call with investors. But it was a listen-only call. Enraged investors weren't allowed to ask questions. It lasted just fifteen minutes.

In carefully scripted remarks, Maounis began by telling his investors that while Amaranth employees had lost a lot of their own money that month, they had lost even more for investors. "We feel bad about losing our own money. We feel much worse about losing your money."

His message: it wasn't Amaranth's fault. He blamed "highly unusual market behavior" that not only had reduced the value of Amaranth's holdings, but also had made it impossible financially for them to get out of their positions. The company's risk models had discounted losses "associated with such scenarios." His traders had assured him they could get out of their holdings quickly, if necessary, and without too much loss. "But sometimes even the highly improb-

.able happens. That is what happened in September." Then Maounis announced that he was eliminating energy trading entirely from his strategy mix. He told investors he still hoped to stay in business.

Talks lasted several days with Citigroup. The head of its hedge fund business wanted to do a deal. But ultimately Citigroup's board was not having any part of Amaranth.

It was now clear: the firm was going down.

If Maounis had come out, even then, and said that he was going to rebuild, employees would still have been behind him, laments a former employee. "I'm sure that he would have had about 90 percent of the people he talked to say, 'Nick, I'm here.'"[16]

But that didn't happen. Maounis' relations with his staff, always distant but friendly, now changed dramatically. Ensconced in his office, he rarely spoke to employees anymore, and refused to hold another staff meeting to explain the firm's situation.

Maounis was out of touch, and people resented it. Later, as some people left, he went to talk to them about sticking around and trying to start a new firm. They rebuffed him.

"He didn't talk to me for the last month and a half—now he's talking to me?" one trader approached by Maounis told another employee. "I don't want to talk to him."[17]

The energy team dwindled as its portfolio shrank. The natural gas holdings were gone, and the team began selling off electricity, base metals, oil, and other holdings.

By September 27, Brian Hunter was gone from Amaranth—fired. But Maounis wouldn't do it. That job was left to Winkler.

If Hunter ever apologized for the losses or expressed remorse, it's not something his colleagues readily remember. But one night as he was leaving the office during the firm's final hectic days, Hunter passed by some of Amaranth's executives and stopped in the doorway. Then he looked up at the ceiling, a sheepish grin on his face, and shrugged, as if to say, *Shit happens!*

A little over two years after starting at the hedge fund, his career there was over. The basketball-playing, hockey-loving young Cana-

234 | BARBARA T. DREYFUSS

dian with the rash trading style had taken investors on a roller-coaster ride as he had sought to make billions and best John Arnold. In his wake, he left tears, anger, and financial catastrophe. At its peak in August, Amaranth LLC had assets totaling $9.668 billion.[18] But four weeks later, more than $6 billion had vanished.[19]

Hunter lost tens of millions of dollars of his own deferred compensation at Amaranth—but nevertheless departed a very wealthy man. He returned to Calgary, and soon moved his family into their new stone-and-wood home that looked out at the Rockies. And in the weeks and months ahead, he delved back into energy trading.

Amaranth, meanwhile, was overwhelmed by redemption demands from investors. Maounis put a clamp on them. He wrote investors on September 29 that the firm was halting redemptions for that month and the next, so that the firm could have an orderly sale of assets and maximize investors' returns. It was a blow to investors such as SDCERA that had requested their money back days earlier.

In his letter Maounis couldn't help adding that Amaranth would continue to pursue alliances that might allow the firm to continue operating. He admitted, however, he had nothing to announce in that regard. He ended by updating his investors on how much the firm had lost. It was down an estimated 65 percent to 70 percent for September. For the year, it was down 55 percent to 60 percent. But it hadn't had time to fully determine its losses, Maounis told investors. Events had happened too fast for that.

Despite Maounis' hope of keeping the firm going, after the collapse of the Citigroup deal no other firm was interested. Two days after Maounis' letter to investors, Amaranth hired Fortress Investment Group LLC, another hedge fund, to help it dispose of its investments. It was brought in as a watchdog to assure investors that Amaranth was selling assets in an orderly way aimed at getting the best prices under the circumstances. Amaranth employees did the actual selling.

A few days after the announcement was made about liquidating, San Diego County pension fund representatives met with Amaranth executives, who told them that only about $70 million of the pension fund's original investment of $175 million remained. Furthermore, what little money was still at Amaranth would be distributed among all investors later on.

The official dissolution of Amaranth had begun.

As Amaranth's offices were being shuttered, John Arnold and Bo Collins sat down in a posh restaurant for lunch, as they did once or twice a year. It had been a momentous year for both.

They talked about Amaranth and the roller-coaster ride in natural gas prices that year. Collins wondered about Hunter's seeming obsession with Arnold, the talk he had heard from brokers. "Did anything ever happen between you?" he asked Arnold. The Texas trader couldn't think of anything.

Collins had just finished shutting down his hedge fund, losing millions for his investors, including endowments and pension funds. Arnold assured him that he had had the right view of prices. His positions were just too big for his firm, given Hunter's trades.

By contrast, Arnold had had the financial wherewithal and the support of his investors to endure the virulent price swings. As the value of Hunter's enormous energy holdings collapsed and winter prices tanked, John Arnold had scored his largest win ever.

But he too had played a very risky game. His firm had suffered heavy losses until prices finally turned. And if he had ultimately been wrong—if an August hurricane had hit or if some other event had occurred to drive up the prices of Hunter's holdings—Arnold might have been the one winding down his firm.

Later, while Hunter was on the stand in one of the endless investigations and lawsuits resulting from the collapse of Amaranth, he admitted he worried about Arnold's trading prowess. Asked why, Hunter looked straight at his attorney. "He's probably the best natural gas trader in the world," he said quietly.

EPILOGUE

Brian Hunter spent little time reflecting on what had happened at Amaranth. Within six months he was brazenly circulating a prospectus to investors for his own hedge fund, Solengo Capital, which he planned to grow into a multibillion-dollar commodities firm. He assured potential investors that Solengo's "model is designed to minimize the risk associated with leverage, liquidity, credit and operations."[1] To monitor his new firm's risk he hired Karl Koster, who along with David Chasman had designed and implemented Amaranth's energy risk management software.

He leased office space not only in Calgary but, in a cheeky move, in Greenwich as well. He hired eleven people, including two energy traders from Amaranth, and brought in a friend from TransCanada. Solengo was going to be portfolio manager friendly, Hunter told his staff, designed to "facilitate their lifestyles and needs." They would have total discretion to build their own trading desk however they thought best.

After purchasing furniture and computers, and developing trading strategies and risk management systems, he set up a trading floor equipped with ten computer workstations. It cost him more than $1.7 million, money out of his own pocket.[2]

Even more remarkable than Hunter's hubris was the fact that investors flocked to his firm. He soon had twenty-five investors lined up, who pledged to invest more than $800 million as soon as the firm was operational.

But Hunter's investors and employees scattered in the summer of 2007 after the Federal Energy Regulatory Commission and Commodity Futures Trading Commission in July charged him and Amaranth with natural gas price manipulation. The CFTC accused Hunter of attempted manipulation on two settlement days. It sought fines and wanted to ban him from commodity trading. Most problematic for Hunter's immediate efforts to set up his own fund, however, was the FERC case, because FERC accused him of successfully manipulating the energy market. That opened him up not only to the $30 million in civil penalties FERC sought but also to the possibility of private lawsuits by people arguing they had been hurt by his actions.

Solengo's investors and business partners pulled out. Solengo's directors resigned. They weren't much bothered, Hunter noted, by the CFTC's accusations of attempted manipulation, nor by the report issued by a Senate panel "criticizing my trading activities."[3] But potential investors were worried that Solengo could end up liable for fines and other penalties, he explained.

Canadian government agencies indicated that Hunter likely would not be allowed to register his firm because of the charges. And Hunter was stymied in creating an offshore fund in the Cayman Islands, because that hedge fund haven required a firm to have directors before registering.

A land deal Hunter had been working on also collapsed, when his business partners grew concerned about the repercussions of the FERC case. Another business venture, a self-storage business in Calgary, also fell apart due to similar worries.[4]

Four months later, Hunter received another blow. A New York State Supreme Court judge ruled against him in his case against Deutsche Bank. He had sued Deutsche Bank in 2004, alleging it ousted him without cause and denied him bonus money he had earned. The court said bonuses were solely at the discretion of the employer. Hunter appealed the decision, but his arguments were unanimously rejected by the appellate court in late 2008.

Hunter and several associates, working out of the office space he had leased for Solengo, decided to consult instead for another hedge fund. They started working for Peak Ridge Capital Group, a Boston-based firm that runs several hedge funds. But that effort soured, and by early 2010 a spokesman for Peak Ridge said Hunter was no longer with the firm.[5]

That was the same time in January Hunter received a devastating ruling from a FERC judge. He was found guilty of manipulating natural gas futures prices by FERC administrative law judge Carmen A. Cintron. She determined that Hunter had intentionally manipulated the settlement prices on expiring futures contracts on February 24, March 29, and April 26. Hunter's "trading was specifically designed to lower the NYMEX price in order to benefit his swap positions on other exchanges" including ICE, she wrote. His trading created prices not in line with normal supply and demand, she concluded.

In his defense, Hunter had argued that his actions on two of those days were part of complicated strategies to make money or reduce his holdings, not attempts at price manipulation. With regard to the March trading day at issue, he claimed the government's case was bogus because he had been thousands of miles away on vacation.

But Cintron rejected Hunter's explanations as "not credible." She charged that Hunter's arguments revealed numerous contradictions, selective memory loss, and other problems. "Hunter's violations were serious, willful and harmful," she ruled.[6]

Her decision went to the full commission for review. After analyzing the judge's decision and the extensive case record, the commission announced on April 21, 2011, that it agreed with the judge. It fined Hunter $30 million—to discourage him and others from future market manipulation.

The case against Hunter was the FERC's first fully litigated price manipulation prosecution using its recently expanded regulatory powers. Oversight of the energy and electricity industry began in 1920, when the Federal Power Commission was created to coordinate the hydroelectric power industry. Its authority later was extended to the sale and transportation of natural gas and electricity and other aspects of the industry. In 1977 these powers were shifted to the newly created FERC. At the time, the FERC's enforcement was largely focused on making sure utilities followed the rules and paid their fees. But this changed radically in the wake of the crippling California energy crisis fomented by Enron and other merchant energy companies, when the FERC ramped up its investigation into price and supply manipulation. In 2005, Congress enhanced the FERC's authority and gave it power to impose civil penalties.

The Hunter case also marks the FERC's first foray into financial energy trading, which had previously been the bailiwick of the CFTC. The FERC claimed authority in this particular case on the grounds that many physical gas contracts are tied to the settlement prices of futures contracts. Hunter tried to block FERC's investigation by arguing in federal court that it lacked jurisdiction over financial energy trading, and has sought to overturn its decision on the same grounds.

The CFTC case is still in federal court in New York.

In the summer of 2009, the FERC held a two-week hearing on the price manipulation charges against Hunter, including four days when Hunter took the stand. The government's lead lawyer, Todd Mullins, suggested during the proceeding that a fixation on John Arnold and his trading in the close may have spurred Hunter and his colleagues to try to manipulate gas prices. "They were young men—Mr. Hunter was 32 at the time—managing billions of dollars, earning good chunks of it along the way," Mullins said. "I think they were riding pretty high from making all that money around the hurricanes . . . I think they were feeling pretty smart, pretty sophisticated about these markets, and they thought they could play a little game. I think they thought other people were manipulating the settlement . . . they talk a lot about these other firms doing it, and I think they thought they could do it."[7]

Hunter's legal team argued he was being singled out for prosecution, that others had traded equally big positions in the close. "Why isn't Centaurus here with John Arnold?" demanded Matthew Menchel, Hunter's lawyer. "Why isn't Sempra here? Their trading was as big, if not bigger, and more frequent in the close than Amaranth was and Mr. Hunter was."[8]

In her decision, Judge Cintron rejected the argument that Arnold and Sempra be charged too. She noted that while they also traded heavily on NYMEX in the close, they were not positioned to benefit from it in the same way as Amaranth, which held large positions elsewhere, such as on ICE, that were tied into the NYMEX price.[9]

Whether or not he made money trading in the close, John Arnold did earn a windfall from the mammoth bets he placed on winter prices falling. Centaurus earned a 317 percent return in 2006, when gas prices collapsed.[10] *Trader Monthly* estimated that Arnold personally earned $1.5 billion to $2 billion. He soared to the top of the magazine's list of highest-paid hedge fund traders in 2006, surpassing T. Boone Pickens, Steve Cohen, and Paul Tudor Jones.[11] By 2009, his firm was managing $5 billion and had seventy employees.[12] Forbes described him as the youngest self-made American billionaire that year, when it listed the world's richest people.[13] In spring 2012 Arnold closed his hedge fund, withdrew from energy trading, and announced he would focus on running his charitable foundation.

For T. Boone Pickens 2006 was also a profitable year. What he termed uncharacteristic bets that natural gas prices would nosedive earned him more than $420 million.[14]

Nick Maounis continued to oversee the unwinding of Amaranth, especially its more illiquid holdings, a real estate venture, and private equity financing. Two weeks after J. P. Morgan and Citadel bought Amaranth's energy positions, J. P. Morgan sold its remaining share of the deal to Citadel, raking in a profit of more than $725 million.[15]

In November 2007, Maounis filed a lawsuit against JPMorgan Chase & Co. and its clearing broker subsidiary, J. P. Morgan Futures, charging they had blocked Amaranth's energy book sale to Goldman Sachs because JPMorgan Chase wanted to step into the deal. By its actions, he argued, JPMorgan Chase forced additional losses on Amaranth. Without these, Maounis claimed in a November 13, 2007, letter to his investors, Amaranth's trading losses would have been survivable. He sued JPMorgan Chase for $1 billion in damages and lost in state court, but appealed the decision.

Although embroiled in lawsuits, Maounis didn't retreat from investing. He followed the path of other failed hedge fund owners and started another firm. In late 2008, he opened Verition Fund Management LLC, initially trading his own money. The firm's name derived from the Latin word for truth. It was located in the building that had housed Amaranth. When he eventually opened his fund to outside investors, Maounis promised to give former Amaranth clients a special deal—they wouldn't have to fork over a 20 percent incentive fee for three years. That was assuming, of course, the firm made money. And he promised not to trade in natural gas.[16]

In August 2009 Maounis settled the CFTC and FERC price manipulation charges against Amaranth, agreeing that the bankrupt firm would pay $7.5 million. Charges against Matthew Donohoe by the FERC were also included in the settlement agreement. Maounis told Amaranth investors that the fine was less than the legal costs of fighting the cases. While not admitting or denying the charges, Amaranth and Donohoe agreed not to publicly argue that the charges were false. Amaranth and Donohoe also admitted that if Amaranth had not traded in the close, the settlement price likely would have been different and the fund's profits lower. In contrast to Hunter's argument that the FERC had no authority to bring charges against him, Amaranth and Donohoe formally accepted the FERC's jurisdiction over the issue.[17]

While these agencies questioned Hunter's trading during the settlement period, neither raised concern about his dominating trades throughout the year or their impact on prices. But a private lawsuit filed in federal court on behalf of other natural gas traders did. It charged Amaranth used its dominant position in gas contracts to profit by artificially inflating the summer and winter spreads. The lawsuit also accused Hunter and Amaranth of price manipulation on the same three settlement days as the FERC case. The case was granted class action status by a federal judge, involving more than one thousand traders as potential claimants. In late 2011 Amaranth agreed to pay more than $70 million to settle the case, although Amaranth, Maounis, and Hunter denied all the allegations.[18]

After the sale of Amaranth's energy holdings, the COO, Charles Winkler, and the human resources head, Stanley Friedman, set up a placement service within the firm to help the remaining employees find jobs. Connecticut's governor sent an official to see if the state could be of help. There was a staggered exit plan, and by December all but thirty technology, accounting, and legal staffers were gone. Most found jobs at hedge funds, banks, and other investment firms. They formed an alumni group, maintained a website to keep in touch, and met a few times a year.

The exit plan didn't go smoothly with all employees, however. Two—energy trader Hai Chen and a base metals trader, Harry Sardanis—were upset that Maounis was paying off investors and not them. They had made millions for the firm and deserved their bonuses regardless of Hunter's actions, they argued in a lawsuit filed in September 2007. Chen said he was owed $37.5 million and Sardanis said he was due $18 million. Maounis, Chen, and Sardanis settled the suit. Terms were not disclosed.[19]

Only one institutional investor refused to accept what little money it got back from Amaranth and quietly move on—the San Diego County Employees Retirement Association. Its executives argued that they hadn't withdrawn their money before the blowup only because of lies from Amaranth management.

In March 2007 the retirement fund sued Amaranth, Maounis, Jones, Winkler, and Hunter, charging it had been led astray by Amaranth executives about the risks of the investment strategy. Amaranth countered that the contracts signed by the pension fund had clearly spelled out the risks. The investor agreements warned that Amaranth was "a speculative investment that involves risk, including the risk of losing all or substantially all of the amount invested." The documents also explained that Amaranth executives could decide not to diversify holdings and could invest borrowed money, increasing risk.[20] SDCERA had had ample warning about the dangers of hedge fund investing, Amaranth argued, and the pension fund chose to take the risk. SDCERA acknowledged the warnings, but retorted that it had been lulled by promises of stringent risk management.

In 2010, a federal court in New York agreed with Amaranth and dismissed the case, saying the hedge fund had warned its investors "loud and clear" that they risked significant losses by investing in the fund. SDCERA appealed and then reached an undisclosed agreement with Amaranth executives before the appeals court ruled.

Despite the experience with Amaranth, SDCERA's chief investment officer, David Deutsch, continued to express support for hedge fund investing. But he promised to rely less on outside consultants and vowed to better monitor investment risks.[21] The pension fund fired Rocaton as its consultant.

But in December 2008 SDCERA's investment board made a dramatic about-face in investment strategy. It halved the $1 billion it had previously allocated to alternative risky investments, including hedge funds. The decision came after the fund that year lost almost 12 percent of the money it had invested in swaps and hedge funds. The losses dragged the fund's overall performance down below returns of the average large pension fund.[22]

That year the pension plan had invested $78 million with two hedge fund managers, Paul Greenwood and Stephen Walsh, but soon grew suspicious of what the two were doing with the money. By year's end, SDCERA wanted its money back. But before that could happen, the two hedge fund managers were dragged off by the FBI[23] and charged with stealing over half a billion dollars from pension funds and endowments.[24] Shortly after that SDCERA's David Deutsch quit, citing "philosophical differences" with pension board members over investment strategies.[25]

As of February 2010, the pension fund had recouped only $84 million of its initial $175 million investment.[26]

When Amaranth collapsed, it became clear that consumers had paid a heavy toll for Hunter's trading. At the beginning of August, average gas contracts for the upcoming heating season were as high as $10.88; by mid-October they were down to an average of $7.71 per MMBtu.

Arthur Corbin, president of the Municipal Gas Authority of Georgia, estimates Amaranth's trading cost it $18 million, because the authority bought contracts for winter gas in mid-2006, when prices were very high. These costs were passed on to its customers.

It wasn't just sophisticated traders that got hurt by Amaranth, says Jeff Billings, the gas authority's risk manager. "It was anybody trying to hedge gas for industrial [use] or cities—anyone using these financial instruments to take out volatility and manage costs."[27]

Although prices dropped after Amaranth's demise, the amount of speculative money in energy commodities grew and played a significant role in keeping prices volatile. FERC officials cited speculators as a significant reason for the 2008 commodity hike, in a study titled "Physical Fundamentals Alone Cannot Explain Unprecedented Summer Natural Gas Prices."[28]

It hasn't been easy for companies such as Bob Easterbrook Jr.'s steel-hardening firm to manage its costs. After Amaranth's collapse, Easterbrook watched natural gas prices swing up and down dramatically. To protect himself against double-digit prices, Easterbrook purchased futures contracts when they were between $7.50 and $9.00. Then the economic crisis hit, and prices fell below $3.00. "Living with such volatile gas prices is always a crap shoot—not a good thing when you're trying to run a competitive small business," he says.[29]

Amaranth's sudden demise and the simultaneous drop in prices caught the attention of Senator Carl Levin (D-Mich.), chairman of Congress' most important investigative unit, the Senate Permanent Subcommittee on Investigations, and its ranking Republican, Senator Norm Coleman of Minnesota. They had already been investigating the effect of speculation on energy markets and decided to make Amaranth a case study. The subcommittee subpoenaed millions of trading records, internal company documents, and instant messages. Numerous firm and industry traders were interviewed.

In 2007 the subcommittee held two days of hearings and issued an extensive report on Amaranth's trading. In releasing the report, Levin charged that Amaranth's excessive speculation "altered natural gas prices, caused wild price swings, and socked consumers with high prices. It's one thing when speculators gamble with their own money; it's another when they turn U.S. energy markets into a lottery where everybody is forced to gamble with them, betting on prices driven by aggressive trading practices."[30]

As a result of the subcommittee's investigation and pressure from commercial and consumer energy users, Congress in 2008 finally gave the CFTC authority over electronic trading. Two years later, in the wake of the financial crisis, Congress passed the Dodd-Frank bill, which among other things extended the CFTC's authority to over-the-counter trading and gave it power to limit the speculative positions of swaps traders.

But how much control the regulators end up having over markets remains to be seen, as financial firms continue their efforts to weaken and delay regulations that can crimp commodity speculation. With Wall Street's political clout, this will be an ongoing issue.

Speculators are getting too rich to just give it all up readily. Even the painfully shy John Arnold decided to make a rare public statement on the issue of curbing energy trading. At a CFTC hearing when the idea first surfaced back in 2009, he argued that limits on energy traders would actually cause markets to become even more volatile. Controlling speculators, Arnold insisted, was just not a good idea.[31]

AUTHOR'S NOTE AND ACKNOWLEDGMENTS

Writing a book about the internal machinations of a hedge fund, one that I did not work at, would have been impossible without enormous help from many people who did work there or otherwise witnessed the story firsthand. I want to express my deep gratitude to the many former Amaranth employees, traders and investors at competing firms, and current and former friends and colleagues of key players in this story who spoke with me. Unfortunately, most don't want me to thank them by name. They continue to work on Wall Street and have contact with their former colleagues, acquaintances, and friends, and so they worry about angering them in some way. But they generously shared what they saw and heard, some talking with me for hours at a time.

Former Amaranth employees were angry about what had happened. When Amaranth collapsed, many lost not only their job but a lot of their money, which had been invested in the firm. Despite this, everyone I spoke with was very professional and thought carefully about what they remembered. They did not try to personally wound someone; anecdotes had to be coaxed out of them. They made clear what they had witnessed directly and what they had only heard about. They distinguished between their interpretation of someone's motives or concerns and what they had heard directly from the person involved.

Neither Brian Hunter nor John Arnold, although repeatedly asked, would particpate in an interview with me about the events described in the book. Both were sent extensive excerpts, and while

John Arnold did review materials that were sent to him, I never heard back from Brian Hunter. But many of their former co-workers, friends, teachers, teammates, energy trading competitors, and admirers were willing to speak both on and off the record about them. There was also a wealth of information on Brian Hunter's thinking to be found in the instant messages and emails released by the Senate Permanent Investigations Subcommittee and the FERC, along with depositions and other emails that were part of the record of numerous court cases. Hunter also spent four days on the stand at the FERC hearing in 2009, describing himself, his trading, and his life at Amaranth. John Arnold was intensively questioned by the FERC and the CFTC when both were investigating Enron. The FERC has released Arnold's deposition, along with numerous Enron emails. He was also deposed in the *Antara vs. Enron* case, and the Senate Permanent Investigations Subcommittee released an email exchange between him and Brian Hunter.

The Senate Permanent Investigations Subcommittee investigation also provided detailed documentation on the day-by-day trading of the firm, its holdings on NYMEX and ICE, communications between NYMEX and Amaranth executives, and internal reports by NYMEX and JPMorgan Chase about Amaranth, all of which were invaluable in piecing together the narrative of Amaranth's demise.

I would particularly like to thank the very generous Madison Galbraith for taking me to the floor of NYMEX and beginning my education in energy trading. Commodities trader Marc Chamberlin was extremely gracious, patient, and helpful in answering my constant stream of questions about energy trading. I am indebted to my former colleagues Jane Shickich Cabes and Carol Coale, who didn't hesitate to help me, and Charlene Lu, an astute analyst whose insights and comments made this book better. Over the years, I have benefited greatly from the keen observations and advice of Jeff Wiggins, and I greatly appreciate his help on this book and his support. Tony Davis, one of the best investigative journalists I know, took time away from his own career to help me get the facts right on this story. Simply out of a desire to see another writer succeed, he took it upon himself to visit places in and near Calgary, delve into Alberta public records, and track down people involved in this story.

I want to thank the natural gas hedgers who shared their stories about Amaranth's impact on their firms and clients, including Bob Easterbrook Jr., Aubrey Hilliard, Larry A. Marshall, Arthur Corbin, Jeff Billings, and Thomas Ihrig. Portfolio manager Michael Masters has done critically important research analyzing the impact of speculation on commodity prices and bringing it to the attention of Congress and regulatory agencies. I thank him for sharing his insights with me.

For help in understanding how Enron operated I would like to thank Professors Frank Partnoy and Vincent Kaminski, Jeff Shankman, Gary Hickerson, and Robert McCullough. I would also like to thank Professor Ludwig Chincarini for insights into Amaranth's leverage, Selena Chaisson for discussions about hedge funds, Kathy M. Klenetsky for reading sections, Professor Robert Elliott for his insights on the history of mathematical finance, and Vanderbilt professors John Siegfried, Stephen Buckles, and James Foster.

I owe a big debt to my first editor at Random House, Tim Bartlett, who believed in me, gave this book its start, and provided sage advice on shaping it. Jonathan Jao, who replaced Tim as my editor, was extremely supportive and insightful. I am deeply grateful for his astute suggestions on developing the story. Sam Nicholson at Random House has deft editing skills. My agent, Deborah Grosvenor, saw the importance of this story, guided me in proposal writing, and had my back from the beginning. I was very lucky to work with her. Jacqui Salmon's advice on how to fill out the story was invaluable.

Most of all I want to thank my family: Anna and Justin, for their encouragement, cheerfulness, and understanding when I was tied to my desk and computer; and Bob, for his humor, wise counsel, adroit edits, and constant support.

NOTES

INTRODUCTION

1. Hennessee Group LLC, "Hedge Fund Industry Growth," January 2005, http://www.magnum.com/hedgefunds/articles/2005/050101.pdf, accessed May 9, 2011.
2. Ibid.
3. Ibid.
4. Rosanne Pane and Srikant Dash, "Standard and Poor's Indices Versus Active Funds Scorecard, Fourth Quarter 2002," *Standard & Poor's*, January 21, 2003.
5. Hennessee Group LLC, "Hedge Fund Industry Growth."
6. "US Hedge Fund Manager Earned $1 Billion in 2004," *Finfacts*, May 27, 2005, www.finfacts.com/irelandbusinessnews/publish/article_10001985.shtml.
7. Riva D. Atlas, "The Top Hedge Funds Are Stumbling but Manager Salaries Aren't," *New York Times*, May 27, 2005.
8. Nathan Vardi, "Top 5 Hedge Fund Managers Bank $8.3 Billion," http://video.forbes.com/fvn/lifestyle/zenvo-danish-supercar?partner=playlist, March 1, 2012.
9. Benjamin M. Friedman, "Is Our Financial System Serving Us Well?" *Daedalus*, Fall 2010, 20.
10. John Baffes and Tassos Haniotis, "Placing the 2006/08 Commodity Price Boom into Perspective," World Bank, July 2010. Another study, by M. Lagi, Yavni Bar-Yam, K. Z. Bertrand, and Yaneer Bar-Yam titled "The Food Crises: A Quantitative Model of Food Prices Including Speculators and Ethanol Conversion," released September 21, 2011, by the New England Complex Systems Institute, is even more definitive. The report concludes that sharp jumps in food prices in 2007–8 and 2010–11 were caused primarily by speculation and the emphasis on biofuels.
11. "Record Number of Hedge Funds Liquidate in 2008," Hedge Fund Research, Inc., www.hedgefundresearch.com/pdf/pr_20090318.pdf.
12. Barbara Bovbjerg, Government Accountability Office, "Defined Benefit Pension Plans, Plans Face Challenges When Investing in Hedge Funds and Private Equity," statement before the Department of Labor's Advisory Council on Employee Welfare and Pension Benefits Plans, August 31, 2011.

13. CFTC Commissioner Bart Chilton, "Please Listen Carefully, Menu Options Have Changed," Speech at Trade Tech 2012, New York, March 8, 2012.
14. Boston Consulting Group, "Organizational Study and Reform," study done for the Securities and Exchange Commission, March 10, 2011.
15. Bovbjerg, "Defined Benefit," 1.

CHAPTER 1: GOING ALL IN

1. Details of the trading done by Hunter and Arnold are in charts, graphs, and text in the Hearing, Staff Report, and Appendices of the Permanent Subcommittee on Investigations of the Committee on Homeland Security and Governmental Affairs, U.S. Senate, "Excessive Speculation in the Natural Gas Market," 2007, 325–32.

CHAPTER 2: THE MAN FROM CALGARY

1. Matthew Menchel, opening statement, FERC hearing in the matter of Brian Hunter, Federal Energy Regulatory Commission, August 18, 2009.
2. Donald MacKenzie, "An Equation and Its Worlds: Bricolage, Exemplars, Disunity and Performativity in Financial Economics," *Social Studies of Science* 33, 6 (December 2003): 854.
3. Frank Partnoy, *Infectious Greed* (New York: Henry Holt, 2003), 86.
4. Ibid., 37–38.
5. Ibid., 26.
6. "Volcker Spares No One in Broad Critique," WSJ.com, September 23, 2010.
7. Partnoy, *Infectious Greed*, 85.
8. Author interview.
9. Author interview.
10. Gyle Konotopetz, "TransCanada Boss Pursues Pipe Dreams," *Business Edge News Magazine*, September 30, 2004.
11. Ibid.
12. "Exit Marketing," *Pipeline & Gas Journal*, January 2003.
13. Author interview.
14. Bethany McLean, "The Man Who Lost $6 Billion," *Fortune*, July 8, 2008.
15. Scott Patterson, *The Quants* (New York: Crown Business, 2010), 6, 147.
16. Scott Patterson and Serena Ng, "Deutsche Bank Fallen Trader Left Behind $1.8 Billion Hole," *Wall Street Journal*, February 6, 2009.
17. Majority and Minority Staff Report, "Wall Street and the Financial Crisis: Anatomy of a Financial Collapse," Senate Permanent Subcommittee on Investigations report, April 13, 2011.
18. "Derivative House, Interest Rate Derivatives, Credit Derivatives House and Energy/Commodity Derivatives House of the Year—Deutsche Bank," *Risk Magazine* 16, 1 (January 2003).
19. Ibid.
20. *Brian J. Hunter v. Deutsche Bank AG, New York Branch*, Supreme Court of the State of New York, New York County, Index No. 602791/2004, 4.
21. Ibid., plaintiff's response to defendant Deutsche Bank, 11.
22. Author interviews.

23. *Brian J. Hunter v. Deutsche Bank AG*, 7.

24. Author interview.

25. Deposition of Kevin Rogers, re: *Brian J. Hunter v. Deutsche Bank AG*, August 29, 2006.

26. Author interview.

27. *Brian J. Hunter v. Deutsche Bank AG*, 9.

28. Deposition of Kevin Rogers, 319–22.

29. Ibid., 445.

30. Elizabeth Mehren, "Nor'easter Blankets Northeast in Snow, Ice," *Los Angeles Times*, December 7, 2003; National Climate Data Center, Global Hazards and Significant Events, December 2003, Severe Winter Weather, http://lwf .ncdc.noaa.gov/oa/climate/research/2003/dec/hazards.html.

31. "CFTC, FERC Find No Evidence of Manipulation in Winter Spike," *Natural Gas Week*, September 6, 2004.

32. Author interview.

33. Deposition of Kevin Rogers, 371–74.

34. According to traders familiar with his trading at the time.

35. Deposition of Kevin Rogers, 399–402.

36. Ibid., 307. Hunter's complaint states that losses during the first week of December 2003 were approximately $51.2 million.

37. Ibid., 430.

38. Decision and Order, Supreme Court of the State of New York, *Brian J. Hunter v. Deutsche Bank AG*, November 7, 2007, Case 1:07-cv-06682.

39. *Brian J. Hunter v. Deutsche Bank AG*, 10-11.

40. Deposition of Kevin Rogers.

41. Ibid., 359–60.

42. Deposition of Brian J. Hunter, re: *Brian J. Hunter v. Deutsche Bank AG*, May 6, 2006, 427–28.

43. Author interview with Deutsche Bank employee.

CHAPTER 3: LONE STAR GAMBLER

1. Bethany McLean and Peter Elkind, *The Smartest Guys in the Room* (New York: Portfolio, 2003), 223.

2. David Barboza, "Corporate Conduct: The Trader; Enron Trader Had a Year to Boast of, Even If . . ." *New York Times*, July 9, 2002.

3. Clinton Free and Norman Macintosh, "Management Control Practice and Culture at Enron: The Untold Story," Canadian Accounting Association Annual Paper, August 2006.

4. Author interview.

5. Author interview with former Enron executive.

6. Deposition of John Arnold before the Commodity Futures Trading Commission, in the matter of Enron Corp., Ref. No.4916. August 19, 2002, section 52.

7. Ibid.

8. Loren Fox, *Enron: The Rise and Fall* (Hoboken, NJ: John Wiley & Sons, 2003), 12.

9. The history of natural gas deregulation comes from the website naturalgas

.org, maintained by the Natural Gas Supply Association. How Ken Lay positioned Enron to take advantage of deregulation is detailed in Fox, *Enron*, and McLean and Elkind, *Smartest Guys*.

10. Fox, *Enron*, 23.
11. McLean and Elkind, *Smartest Guys*, 61.
12. Fox, *Enron*, 39.
13. Author interview.
14. Public Citizen, "Blind Faith: How Deregulation and Enron's Influence over Government Looted Billions from Americans," December 2001.
15. Author interview.
16. Author interview.
17. Author interview.
18. Deposition of John Arnold before the Commodity Futures Trading Commission, section 57.
19. Author interview.
20. Author interview.
21. Author interview.
22. Deposition of John Arnold before the Commodity Futures Trading Commission, section 128.
23. Author interviews.
24. Email, August 8, 2001, from John Arnold to Jennifer Fraser.
25. Majority Staff Memorandum, Senate Committee on Governmental Affairs, November 12, 2002.
26. McLean and Elkind, *Smartest Guys*, 223.
27. Robert McCullough, "Regulations and Forward Markets, Lessons from Enron and the Western Market Crisis of 2000–2001," McCullough Research, May 8, 2006.
28. Deposition of John Arnold before the Commodity Futures Trading Commission, section 153.
29. Ibid., section 185.
30. A former Enron trader who followed Arnold's activity closely estimates the notional value of his trades as at least $1 billion per day and says they involved hundreds of thousands of contracts. A similar dollar figure is given in McLean and Elkind, *Smartest Guys*, 223.
31. "Final Report on Price Manipulation in Western Markets," Docket No. PA02-2-000, Staff of the Federal Energy Regulatory Commission, March 2003.
32. Richard Oppel Jr., "Panel Finds Manipulation by Energy Companies," *New York Times*, March 27, 2003.
33. Deposition of John Arnold before the Commodity Futures Trading Commission, section 34.
34. Ibid., section 265.
35. Ibid., section 318.
36. Author interview.
37. Deposition of John Arnold before the Commodity Futures Trading Commission, section 110.
38. Ibid., sections 150–1.

39. Author interviews.
40. Author interview with several former Enron officials regarding the meeting; deposition of John Arnold before the Commodity Futures Trading Commission, for the facts on how much he gained and lost.
41. U.S. Energy Information Administration, *Natural Gas Weekly Market Update*, January 22, 2001.
42. Author interview.
43. Deposition of John Arnold before the Commodity Futures Trading Commission, sections 341–47.
44. McCullough, "Regulations"; testimony of Michael Maggi to the CFTC and FERC, June 18, 2002.
45. *Official Employment-Related Issues Committee of Enron Corp. vs. John D. Arnold et al.*, U.S. Bankruptcy Court, Southern District of Texas, Order of the Court, Dec. 9, 2005.
46. Deposition of John Arnold before the Commodity Futures Trading Commission, section 110.
47. Author interview with Professor Frank Partnoy.
48. *Enron North America v. Antara Resources, Inc.*, oral and videotaped deposition of John Arnold, May 6, 2005.
49. Author interview with George Lugrin, Westmoreland Hall, P.C., counsel for Antara Resources, April 21, 2009.
50. Jeffrey Ryser, "Two Former Enron Trading Experts Share Dais and Ideas on Energy Market," *Platts Power Markets Week*, February 13, 2006.
51. Author interview.
52. CFTC Hearing on Speculative Position Limits in Energy Futures Markets, August 5, 2009, attended by the author.
53. Stephen Taub, "Centaurus' Arnold Lost 3.27 Percent in 2010," *Institutional Investor*, January 18, 2011.
54. Author interview.
55. Gregory Zuckerman and Henny Sender, "Oil Has Become Speculator's Paradise," *Wall Street Journal*, August 23, 2004.
56. Author interview.

CHAPTER 4: A FUND FOR EVERYONE

1. Peter Landau, "Alfred Winslow Jones: The Long and Short of the Founding Father," *Institutional Investor*, August 1968.
2. Ibid.
3. Carol Loomis, "The Jones Nobody Keeps Up With," *Fortune*, April 1966.
4. Barton Biggs, *Hedge Hogging* (Hoboken, NJ: John Wiley & Sons, 2006), 82–84. In 1964 as an analyst at E. F. Hutton, Biggs also ran a portfolio for A. W. Jones. Biggs earned half his yearly payout from commissions from Jones. He spent thirty years at Morgan Stanley as its chief investment strategist and a member of its executive committee, before running his own hedge fund until his death in 2012.
5. Ibid., 83.
6. Ibid.

7. Loomis, "Jones."

8. Alan Rappeport, "A Short History of Hedge Funds," CFO.com, March 27, 2007, http://www.cfo.com/article.cfm/8914091/c_2984367.

9. The Securities Investment Promotion Act of 1996, Report of the Committee on Banking, Housing and Urban Affairs, U.S. Senate, Report 104-293, 104th Congress, 2d Session, June 26, 1996.

10. Staff report to the Securities and Exchange Commission, "Implications of the Growth of Hedge Funds," September 2003.

11. Amaranth September 2005 update to investors.

12. Amaranth confidential private placement memorandum, Number 153, for the exclusive use of San Diego County Employees Retirement Association, March 2003.

13. Author interview.

14. Biggs, *Hedge Hogging*, 87.

15. Sebastian Mallaby, *More Money than God* (New York: Penguin, 2010), 141.

16. Author interview.

17. Author interview.

18. Author interview.

19. Roger Lowenstein, *When Genius Failed* (New York: Random House, 2000), 146.

20. Nicholas Dunbar, *Inventing Money* (Chichester: John Wiley & Sons, 2000), 187.

21. The President's Working Group on Financial Markets, "Hedge Funds, Leverage and the Lessons of Long-Term Capital Management," April 1999.

22. Lowenstein, *Genius*, 236.

23. Author interview.

24. Sanford C. Bernstein & Co., "The Hedge Fund Industry—Products, Services, or Capabilities," Bernstein Research Call, May 19, 2003, 5.

25. Jenny Anderson, "US Regulators Grow Alarmed over Hedge Fund Hotels," *International Herald Tribune*, January 1, 2007.

26. Greenwich Associates, "Hedge Funds: The End of the Beginning?" 2004.

27. Christopher B. Philips, "Understanding Alternative Investments: A Primer on Hedge Fund Evaluation," Vanguard Investment Counseling and Research, 2006, 2.

28. Ian McDonald, "Invesco Plans Aggressive Offering That Looks a Lot Like a Hedge Fund," TheStreet.com, July 12, 2000.

29. Securities and Exchange Commission, "Implications of the Growth of Hedge Funds."

30. Author interview.

31. Douglas Elliott's comments were made at the "Living on the Hedge" conference, Brookings Institution, February 12, 2009. Elliott was an investment banker for over twenty years and now is a fellow at the Brookings Institution.

32. Greenwich Associates survey of hedge funds conducted in 2003.

33. Douglas Elliott, author interview.

34. Anderson, "US Regulators."

35. Jesse Eisinger, "Wall Street Requiem," *Conde Nast Portfolio*, November 2007.

36. Nicholas Chan, Mila Getmansky, Shane M. Haas, and Andrew W. Lo, "Systemic Risk and Hedge Funds," in Mark Carey and René M. Stulz, eds., *The*

Risks of Financial Institutions (Chicago: University of Chicago Press, 2006), 235–41.
37. Philips, "Understanding," 20.
38. Ben Rooney, "Hedge Fund Graveyard: 693 and Counting," CNNMoney .com, December 18, 2008. A report for the Milkin Institute by James Barth, Tong Li, Triphon Phumiwasana, and Glenn Yago, "Hedge Funds: Risks and Returns in Global Capital Markets," December 2006, found that 766 hedge funds closed in 2005.

CHAPTER 5: AMARANTH

1. Author interview with Greenwich resident who attended the events described in the following paragraphs.
2. Author interview.
3. Author interview.
4. Nassim Nicholas Taleb, *The Black Swan* (New York: Random House, 2007), 44.
5. Amaranth's CP Leveraged Funds due diligence report 2001. All the Amaranth due diligence reports cited were prepared by JPMorgan Chase.
6. Author interview with former Paloma executive.
7. Amaranth's CP Leveraged Funds due diligence report, 2001.
8. Ibid., 2004.
9. Ibid., 2001.
10. Ibid.
11. Author interview with former employees.
12. Author interview with former Citadel employee.
13. Enron Corporation emails released by the FERC, Harry Arora to Shaka Jaggi, November 29, 2001, www.enron-mail.com/email/arora-h/sent_items/RE_5151.html.
14. Affidavit of Hai Chen in Support of Motion for Prejudgment Remedy, *Hai Chen and Harry Sardanis v. Nicholas M. Maounis and Amaranth Group, Inc.*, U.S. District Court, District of Connecticut, 07-cv-01416.
15. Bonus summary letter from Amaranth to Hai Chen, March 18, 2003, reports an 11 percent return in 2002 for investors. Amaranth's CP Leveraged Funds due diligence report, 2004, states 15.3 percent for 2002.
16. Confidential Private Placement Memorandum, Amaranth Partners LLC, March 2003, for the exclusive use of San Diego County Employees Retirement Association, Memorandum Number 153.
17. *Hai Chen and Harry Sardanis v. Nicholas M. Maounis and Amaranth Group, Inc.*, 7.
18. Amaranth's CP Leveraged Funds due diligence report, 2004.
19. Ibid.
20. Author interview.
21. Amaranth's CP Leveraged Funds due diligence report, 2004.
22. *Risk Magazine* 16, 1 (January 2003).

CHAPTER 6: WIDOW MAKER

1. Author interview.
2. Author interview.
3. Author interview with staff at Sophia's Costumes.
4. Testimony of Brian Hunter, FERC hearing in the matter of Brian Hunter, August 19, 2009, page 384.
5. Interviews with former Amaranth employees.
6. Amaranth's CP Leveraged Funds due diligence report, 2004, says 10.4 percent. However, a confidential compensation letter sent to Hai Chen, May 10, 2005, by Nick Maounis, submitted in the court case *Hai Chen and Harry Sardanis v. Nicholas Maounis and Amaranth Group, Inc.* stated that the firm had generated net average return for investors of 8.1 percent in 2004.
7. Estimates vary. Amaranth's CP Leveraged Funds due diligence report states just over $6.19 billion under management as of the end of 2004. The confidential compensation letter to Hai Chen, dated May 10, 2005, cited above, states the firm had $6.7 billion.
8. *San Diego County Employees Retirement Association v. Nicholas Maounis, Charles H. Winkler, Robert W. Jones, Brian Hunter and Amaranth Advisors, LLC*, U.S. District Court, Southern District of New York, 2007-cv-02618, 18.
9. Author interview with former SAC employee.
10. *San Diego County Employees Retirement Association v. Nicholas Maounis.*
11. Deposition of Nicholas Maounis, included as exhibit attached to Federal Energy Regulatory Commission, Order to Show Cause and Notice of Proposed Penalties, Issued July 26, 2007.
12. Swamplot–Houston's Real Estate Landscape, "Big and Modern on Lazy Lane," Swamplot.com, March 11, 2006. http://swamplot.com/big-and-modern-on-lazy-lane-john-arnold-tries-house-trading/2008-03-11.
13. Leah McGrath Goodman, *The Asylum* (New York: HarperCollins, 2011), 316.
14. Author interview.
15. Kate Sayen Kirkland, *The Hogg Family and Houston* (Houston: University of Texas Press, 2009), preface.
16. Lisa Gray, "Former Enron Trader to Raze Historic Home," *Houston Chronicle*, May 3, 2005.
17. Author interview.
18. Author interview with participants.
19. Interview with former NYMEX official.
20. Author interview.
21. Author interview.
22. Amaranth's CP Leveraged Funds due diligence report, 2004, updated December 27, 2005.
23. Bill Feingold, Schaeffer Research, September 18, 2006.
24. Amaranth's CP Leveraged Funds due diligence report, 2004, updated December 27, 2005.
25. Author interview with former Amaranth employee.
26. Federal Energy Regulatory Commission, Order to Show Cause, 70. Also

from the Hearing, Staff Report and Appendices of the Permanent Subcommittee on Investigations of the Committee on Homeland Security and Governmental Affairs, U.S. Senate, "Excessive Speculation in the Natural Gas Market," 2007, 265.

CHAPTER 7: PITCHING TO GRANDMA

1. The description of the meeting and quotes from presentations, comments, and questions are taken from a video of the meeting.
2. "San Diego County Employee Retirement Association: The Quest for 'Alpha,'" report by the San Diego Grand Jury 2006–7, filed May 15, 2007, Appendix A.
3. Ibid.
4. Frances Denmark, "Making Waves," *Institutional Investor's Alpha Magazine*, January/February 2006.
5. San Diego County grand jury report. David Deutsch later disputed that percentage after Amaranth collapsed. Deutsch said only 8 percent was in risky investments. The rest was invested in products that would ensure consistent low-risk profits, he claimed. But he didn't deny these investments were also managed by hedge funds.
6. San Diego County grand jury report.
7. SDCERA, Comprehensive Annual Financial Report for the fiscal year ended June 2005, on the website of the SDCERA.
8. Author interview.
9. Denmark, "Making Waves."
10. Maureen Whalen, "Hedging Bets on Employees' Futures: Is Investing Pension Fund Assets in Hedge Funds a Breach of Fiduciary Duty?" 2008, http://works.bepress.com/maureen_mcgreevy/2.
11. Susan L. Barreto, "Calpers' Hedge Fund Program Returns 8.6%," *Reuters-Hedgeworld*, July 26, 2005.
12. Government Accountability Office, "Defined Benefit Pension Plans," August 2008, 3.
13. Keystone State Capital Corporation, "Pension Investment in Hedge Funds," April 7, 2008.
14. William Klunk, "Pension Funds Investing in Hedge Funds," Congressional Research Service, Order Code RS22679, June 15, 2007.
15. 2006 NACUBO Endowment Study, National Association of College and University Business Officers.
16. Tomoeh Murakami Tse, "Public Pensions Systems Betting on Hedge Funds," *Washington Post*, July 24, 2007.
17. Ross Kerber, "Galvin Says Cahill Relies Too Much on Hedge Funds," *Boston Globe*, March 21, 2006.
18. Kelly DePonte, "Fund of Funds: A Brief History," Probitas Partners, www.probitaspartners.com/pdfs/FoF%20History%202005.pdf.
19. Securities and Exchange Commission, "Implications of the Growth of Hedge Funds."
20. Biggs, *Hedge Hogging*, ix.

21. Author interview.
22. Author interview.
23. Seth Hettena, "Hedge Fund Champion Leaves County Pension Amid Losses, Tension," *Voice of San Diego*, March 5, 2009.
24. *SDCERA v. Nicholas M. Maounis, Charles H. Winkler, Robert W. Jones, Brian Hunter and Amaranth Advisors, LLC*, U.S. District Court, Southern District of New York, 07-cv-2618, March 29, 2007.
25. San Diego County grand jury report.
26. Patrick Hosking, "Investor Paid Out Extra Penalties to Quit Amaranth," *Times* (London), October 13, 2006.

CHAPTER 8: THE $100 MILLION MAN

1. Amaranth's CP Leveraged Funds due diligence report 2005.
2. Amaranth September 2005 update to investors.
3. Author interview.
4. Amaranth's CP Leveraged Funds due diligence report, 2006.
5. Ibid., 2004, updated December 2005.
6. Document in file folder, *Brian J. Hunter v. Deutsche Bank AG*.
7. Amaranth September 2005 update.
8. *Centaurus Energy Masterfund LP v. BP Corporation North America, Inc.*, U.S. District Court, Southern District of New York, 06-cv-07856, September 29, 2006.
9. Interviews with several commodity traders.
10. Ann Davis, "The Energy-Trading High Wire," *Wall Street Journal*, March 21, 2006.
11. Alexei Barrionuevo, "Energy Trading Without a Certain 'E,'" *New York Times*, January 15, 2006.
12. Author interview with an investor in the fund.
13. Charge/Mortgage of Land, Land Titles Act, December 10, 2004, and Encumbrances, Liens & Interests, Alberta Government Services, Land Titles Office.
14. Affidavit of David Chasman, June 5, 2009, before the Federal Energy Regulatory Commission.
15. FERC, Order to Show Cause, 70–71.
16. Ibid., 70.
17. Ibid., 70–71.
18. Author interviews.
19. Amaranth Monthly Investor Update, Snapshot for January 2006.
20. Testimony of Brian Hunter, FERC hearing, August 21, 2009, 773–74.
21. Ibid., August 18, 2009, 367.
22. Ibid., 335.
23. Author interviews with office management staff and firms renting office space.
24. Testimony of Brian Hunter, FERC hearing. August 18, 2009, 336–37.
25. Ibid., August 19, 2009, 435–36.
26. Ibid., 523.
27. Ibid., 524.

28. Senate Permanent Subcommittee on Investigations, June 25, 2007, 268, 272.
29. Testimony of Vincent Kaminski, FERC hearing, August 25, 2009.
30. Leah McGrath Goodman, "The Reckoning of Centaurus Billionaire John Arnold," *Absolute Return + Alpha*, February 1, 2011.
31. Author interview.
32. Testimony of Brian Hunter, FERC hearing, August 19, 2009, 437–38, 443.
33. Prepared direct testimony of Harpreet Singh Arora, Exhibit S2, FERC hearing.
34. Author interview.
35. Hunter earned $320 million in February, although the firm took $81 million out for a reserve fund, crediting him with profits of $239 million. Testimony of Brian Hunter, FERC hearing, August 19, 2009, 504.

CHAPTER 9: KING OF GAS

1. Chart, "Repeat High Volume Traders Identified Using Dr. Kaminski's Methodology," RES Demonstrative 4, submitted into evidence in FERC hearing.
2. Instant message between Brian Hunter and David Chasman, April 26, 2006, FERC, Order to Show Cause.
3. Prefiled testimony of Vincent Kaminski, FERC hearing, exhibit S1.
4. Testimony of Brain Hunter, FERC hearing. August 19, 2009, 444–445. FERC, Order to Show Cause, 32.
5. Prepared Direct Testimony of Harpreet Singh Arora before the Federal Energy Regulatory Commission, exhibit S2.
6. *CFTC v. Amaranth Advisors, Amaranth Advisors Calgary and Brian Hunter*, complaint, U.S. District Court, Southern District of New York, 07-civ-6682, 7.
7. Testimony of Eric Bolling, FERC hearing, August 24, 2009, 1106.
8. The number of contracts sold by Hunter varies. The FERC Order to Show Cause, 42, shows 3,111 contracts sold during the settlement period. The exhibit RES 2-1, prepared direct testimony of Michael Quinn in FERC hearing, shows Amaranth's net trading activity during the settlement period as being 2,901 contracts.
9. Initial Decision, Brian Hunter IN07-26-004, FERC, Administrative Law Judge Carmen Cintron, issued January 22, 2010.
10. Prepared direct testimony of Michael Quinn, FERC hearing.
11. Initial Decision, Brian Hunter IN07-26-004.
12. *CFTC v. Amaranth Advisors*, 8.
13. Motion for Summary Disposition and Answer of Amaranth Advisors LLC, Amaranth Advisors Calgary UPC, Amaranth Management Limited Partnership, Amaranth Partners LLC, Amaranth Capital Partners LLC, and Amaranth Group Inc. to FERC's Order to Show Cause 85, and Brian Hunter's Memorandum in Response to the FERC's Order to Show Cause and Notice of Proposed Penalties, 30.
14. Email from Steven Johnson, managing director, Amaranth, to investors, March 29, 2006, at 10:49 a.m.
15. *SDCERA v. Nicholas Maounis et al.*, 18–19.
16. Testimony of Brian Hunter, FERC hearing, August 19, 2009, 476-77.
17. Deposition of Hai Chen, in *Hai Chen and Harry Sardanis v. Nicholas M.*

Maounis and Amaranth Group, Inc., U.S. District Court, District of Connecticut, 2008.

18. Senate Permanent Subcommittee on Investigations report, 275, 283.
19. The investigation by the Senate Permanent Subcommittee on Investigations analyzed in great detail all of Amaranth's trading throughout these months. It looked at how prices moved when Amaranth made its huge purchases or sold heavily. It concluded, "Because Amaranth was overwhelmingly the predominant buyer of January/November spread, Amaranth's actions must be considered to be the predominant cause of the increase in the January/November price spread . . . the significant growth in Amaranth's positions in other winter and summer contracts during this period is further evidence that Amaranth's large buys of winter contracts and large sales of summer contracts were the major cause of the widening difference in price between the winter and summer contracts. Amaranth's trades were not the sole cause of the increasing price spreads between summer and winter contracts: rather they were the predominant cause."
20. Instant message between Brian Hunter and unnamed trader on April 27, 2006, beginning at 2:35 p.m., Exhibit 22, instant messages and emails released by the Senate Permanent Subcommittee on Investigations, 921.
21. Author interview.
22. Author interview with hedge fund owner.
23. Absolute Return Symposium 2006, *HedgeFund Intelligence Ltd.*, November 28, 2006.
24. Senate Permanent Subcommittee on Investigations report, 261.
25. Senate Permanent Subcommittee on Investigations report, 263.
26. "Natural Gas Prices Buoyed by Petroleum Strength, Hurricane Concerns," *Intelligence Press*, April 7, 2006, http://www.rigzone.com/news/article.asp?a _id=31100.
27. McGrath Goodman, *The Asylum*, 332.
28. Author interview.
29. Author interview.
30. Author interview.
31. Instant message between Brian Hunter and an unnamed trader, April 13, 2006, 3:13 p.m., exhibit 22, Senate Permanent Subcommittee on Investigations report, 921.
32. Instant message between Brian Hunter and unnamed trader, April 13, 2006, 1:32 p.m., exhibit 9, Senate Permanent Subcommittee on Investigations report, 721.
33. FERC, Order to Show Cause, 82.
34. Testimony of Brian Hunter, FERC hearing, August 21, 2009, 780.
35. Affidavit of David Chasman, June 5, 2009, before the Federal Energy Regulatory Commission.
36. Testimony of Matthew Donohoe, FERC hearing, August 21, 2009, 801.
37. Email between Brian Hunter and Manos Vourkoutiotis, testimony of Brian Hunter, FERC hearing, August 21, 2009, 799–801.
38. Testimony of Brian Hunter, FERC hearing, August 21, 2009, 782.
39. Testimony of David Chasman, FERC hearing, September 2, 2009, 2415.
40. Deposition of Rob Jones, included as exhibit in FERC Order to Show Cause.

41. Ibid.
42. Initial Decision, Brian Hunter IN07-26-004.
43. Instant message between Brian Hunter and David Chasman, April 26, 2006, 12:40 p.m.
44. Instant message between Brian Hunter and a trader, TRDRxtra, April 26, 2006, 1:22 p.m.
45. Exhibit Res 2-44, Net "Impact" of the Top 10 Net Buyers and Top 10 Net Sellers During At-Issue Settlement Periods, FERC hearing in the case of Brian Hunter.
46. Testimony of Brian Hunter, FERC hearing, August 19, 2009, 401.
47. Testimony of Brian Hunter, FERC hearing, August 21, 2009, 846–47.
48. FERC, Order to Show Cause, 29.
49. Expert Report of Anthony Saunders, PhD, presented May 8, 2009, on behalf of Amaranth in *Amaranth LLC, Amaranth LLC and Amaranth Advisors LLC v. J. P. Morgan Chase & Co., J. P. Morgan Chase Bank, N.A. and J. P. Morgan Futures, Inc.*, Supreme Court of the State of New York, case No. 603756/07.
50. Amaranth Performance and Net Asset Value Report—September 2006 YTD, Amaranth Snapshot, April 30, 2006, sent to investors.
51. Senate Permanent Subcommittee on Investigations report, 275.
52. Instant message between Brian Hunter and unnamed trader, April 27, 2006, at 2:35 p.m., exhibit 22, Senate Permanent Subcommittee on Investigations Report, 921.
53. Instant message between Brian Hunter and CRAIGSCHOR, April 25, 2006, at 12:14 p.m., exhibit 9, Senate Permanent Subcommittee on Investigations report, 724.

CHAPTER 10: PAYING THE (INFLATED) TAB

1. Author interview.
2. U.S. Energy Information Administration, *Natural Gas Weekly Updates*, February 16, February 23, March 9, March 23, May 11, 2006.
3. Author interview.
4. Mark N. Cooper, PhD, "The Role of Supply, Demand and Financial Commodity Markets in the Natural Gas Price Spiral," prepared for the Midwest Attorneys General Natural Gas Working Group, March 2006.
5. President Franklin D. Roosevelt, Message to Congress, February 9, 1934.
6. Graham Purcell and Abelardo Lopez Valdez, "The Commodity Futures Trading Commission Act of 1974: Regulatory Legislation for Commodity Futures Trading in a Market-Oriented Economy," *South Dakota Law Review* 21 S.D.L. Rev. 555 (1976).
7. Author interview.
8. Author interview with Michael Greenberger.
9. John Dunbar, "Obama Targets 'Enron Loophole,'" *Los Angeles Times*, June 23, 2008.
10. Robert Shapiro and Nam Pham, "An Analysis of Spot and Futures Prices for Natural Gas: The Roles of Economic Fundamentals, Market Structure, Speculation and Manipulation," August 2006.
11. Ibid.

12. Testimony of Paul Cicio, Industrial Energy Consumers of America, in hearing before the Commodity Futures Trading Commission, August 5, 2009.
13. Shapiro and Pham, "Analysis."
14. Cooper, "Role," 57.
15. Ann Davis, "Power Banking: Morgan Stanley Trades Energy Old-Fashioned Way: In Barrels," *Wall Street Journal*, March 2, 2005.
16. Ibid.
17. Barrionuevo, "Energy Trading."
18. Peter C. Fusaro and Gary Vasey, Energy Hedge Fund Center press release, May 15, 2006.
19. Cooper, "Role," 14.
20. Testimony of Jeffrey H. Harris, Chief Economist of the CFTC, before the Commodity Futures Trading Commission Hearing to Examine Trading on Regulated Exchanges and Exempt Commercial Markets, September 18, 2007.
21. Written Testimony of Jeffrey Harris, chief economist of the CFTC, and John Fenton, Director of Market Surveillance of the CFTC, before the House Committee on Agriculture, Subcommittee on General Farm Commodities and Risk Management, May 15, 2008.
22. ICE Form 10-k, cited by the Senate Permanent Subcommittee on Investigations report.
23. Cicio testimony.
24. Author interview.
25. Author interview.
26. Author interview and newsletters of Aubrey Hilliard.

CHAPTER 11: "GONNA GET OUR FACES RIPPED OFF"

1. Merrill Lynch and CapGemini, *Wealth: How the World's High-Net-Worth Grow, Sustain and Manage their Fortunes*, (Mississauga: John Wiley & Sons Canada Ltd., 2008) 129.
2. Amaranth April statement, issued May 11, 2006, does not mention whether or not it includes the 2 percent expense fee.
3. Amaranth April 2006 update to investors.
4. Amaranth snapshots at January 31, 2006, February 28, 2006, March 31, 2006, which show the percentage that energy was of the profits. The total profits per month came from Amaranth's Performance and Net Asset Value Report, September 2006 YTD.
5. Expert Report of Anthony Saunders, PhD, *Amaranth LLC v. J. P. Morgan Chase*.
6. Author interview.
7. Instant message between Brian Hunter and David Chasman, May 1, 2006, beginning at 12:36 p.m. Chasman explained what he meant in his June 12, 2009 deposition for the FERC hearing.
8. Email exchange between Nick Maounis and Rob Jones, Exhibit Number S-20, FERC hearing in the matter of Brian Hunter.
9. Testimony of David Chasman, FERC hearing, September 2, 2009, 2431–34.
10. Ibid., 2452–53.

11. Author interview.
12. Senate Permanent Subcommittee on Investigations report, 926.
13. Ibid., 288.
14. Ibid., 279.
15. Amaranth update to investors, May 2006.
16. Instant message exchange between Brian Hunter and another trader, May 12, 2006, beginning at 2:53 p.m., exhibit 22, Senate Permanent Subcommittee report, 932.
17. Testimony of Shane Lee, June 25, 2007, Hearing of the Senate Permanent Subcommittee on Investigations.
18. Senate Permanent Subcommittee on Investigations report, 286.
19. Deposition of David Chasman, included as exhibit with FERC Order to Show Cause.
20. Senate Permanent Subcommittee on Investigations report, 291.
21. Ibid., 941–42.
22. Instant message between Brian Hunter and unnamed trader, May 25, 2006, beginning at 1:10 p.m., exhibit 22, Permanent Subcommittee on Investigations report, 943.
23. Author interview.
24. Amaranth timeline, internal J. P. Morgan chronology, Senate Permanent Subcommittee on Investigations report, 842.
25. Expert Report of Anthony Saunders, PhD., *Amaranth LLC v. J. P. Morgan Chase.* FERC Order to Show Cause, said the losses were more than $1 billion that month. Amaranth's Performance and Net Asset Value Report, September YTD, said that losses were $974,202,000, but that only included Amaranth LLC entity, not other accounts that held funds, such as the deferred bonus monies and Amaranth Global Equities.
26. Senate Permanent Subcommittee on Investigations report, 292.
27. Author interview.
28. Author interview.
29. Senate Permanent Subcommittee on Investigations report, 298.
30. Ibid., 299.
31. Ibid., 297–98.
32. Testimony of David Chasman, FERC hearing, September 2, 2009, 2451.
33. Author interview.
34. Email between Brian Hunter and Shane Lee on May 26, 2006, starting at 10:40 p.m., exhibit 9, Senate Permanent Subcommittee on Investigations report, 732.
35. Amaranth's Forward Curve on May 25, 2006–all natural gas contracts and Amaranth's Forward Curve on May 26, 2006.
36. Amaranth June 2006 update sent to investors.
37. Ludwig Chincarini, "A Case Study on Risk Management: Lessons from the Collapse of Amaranth Advisors LLC," *Journal of Applied Finance,* Spring/Summer 2008.
38. Author interview.
39. Author interview.
40. Author interview.
41. Author interview.

42. Author interview.
43. Author interview.
44. Author interview.
45. *SDCERA v. Nicholas M. Maounis et al.*, page 26.
46. Ibid., 26, 27.
47. Memorandum to the State Investment Council from William G. Clark, Director of the New Jersey Division of Investment.
48. Deposition of Brian Hunter, FERC Order to Show Cause, 119.
49. Author interviews.
50. Timeline summarizing JPMorgan Chase's interactions with Amaranth 2003 through September 21, 2006, prepared by JPMorgan Chase.
51. Deposition of Brian Hunter, FERC Order to Show Cause.
52. Deposition of Steven Johnson, FERC Order to Show Cause.
53. Deposition of Charles Winkler, FERC Order to Show Cause.
54. Amaranth update to investors, June 2006.
55. Senate Permanent Subcommittee on Investigations report, 297.
56. Amaranth snapshot at June 30, 2006, and Amaranth June 2006 update.
57. Instant message between Brian Hunter and unnamed trader on June 2, 2006, beginning at 3:10 p.m., exhibit 22, Senate Permanent Subcommittee on Investigations report, 945.
58. Author interviews with traders.
59. Author interviews.
60. Instant message between Brian Hunter and unnamed trader, June 13, 2006, starting at 10:10 a.m., exhibit 22, Senate Permanent Subcommittee on Investigations report, 975.
61. Emails between Brian Hunter and Shane Lee, Sunday, June 18, 2006, starting at 7:09 p.m., exhibit 9, Senate Permanent Subcommittee on Investigations report, 750.
62. Permanent Subcommittee on Investigations report, 300.
63. Instant messages between Brian Hunter and unnamed trader on June 14, 2006, beginning at 3:21 p.m., exhibit 22, Senate Permanent Subcommittee on Investigations report, 983.
64. Instant message exchange between Brian Hunter and Shane Lee, June 15, 2006, beginning at 12:45 p.m., exhibit 9, Senate Permanent Subcommittee on Investigations report, 747.
65. Author interview.
66. U.S. Energy Information Administration, Natural Gas Weekly Update, July 27, 2006.
67. Amaranth's Forward Curve on July 18, 2006, all natural gas contracts, Senate Permanent Subcommittee on Investigations report, 618.
68. Email exchange between Brian Hunter and Shane Lee, July 27, 2006, beginning at 11:30 p.m., exhibit 9, Senate Permanent Subcommittee on Investigations report, 763.
69. Email exchange between Brian Hunter and Brad Basarowich, July 28, 2006, beginning at 11:23 p.m., exhibit 9, Senate Permanent Subcommittee on Investigations report, 765.
70. Amaranth's forward curve on July 24-31, 2006, Senate Permanent Subcommittee on Investigations report, 622–27.

71. Senate Permanent Subcommittee on Investigations report, 294.
72. Senate Permanent Subcommittee on Investigations report, 301–07.
73. Senate Permanent Subcommittee on Investigations report, 345.
74. Instant message exchange between Hunter at Amaranth and Cathy at Aeco, July 31, 2006, beginning at 4:02 p.m., exhibit 9, Senate Permanent Subcommittee on Investigations report, 768.
75. Author interview.

CHAPTER 12: PUMP AND DUMP

1. Amaranth July 2006 update.
2. *SDCERA vs. Nicholas Maounis et al.*, complaint, 29.
3. Ibid., 30-1.
4. Memorandum to the State Investment Council from William G. Clark, Director, regarding Amaranth.
5. U.S. Energy Information Administration, *Natural Gas Weekly Update*, August 3, 2006.
6. "NOAA continues to predict above-normal hurricane season," *NOAA Magazine Online*, August 8, 2006.
7. Author interview.
8. Author interview.
9. Senate Permanent Subcommittee on Investigations report, 274.
10. Author interview.
11. Email from Brian Hunter to Steven Ardovini, Aug. 16, 2006, exhibit 9, Senate Permanent Subcommittee on Investigations report, 770.
12. Email from Steven Ardovini to Brian Hunter, Aug. 16, 2006, exhibit 9, Senate Permanent Subcommittee on Investigations report, 770.
13. Letter from NYMEX Senior Director Anthony Densieski to Amaranth Chief Compliance Officer Mike Carrieri, August, 2, 2006.
14. Senate Permanent Subcommittee on Investigations report, 313.
15. Amaranth timeline, prepared by JPMorgan.
16. Email exchange between Brian Hunter and Shane Lee, August 22, 2006, starting at 12:30 a.m., exhibit 9, Senate Permanent Subcommittee on Investigations report, 772.
17. Author interview.
18. Senate Permanent Subcommittee on Investigations report, 325–26.
19. Ibid., 329.
20. Ibid., 330.
21. Ibid., 332.
22. Instant message exchange between Brian Hunter and CRUMMERTD, August 29, 2006, starting at 3:22 p.m., exhibit 22, Senate Permanent Subcommittee on Investigations report, 788.
23. *Amaranth LLC and Amaranth Advisors LLC v. J. P. Morgan Chase.* In testimony at Brian Hunter's FERC hearing in August 2009, Matt Donohoe estimated more than $700 million.
24. Ibid., 13.
25. Letter from Michael Carrieri, Amaranth compliance director, to Anthony Densieski, Market Surveillance, NYMEX, August 30, 2006.

26. *Amaranth LLC and Amaranth Advisors LLC v. J. P. Morgan Chase*, 14.
27. Senate Permanent Subcommittee on Investigations report, 337.
28. Author interview.
29. Author interview.
30. *Amaranth LLC v. J. P. Morgan Chase*, complaint, 12.
31. Testimony of Shane Lee to the Senate Permanent Subcommittee on Investigations, Monday, June 25, 2007.
32. Author interview of former Amaranth employee.
33. Email exchange between Brian Hunter and Shane Lee, September 7, 2006, starting at 1:44 p.m., exhibit 9, Senate Permanent Subcommittee on Investigations report, 795.
34. Exhibit 7b, FERC hearing in the matter of Brian Hunter.
35. Testimony of David Chasman, FERC hearing, September 2, 2451–52.
36. Exhibits 7b and 8b, FERC hearing in the matter of Brian Hunter.
37. Email from John Arnold to Brian Hunter, September 17, 2006, 9:19 a.m., exhibit 9, Senate Permanent Subcommittee on Investigations report, 798–99.
38. *Amaranth LLC v. J. P. Morgan Chase*, 1–3.

CHAPTER 13: $6 BILLION SQUEEZE

1. Amaranth's CP Leveraged Funds due diligence report 2006.
2. Deposition of Howard Wietschner, April 29, 2009, *Amaranth LLC v. J. P. Morgan Chase*.
3. Ibid.
4. Ibid.
5. Ibid.
6. *Amaranth LLC v. J. P. Morgan Chase*, complaint, 2.
7. Interviews with former employees.
8. Interviews with former employees.
9. Email exchange between Brian Hunter and John Arnold, September 16, 2006, at 5:47 p.m., exhibit 9, Senate Permanent Subcommittee on Investigations report, 798–99. Arnold indicates that Hunter tried to contact him on September 15th.
10. Deposition of Elisha Wiesel, July 29, 2009, *Amaranth LLC v. J. P. Morgan Chase*.
11. Email chain between John Hogan and Carlos Hernandez and Steven Black, starting September 16, 2006 at 9:20 a.m. and going through September 18, 2006, at 5:24 a.m., *Amaranth LLC v. J. P. Morgan Chase*.
12. Email exchange between Brian Hunter and John Arnold, September 16, 2006, at 5:47 p.m., exhibit 9, Senate Permanent Subcommittee on Investigations report, 798–99.
13. *Amaranth LLC v. J. P. Morgan Chase*, complaint, 15.
14. Deposition Nicholas Maounis, May 20, 2009, *Amaranth LLC v. J. P. Morgan Chase*, 136–39.
15. Email exchange between Brian Hunter and Michael Hoss, September 16, 2006, starting at 11:18 p.m., *Amaranth LLC v. J. P. Morgan Chase*, lawsuit evidence.
16. *Amaranth LLC v. J. P. Morgan Chase*, complaint, 15–6.

17. Deposition of Elisha Wiesel, July 29, 2009, *Amaranth LLC v. J. P. Morgan Chase*.
18. Email from John Arnold to Brian Hunter, September 17, 2006, 9:19 a.m., exhibit 9, Senate Permanent Subcommittee on Investigations report 798–99.
19. Email from Brian Hunter to John Arnold, September 17, 2006, 9:30 a.m., exhibit 9, Senate Permanent Subcommittee on Investigations report, 798–99.
20. Hearing before the Permanent Subcommittee on Investigations, Monday, June 25, 2007, U.S. Government Printing Office, Washington, D.C., 2008, 55.
21. *Amaranth LLC v. J. P. Morgan Chase*. The description of this meeting comes from Amaranth documents. JPMorgan Chase agrees that Greenberg met with Winkler and asked why Amaranth had given other firms first crack at the energy book deal before offering it to JPMorgan.
22. Email from Stuart Tucker to Richard Berliand, September 18, 2006, at 12:16 a.m., *Amaranth LLC v. J. P. Morgan Chase* lawsuit evidence.
23. Author interviews with former Amaranth employees.
24. Deposition of Nicholas Maounis, May 20, 2009, *Amaranth LLC v. J. P. Morgan Chase*.
25. Deposition of Howard Wietschner, April 29, 2009, *Amaranth LLC v. J. P. Morgan Chase*.
26. Deposition of George Taylor, May 12, 2009, *Amaranth LLC v. J. P. Morgan Chase*.
27. Deposition of Howard Wietschner, April 29, 2009, *Amaranth LLC v. J. P. Morgan Chase*.
28. Deposition of Parker Drew, June 9, 2009, *Amaranth LLC v. J. P. Morgan Chase*.
29. Deposition of Nicholas Maounis, May 20, 2009, *Amaranth LLC v. J. P. Morgan Chase*.

CHAPTER 14: "YOU'RE DONE"

1. The New York Supreme Court, Appellate Division, decision found that Goldman Sachs wanted its money in advance. But Amaranth disputes this, saying that Goldman was willing to receive its payment over several days as Amaranth received collateral back from J. P. Morgan Futures.
2. New York Supreme Court, Appellate Division, First Department, decision, Catterson, J. Nov. 5, 2009, Case # 603756/07.
3. Email cited in deposition of Stuart Tucker, J. P. Morgan risk manager in *Amaranth LLC v. J. P. Morgan Chase*.
4. Deposition of Rob Jones, May 21, 2009, *Amaranth LLC v. J. P. Morgan Chase*.
5. Deposition of Diane Genova, June 11, 2009, *Amaranth LLC v. J. P. Morgan Chase*.
6. Deposition of Elisha Wiesel, July 29, 2009, *Amaranth LLC v. J. P. Morgan Chase*.
7. *Amaranth LLC v. J. P. Morgan Chase*, complaint, 6.
8. Remarks by Nicholas Maounis, investor conference call, Friday, September 22, 2006.
9. Author interview.
10. Expert Report of Anthony Saunders, PhD, *Amaranth LLC v. J. P. Morgan Chase*, 4.

11. *Amaranth LLC v. J. P. Morgan Chase*, complaint. In a response, J. P. Morgan denies the statement attributed to Black and Winters.
12. Mallaby, *More Money Than God*, 320.
13. Supreme Court, Appellate Division, First Department ruling, Order, November 5, 2009, *Amaranth LLC et al. v. J. P. Morgan Chase*.
14. Letter to investors, Nick Maounis, September 20, 2006.
15. Katherine Burton and Jenny Strasburg, "Hot Trader Led to Biggest Hedge-Fund Collapse," *Bloomberg News*, December 17, 2006.
16. Author interview.
17. Author interview.
18. The CP Leveraged Fund 2006.
19. Amaranth LLC Performance and Net Asset Value Report, September YTD.

EPILOGUE

1. Private Placement Memorandum, Solengo Capital, 3.
2. Supplemental Declaration of Brian Hunter in Further Support of Plaintiff's Motion for a Preliminary Injunction and Declaratory Relief, *Brian Hunter v. FERC*, U.S. District Court, District of Columbia, 07-civ-1307, August 3, 2007.
3. Supplemental Declaration of Brian Hunter.
4. Supplemental Declaration of Brian Hunter.
5. Author interview.
6. Initial Decision, Brian Hunter IN07-26-004.
7. Statement of Todd Mullins, FERC hearing, August 18, 2009, 196–97.
8. Opening Statement of Matthew Menchel, FERC hearing, August 18, 2009.
9. Initial Decision, Brian Hunter IN07-26-004, 27.
10. Leah McGrath Goodman, then Editor-At-Large at *Trader Monthly Magazine*, reported the profit statistic, which came from Centaurus employees, in the magazine.
11. Andrew Ross Sorkin, "A Billion-Dollar Year for Top Hedge Fund Managers," DealBook nytimes.com, April 10, 2007.
12. Testimony of John D. Arnold, CFTC Hearing to Discuss Position Limits, Hedge Exemptions and Transparency for Energy Markets, August 5, 2009.
13. Steve Bertoni, "The World's Youngest Billionaires," Forbes.com, March 10, 2009.
14. Harry Hurt III, "Fortune Hunter," *Portfolio*, May 2007.
15. *Amaranth LLC v. J. P. Morgan*, 9.
16. Katherine Burton, "Amaranth Founder Maounis to Start New Multistragey Hedge Fund," *Bloomberg*, May 10, 2008. Jenny Strasburg, "Former Amaranth Chief Returns to the Stage," *Wall Street Journal*, June 26, 2010.
17. FERC, Order Approving Uncontested Settlement, Issued August 12, 2009. Details are enumerated in Exhibit A, Joint Explanatory Statement issued with the Order.
18. Final Order and Judgment, Amaranth Natural Gas Commodities Litigation, U.S. District Court, Southern District of New York, 07-cv-06377.
19. *Hai Chen and Harry Sardonis v. Nicholas M. Maounis and Amaranth Group, Inc.*

20. Memorandum of Law in Support of Motion to Dismiss the Complaint by Defendant Amaranth Advisors LLC, *SDCERA v. Nicholas M. Maounis.*

21. Joel Chernoff, "Alpha Engine Portfolio Revving Up Controversy," *Pensions and Investments*, October 30, 2006.

22. Seth Hettena, "Hedge Funds County Once Championed Now Prove Too Risky," *Voice of San Diego*, December 19, 2008.

23. SDCERA press release, March 12, 2009.

24. "Two Investment Managers Arrested on Fraud Charges," Department of Justice press release, February 25, 2009.

25. Seth Hettena, "Hedge Fund Champion Leaves County Pension Amid Losses, Tension," *Voice of San Diego*, March 5, 2009.

26. Communication to author from Johanna Schick, investment office, SDCERA.

27. Author interviews.

28. State of the Markets Report, Division of Energy Market Oversight, FERC, August 2009.

29. Author interview.

30. "Investigations Subcommittee Releases Levin-Coleman Report on Excessive Speculation in the Natural Gas Market," Media release, June 25, 2007.

31. Testimony of John D. Arnold, CFTC hearing, August 5, 2009.

INDEX

Chasman, David, 151, 175, 180
  attempt to reign in Hunter, 152–53,
    173–74, 175
  background, 129–30
  Hunter and, 130–31, 151, 154, 175,
    180
  as risk manager of Amaranth's natural
    gas portfolio, 129–31, 151,
    152–53, 173–74, 175, 180, 181,
    183, 237
Chen, Hai, 91, 243
Chestermere, Alberta, 10, 11, 12
Cicio, Paul, 168
Cintron, Carmen A., 239, 240–41
Citadel Investment Group, 85, 86, 87,
    88, 226, 228, 241
Citigroup, 232–33
Coale, Carol, 191–92
Cohen, Steven, 79, 102, 241
collateral cost (margin payment), 109
Collins, Robert "Bo," 21, 107–11, 129,
    134, 147, 148, 149. See also
    MotherRock
  Arnold and, 108
  Hunter and, 107–11, 154
  Hunter targets, 196
  MotherRock's slide and closing,
    191–92, 195, 196, 208, 234
  natural gas speculation, 2006, 150–51,
    175, 177, 185–87, 189–91, 209
  trading practices, 138
  "widow maker" and, 109, 110, 195
commercial banks
  derivatives traded by, 25
  repeal of Glass-Steagall Act and, 24
  securities business and, 24
commodities, xxiv. See also natural gas;
    New York Mercantile Exchange
  anonymity of investors, 7–8
  banks trading in (clearing brokers), 75
  banning of options on agricultural
    products, 15
  brokers, 75, 149, 200
  exchanges, 31
  expansion of futures market, 69
  first computer-based commodity
    trading operation, 41
  futures exchanges, history, 162
  Goldman Sachs in trading, 167
  hikes in food and oil, speculation and,
    xxvi, 5

  hikes in natural gas prices, speculation
    and, 5, 59, 158–61, 165, 169, 170,
    176, 244–45
  margin requirement on futures, 75
  online investing, Enron and, 51–52
  regulation of, 164
  the settlement day, 140
  shorting, 6
  speculative trading in, xxv, xxvi,
    162–63
  trading at the close and, 140–41,
    142–44, 154, 155
Commodity Exchange Act of 1936, 163
Commodity Futures Modernization Act
    (CFMA), 164–65
Commodity Futures Trading
    Commission (CFTC), 62
  authority over electronic trading
    granted (2008), 245–46
  complaints about price manipulation
    and, 161
  creation of, 163
  exemption of energy swaps from
    oversight, 44–45, 168
  growth of noncommercial traders
    calculated, 168
  Hunter and Amaranth charged with
    natural gas price manipulation, 238,
    240
  manipulation of the silver market and,
    163, 171
  oversight and regulatory powers,
    164–65, 170–71, 245–46
  "pump and dump" strategy and, 205
  review of suspicious trading by
    Amaranth, 155
Corbin, Arthur, 159, 244
Cramer, Jim, xxi
credit default swap trading, xxv–xxvi, 20,
    168. See also derivatives
  Arnold and, 52–53
  exempted from oversight, 44–45
  hedgers and, 166–67
  in natural gas (gas swaps) and Enron,
    41, 43, 44–45, 46, 50, 52, 164
  in natural gas and Hunter, 25, 26, 195
  natural gas prices at Henry Hub
    and, 20
  regulation of, 164, 246
  SDCERA investments in, 244
  Weinstein and, 25

ABOUT THE AUTHOR

BARBARA T. DREYFUSS worked as a research analyst and senior vice president for Prudential Securities for two decades. Her focus was health policy, and she was based in the Washington, D.C. area. She has written for *The American Prospect, Mother Jones, Washington Monthly,* and *The Veteran.* She lives in Cape May, New Jersey.

ABOUT THE TYPE

The text of this book was set in Janson, a typeface designed in about 1690 by Nicholas Kis, a Hungarian living in Amsterdam, and for many years mistakenly attributed to the Dutch printer Anton Janson. In 1919 the matrices became the property of the Stempel Foundry in Frankfurt. It is an old-style book face of excellent clarity and sharpness. Janson serifs are concave and splayed; the contrast between thick and thin strokes is marked.